T3-ALY-315

SAN JOSE
SILICON VALLEY

INNOVATIVE VISION, ENTREPRENEURIAL SPIRIT

Produced in cooperation with
The San Jose Silicon Valley Chamber of Commerce.

Library of Congress Cataloging-in-Publication Data

San Jose Silicon Valley : innovative vision, entrepreneurial spirit /
editorial Coordinator, Lynne Bowman ; corporate profiles writer, Suzan
Lindstrom, feature photographer, Dana L. Grover.— 1st ed.
    p. cm.
    ISBN 1-58192-047-4
    1. San Jose (Calif.)—Economic conditions. 2. Santa Clara County
(Calif.)—Economic conditions. 3. San Jose (Calif.)—Social
conditions. 4. Santa Clara County (Calif.)—Social conditions. 5. San
Jose (Calif.)—History. 6. Santa Clara County (Calif.)—History. 7.
Industries—California—San Jose—History. 8.
Industries—California—Santa Clara County—History. 9. High technology
industries—California—San Jose—History. 10. High technology
industries—California—Santa Clara County—History.   I. Bowman,
Lynne, 1946-   . II. Lindstrom, Suzan, 1949-   . III. Grover, Dana
L., 1943-   .
    HC108.S715 S26 2001
    338.7'62'000979473—dc21

                        2001004878

All Photography by Dana L. Grover, except as listed below:

Photography on page 71 (top) courtesy of San Jose Repertory Theatre

Photography on page 72 (top) courtesy of Opera San Jose

Photography on page 73 (top left, top right) courtesy of San Jose Stage

Photography on pages 106-7, 109, 128 (bottom), 150 (bottom left) courtesy of IBM

Photography on pages 108 (top), 130 (bottom) courtesy of Intel Corporation

Photography on page 128 (top) courtesy of United Way Silicon Valley

Photography on page 129 by Steve Yamaguma/courtesy of Silicon Valley Charity Ball

Photography on page 132 by Robert Fouts

Photography on page 134 courtesy of Palo Alto Medical Foundation

Photography on pages 136 (left), 139, 140 (bottom) courtesy of Kaiser Permanente

Photography on pages 144, 147 (top) by Tom Chargin/courtesy of Santa Clara County Office of Education

Photography on page 146 (top) courtesy of Williams Elementary School, National Blue Ribbon School/
San Jose Unified School District

Photography on page 146 (bottom right) courtesy of Randol Elementary School, National Blue Ribbon School/
San Jose Unified School District

Photography on page 147 (bottom) courtesy of Los Alamitos (Robotics program), National Blue Ribbon School/
San Jose Unified School District

Photography on page 157 by Sharon Hall/courtesy of San José State University

The San Jose Silicon Valley Chamber of Commerce and Community Communications, Inc. would like to express our gratitude to these companies for their leadership in the development of this book.

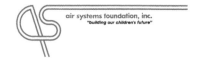

IBM

intel ®

SONY

 >KNIGHT RIDDER>

Ⓢ Spectra-Physics

NEC
NEC Electronics Inc.

 T THERMA

Santa Clara Valley
Water District

VERITAS™

San Jose Silicon Valley

INNOVATIVE VISION, ENTREPRENEURIAL SPIRIT

Editorial Director: Lynne Bowman
Feature Photographer: Dana L. Grover
Corporate Profiles, Lead Writer: Suzan Lindstrom
Additional Corporate Profile Writers: Gary Burchfield,
Richard S. Cox, Danek S. Kaus, Kathy Mayer,
Marvin Ross, Bob Serata, and Barbara Stahura

Community Communications, Inc.
Publisher: Ronald P. Beers

Staff for *San Jose Silicon Valley:
Innovative Vision, Entrepreneurial Spirit*

Acquisitions: Henry S. Beers
Publisher's Sales Associate: Linda Frank
Editor In Chief: Wendi L. Lewis
Managing Editor: Angela C. Johnson
Profile Editor: Amanda J. Burbank
Design Director: Scott Phillips
Designer: Matt Johnson
Photo Editors: Angela C. Johnson and Matt Johnson
Contract Manager: Christi Stevens
National Sales Manager: Ronald P. Beers
Sales Assistant: Sandra Akers
Editorial Assistants: Deb Carroll, Krewe Maynard,
and Eleanor Planer
Proofreader: Carolyn Phillips
Acquisitions Coordinator: Angela P. White
Accounting Services: Stephanie Perez
Print Production Manager: Jarrod Stiff
Pre-Press and Separations: DCR Graphics

CCI

Community Communications, Inc.
Montgomery, Alabama

David M. Williamson, Chief Executive Officer
Ronald P. Beers, President
W. David Brown, Chief Operating Officer

© 2001 Community Communications
All Rights Reserved
Published 2001
Printed in USA
First Edition
Library of Congress Catalog Number: 2001004878
ISBN Number: 1-58192-047-4

Every effort has been made to ensure the accuracy of the
information herein. However, the authors and
Community Communications are not responsible for any
errors or omissions that might have occurred.

TABLE of CONTENTS

FOREWORD

The San Jose Silicon Valley Chamber of Commerce represents a powerful network of small retailers, small manufacturers, mid-size service-sector firms, and large high-tech enterprises—companies that have, together, created Silicon Valley's resilient economy. Representing nearly 2,000 companies, our chamber is the largest non-profit organization representing the entire supply chain of business enterprises throughout the San Jose Metropolitan Area. As a large, urban chamber, we have long-witnessed our region's ups and downs. Our take? Silicon Valley's technological revolution is far from over, and our best days as a successful community lie ahead.

According to the American Electronics Association, one of our leading economic partners, this valley offers:
• The nation's largest high-tech presence and number of jobs
• A combined high-tech payroll of $56 billion, with $22 billion of that in San Jose alone
• An average wage in high-tech of $85,100 in San Jose versus $67,000 in California
• A labor force in which high-tech firms employ one out of every four private sector workers
• At least one computer in 77 percent of all households—the #1 ranking in the entire nation

Of course, the "backbone" of Silicon Valley's economy is more than technology companies. It includes the wealth of assets that are chronicled throughout *San Jose Silicon Valley: Innovative Vision, Entrepreneurial Spirit.* The words and photographs will take you on a journey through the history and growth of the community, including business, technology, education, medicine, sports, arts, and attractions. Readers also will be introduced to many of the companies and organizations that have helped the Silicon Valley become a legendary player in the global economy.

The San Jose Silicon Valley Chamber of Commerce is pleased to present this book to showcase this incredible region. Our community boasts a full vision and vibrant spirit. As the twenty-first century plays out, the Silicon Valley will continue to be the leader in technological innovations that will improve the lives of people all over the world.

—*Jim Cunneen*
President and CEO
San Jose Silicon Valley Chamber of Commerce

Preface

Writing about San Jose is writing about what's possible. What's next. What's coming up so fast it's not clearly visible yet to most of the rest of the world, but is already part of life here.

Even our local history, as you'll see woven through the chapters that follow, is a story of seismic social and economic changes. The Valley, we've come to call it, as if the "Silicon" part is now just assumed, seems to always have been where you came when you wanted the best of what the future offered. Productive land. Gold. Good jobs. An open, accepting society. Public education. San Jose always has been right out there on the edge of some frontier or other, and quite likely will remain so.

Embracing the new is our culture. That's what we do here. It's reflected in technology-based economics—or perhaps more accurately, idea-based economics—and in the astounding richness of our ethnic tapestry. While the rest of the United States is just now waking up to the power and presence of the Hispanic community, for example, San Jose has arrived already at a certain ease with its bilingual roots and character.

Thank you, Connie Yu, for your scholarship and perspective on San Jose's Chinese heritage. Thank you, Susan Ditz, for tapping into your extraordinary Rolodex on our behalf. Thank you, Jake Bowman, for taking on the task of explaining in just a few paragraphs how the Silicon Valley economy works. Thank you, Jim Tucker, for generously making yourself available as a resource. Thank you, Angela, for giving us an excuse to do some thinking, talking, and writing about the only place in the world where all this could have happened. And thank you, dear Reader, for giving these pages a turn. We hope to reward you with glimpse, as you look at San Jose Silicon Valley, at what's coming down the road.

—*Lynne Bowman*

PartOne

1
CHAPTER ONE

THE VALLEY
TRANSFORMED

By Jake Bowman

*Rolling hills of the South Valley overlook Anderson Lake,
where an old ranch barn commands a view of
San Jose's suburban outskirts.*

Four flags commemorate San Jose's historic ruling governments: Spanish, Mexican, California Republic "Bear Flag," and the Stars and Stripes. The flags fly near the corporate headquarters of Adobe Systems, Inc., in downtown San Jose.

It is difficult to imagine how the transformation of the Santa Clara Valley into Silicon Valley was possible. The advent of the "New Economy" was like an explosion, radiating across the valley in the flash of a few decades. Gone was the old ecology of fruit trees and farmland, replaced by a forest of strip malls and housing. In all the stories about sprawl, development, and redevelopment, what's seldom heard is this: it's not the first time this magical valley has been completely transformed.

The invasion of the Spanish was the initial instance in recorded memory that a new economy overhauled the valley's entire way of life. Explorers like Portola and De Anza weren't the only ones to discover a New World when they arrived in the eighteenth century. The valley's first entrepreneurial inhabitants, the native Californians, discovered the European economy's demand for furs and game. For millennia, their ancestors had hunted and gathered acorns in the great oak forests of the valley, named Santa Clara by the Spanish missionaries. Their first contact with European colonizers changed that ancient lifestyle forever.

While a few of the locals were employed directly by the Catholic missions of San Jose and Santa Clara, the economic effects of this new regime reverberated throughout the region. The people, who in previous generations never would have left their clan territory, ventured forth in new trade routes that crisscrossed the Bay Area to supply the new Spanish settlement. The local clans of native Californians shared a new identity, the Ohlone, to distinguish themselves from the new arrivals.

El Pueblo de San Jose de Guadalupe, the municipal ancestor of the capital of Silicon Valley, became an agricultural outpost established to feed the garrisons of the San Francisco and Monterey Presidios. In the space of a couple of generations, the very face of the valley was totally transformed, as the great oaks were felled for timber and the land was cleared for fields and pasture.

The Mexican Province of Alta California gave way to the Bear Flag Republic. American annexation soon followed. The Gold Rush transformed the Californian economy again, as immigrants came west from every direction, from the Eastern States and East Asia. But while the rest of the state was building boomtowns, quicksilver mining took hold in the Los Gatos Hills, the Santa Clara Valley sprouted farms and vineyards, and San Jose became the provisional capital of a newly united state.

The American settlement of the Santa Clara Valley completely altered the landscape one more time, covering the valley floor with orchards. Towns like Sunnyvale, with names tailor-made for labels, sprang up around the canneries. The "Valley of Heart's Delight" became an industrial-scale operation in agricultural production, fruit basket of the nation.

After such a tumultuous history of economic revolutions, it shouldn't come as a surprise that the second half of the last century would bring an even more profound transformation. Somewhere between the academic poles of Stanford and Berkeley, around Moffett Field and the NASA-Ames research center, another new economy was born, and all the mineral its forges needed was yet another earthly resource the valley had in abundance: sand.

The valley is still a magical place where the natives take revolutions in stride, a unique place where the people expect change, and thrive on it. According to cybernetic philosophy, these sudden shifts that change all the rules and create new levels of variety and complexity are just "metasystem transitions." No big deal. Revolutionary change is just business as usual around here. ∎

Mission San Jose was founded June 11, 1797 by Father Fermin Francisco de Lasuen on the site of the Ohlone village of Orisome. In 1956, the town of Mission San Jose was incorporated into the city of Fremont, a neighbor of the city that shares the Mission's name.

The Seal of the State of California is planted on the spot where the first state legislature was convened, on December 15, 1849. It was known as the "Legislature of 1,000 Drinks" because Senator Thomas Green would make motions to adjourn the legislature by saying, "Gentlemen, let's have a drink. Let's have a thousand." Some say he offered the drinks at his expense, as part of his strategy to become major general of the state militia.

The First Unitarian Church, across from St. James Park in downtown San Jose, is home to downtown's only labyrinth, sometimes offering walk-in meditation during the lunch hour for busy executives. The First Unitarian labyrinth's design is based on one laid in the floor of Chartres cathedral in France.

Mission Santa Clara de Asis, instituted in 1777, is the historic center of Santa Clara University. The original mission was founded by Franciscan monks of the Catholic church in New Spain. In 1850, when California was admitted as a state, it was Joseph Alemany, a Dominican priest, who took charge of the new diocese. Bishop Alemany transferred the mission to the Jesuit order, who opened a school there the very next year.

The farms of Gilroy are famous for one thing: garlic. "The Garlic Capital of the World" ships the bulk of fresh-market garlic to supermarkets across America. They are also well-known locally for other spicy treats, such as bell peppers and jalapeños.

Santa Clara Valley was known for its orchards before the integrated chip arrived to change the Valley's landscape and name. The rural districts of Morgan Hill maintain this precious agricultural heritage in varieties of cherry, apricot, walnut, almond, plums and prune.

"In 1998, we moved our corporate headquarters from Miami to San Jose to ensure that our company's leaders are in the best possible position to understand the world of the Internet—to be where the most aggressive online innovation is taking place and the most exciting coalitions are forming.

"In San Jose, we are exposed to a breadth of new perspectives, employees, and investment opportunities—none of them available in Miami. We continue to find that the benefits of our location in Silicon Valley are greater than we had expected."

—*Tony Ridder*
Chairman and CEO
Knight Ridder

Top: Fine Victorians line the streets of elegant districts downtown. Right: Palm Haven is a well-loved neighborhood between Willow Glen and the West Side, with stately mansions standing between bungalows along a palm-lined boulevard.

Bird Avenue twists through a neighborhood of Willow Glen known for beautifully restored Victorians.

Top: The pubs and bistros of Murphy Street in downtown Sunnyvale attract Silicon Valley workers who enjoy microbrews and fine cuisine. Right: Main Street in downtown Los Gatos is the main scene for street life and people-watching in this town of only twelve square miles, nestled in the foothills of the Santa Cruz. Far right: In the shadow of one of San Jose's earliest skyscrapers, the Bank America Building, lie the Fountain Alley Victorians, among the last vestiges of old downtown. Fountain Alley is a pedestrian mall, linking the First and Second Street transit center.

Fairmont Hotel, overlooking Cesar Chavez Park and Market Street, has played host to kings, presidents, and countless celebrities on their visits to the valley.

Right: A bench in St. James Park is the perfect place to rest and watch people and cars along Santa Cruz Avenue. Opposite page: Le Petit Trianon Theatre is an acoustic gem, acclaimed by audiences, critics, and performers as the ideal concert hall for small groups, such as the San Jose Chamber Music Society.

Top: The roots of an oak drink the waters at Vasona Lake Park in Los Gatos, where fishing is a popular activity. Right and opposite page: Lexington Reservoir is a training ground for competitive crews, whose champions go on to row for the Ivy League. The Reservoir is also a great place for sailing.

Right: "Music in the Other Park" is a regular summer event in St. James Park, based on the outstanding success of Music in the Park, held at Cesar Chavez. Far right: The Joyce Cooling Band performs in St. James Park. Opposite page: The McKinley Statue in St. James Park simply memorializes the spot where a speech was delivered by the President in 1901.

CHAPTER TWO

REGION OF
DIVERSITY

By Connie Young Yu

*Vietnamese New Year in San Jose starts with
the Tet Parade downtown, and is followed by
a festival at the fairgrounds.*

The Yun Yee Tong and its Lion and Dragon Dance Group are a central attraction of the Tet Parade.

What is typical about San Jose? Nothing and everything. This extraordinary city is defined daily by new pioneers in technology and commerce from all lands. Here, a mix of cultures and ethnic groups has stimulated new ideas, and fostered common interests and cooperation. The result is an exciting, dynamic place to visit, to live, and to work.

In the 1980s, a large influx of engineers and entrepreneurs from all over the world joined forces with pioneer innovators to transform the valley into the technological hub of the world. Along with the booming chip industry, a San Jose lifestyle of diversity and exceptional ambiance developed. The census data of 2000 showed that San Jose had the highest percentage of adults with a college degree of any metropolitan area. Foreign-born immigrants play a large role in this remarkable statistic.

This community redefines America. School children share a myriad of cultural experiences and learn how to celebrate the New Year several different ways. Co-workers may be Korean, Indian, Lebanese, and Muslim. On weekends there might be a Huong dance festival, Portuguese Heritage Day, or an African arts fair. Visit a Chinese American museum, have sushi in Japantown, or shop at a Mexican mall, all in the same day. For dinner, check out the local papers that list restaurants by cuisines of the world, everything your heart desires from Italian to Ethiopian to Moroccan to Peruvian.

The diversity factor is nothing new here. Latinos and Asians have deep roots in Santa Clara Valley. In the nineteenth and early twentieth century their hard work and determination made the valley into an agricultural center. Arriving in the 1850s, Chinese laborers worked on the San Jose-Santa Cruz railroad lines. They cleared huge areas of chaparral for the planting of wheat and alfalfa. They became strawberry growers, orchardists, fruit pickers and packers.

The celebration of Cinco de Mayo in San Jose is the largest of its kind in North America, outside of Mexico.

Immigrants from Europe brought agricultural plantings from their homelands to a welcoming California soil. Italian farmers planted olive trees, apricots, and peaches with amazing results. Unsuccessful in goldmining, French immigrant Louis Pellier introduced the French prune to the valley in the 1850s, making San Jose "the prune capital of the world." Varieties of pears Pellier developed were planted, harvested, and packed by Chinese, Japanese, and Mexican workers and were shipped all over the United States. French settlers, notably Charles Lefranc, Etienne Thee, and Paul Masson, were pioneers in the winemaking industry. Mirassou Vineyards, established by French immigrants, is the oldest family wine business in America.

In the 1860s, the New Almaden Quicksilver Mine employed miners from Cornwall, as well as Irish workers, Swedes, Germans, Spaniards, Chelenos, and Chinese. The mine exists today as a historic park. In the nineteenth century, San Jose had five different Chinatowns, and one was recently unearthed by the expansion of Guadalupe Expressway near downtown. San Jose's Japantown, established in the early 1900s, flourishes today, and during lunchtime its restaurants are crowded with engineers and executives from nearby companies. San Pedro Street has a European atmosphere with outdoor cafes, and, nearby, the historic Fallon House and Peralta Adobe building is open to visitors. San Jose, a city with a fond memory for its heritage, has kept a tangible connection between the agricultural past and its high-tech present.

San Jose's city government is renowned for its foresight and progressive spirit. Norman Mineta, who was interred in a relocation camp for Japanese Americans during World War II, was the first Asian American mayor of a major city. In the 1970s, Janet Gray Hayes was one of the few women mayors of a large American city. Mayors Tom McEnery and Susan Hammer encouraged programs that promoted history and diversity. Ron Gonzales is the first Latino mayor and faces the challenges of San Jose's extraordinary success, that of expansion and new development. ■

The Japanese Friendship Garden is a living monument to San Jose's sister city, Okayama, patterned after her internationally renowned Korakuen Park. Feeding the Koi fish, colorful carp that grow over 30 inches and live over that many years, is the customary activity.

Top: San Jose Buddhist Church Betsuin on North Fifth Street is a temple of the Jodo Shinshu Nishi Hongwanji tradition of Buddhism, and occupies a special place in the heart of Japantown.

Right: One of North America's oldest Taiko drum troupes, San Jose Taiko, performs a unique style of traditional and contemporary drumming at celebrations in San Jose's Japantown.

"We are passionate about serving readers in Silicon Valley and its global electronic community, reporting and writing accurately and fairly, shining a light on injustice, and defending the public's right to know.

"We will reflect the changing demographics of the community in both coverage and hiring, recognizing that diversity is a core component of accuracy. Two stories are central to our mission: the impact of technology and the changing demographic landscape of America. Those two stories create powerful connections between our community and others, both domestic and international."

—*Mercury News* Mission Statement

The Japantown Farmers Market is a weekly event featuring fresh flowers and flavors both familiar and exotic.

Right: The Chavez Family marches in the Cinco de Mayo Parade. Although he was born in Arizona and traveled seasonally as the son of migrant workers, a formative period of Cesar's childhood was spent in San Jose's infamous barrio Sal Si Puedes, whose name translates "Get Out If You Can."

Bottom left: Cesar Chavez Park is a popular place because of the public stage, which is a frequent venue for musical acts, especially during Music in the Park, the Jazz Festival, and Cinco de Mayo.

Bottom right: The fountains are always an attraction for San Jose's smallest residents, no matter what the occasion—especially on sunny days like May 5, also known as Cinco de Mayo.

Iaido, the art of sword-drawing and sword-dancing, is a rarity outside the upper classes of Japan, and a huge hit with the crowd at the Cherry Blossom Festival.

Cupertino's Cherry Blossom Festival began as a commemoration of the sister-city relationship with Toyukawa. It since has become an enormously popular event, featuring martial arts demonstrations and exhibits in origami, flower arrangement, calligraphy, bonsai tree cultivation, and other celebrations of Japanese culture.

The Classical Chinese Lion Dance is traditionally performed by kung fu martial artists who are specially trained in its intricate steps.

Tet, the Vietnamese
New Year, marks the
beginning of the Asian
lunar calendar by the
first full moon before
spring planting, which
is why it is sometimes
called the Spring
Festival. It falls either
in January or
February, depending on
the solar calendar year,
which happens to be
winter in the northern
hemisphere, except San
Jose, where the weather
is almost always
beautiful for Tet.

Left: Laotian women
take part in San Jose
Tet's international fair
celebrating cultures
from all over Indochina.
Far left: Celebrating
the world's annual
rebirth, Tet is revered as
a holiday of fertility
and childhood. Women
wear extravagant
dresses, and everyone
plays in the street
with fireworks.

Heinlenville, one of six Chinatowns in San Jose, was built in 1887. When an earlier Chinese settlement at the present site of the Fairmont Hotel was destroyed by a suspicious fire, John Heinlen, a local businessman, braved death threats to lease property to the displaced Chinese. This area near today's Japantown at Taylor and Sixth became known as Heinlenville. By the 1930s, many of Heinlenville's original residents had passed on. Their children had grown up and integrated into the community at large, and the Chinese Exclusion Act had prevented new arrivals from China. When the Heinlenville estate declared bankruptcy, Heinlenville became the property of the City of San Jose, which razed the whole area, except for Ng Shing Gung, which was dismantled in 1949, and then replicated in 1991. Today NgShing Gung, a community center and house of worship, is located in the San Jose History Park at Kelley Park.

Top: The elaborate
carved and gilded
altar on the second
floor of Ng Shing Gung
formerly housed statues
of five divinities: Kwan
Yin, Goddess of Mercy;
Choi Sun, God of
Prosperity; Cheng
Huan, God of Canton
City; Kwan Gung, God
of War and Justice;
and Tien Hou,
Queen of Heaven.
Left: The first floor
of the original
Ng Shing Gung used
to be a literature and
calligraphy school,
teaching classical
Chinese reading and
writing to the children
of Heinlenville. Now it
features exhibits of the
Chinese-American
history museum,
including a
documentary by Oscar-
winner Jessica Yu.

Left and bottom right: Queens and princesses of Cinco de Mayo wave to their throng of adoring admirers. The holiday originally celebrates the Juarez victory over French forces at the battle of Puebla. However, it has come to symbolize the survival of Mexican culture in the face of foreign pressures in general, with modern traditions such as the aesthetic victory of local custom lowriders over industrial auto design from Detroit.

Opposite page and far left: Dancing and clapping is the soul of the San Jose Kwanzaa celebration, while passionate drumming fills the air. Founded in 1966 by Dr. Maulana Karenga, a professor at California State University, Long Beach, this African-American holiday is celebrated December 26 through January 1, each year in cities throughout the nation. Based on seven principles, one for each day, Kwanzaa is an opportunity for people to connect with their African cultural identity and embrace their history.

As San Jose's Latino cultural center, Mexican Heritage Plaza consists of a traditional central plaza for public gatherings, surrounded by floating gardens called chinampas, a theater for performing arts, a pavilion styled after a pyramid, and a galleria affiliated with the Smithsonian, as well as offices and classrooms.

Left: Every downtown festival brings out the barbeque, whether Thai, Korean, or Texan. Far right: The San Pedro Square Farmers Market brings together many cultures of Californian agriculture, including Japanese, Chinese, Mexican, Portuguese, Dutch, Italian, and Sikh.

The restaurants and sushi bars of Japantown are a popular lunchtime destination. The Japanese community in San Jose has survived, and thrived, despite a tumultuous history during the past century. Today, these restaurants, along with gift shops and other specialty stores, are preserved by the residents, and treasured by the patrons.

Left and far left: The restaurants, shops, and offices reflecting the Southeastern Asian heritage can be found in every neighborhood of downtown. Arriving as refugees from Vietnam in the 1970s, the Vietnamese have established roots in the Silicon Valley, bringing with them the heritage and cultures from their homeland, while becoming a vital part of the community. The current population of Vietnamese and Vietnamese-Americans is ten percent in the San Jose area, with owner- ship of local businesses exceeding 5,000.

*Top: A Victorian
mansion built by one of
San Jose's first mayors,
the Fallon House, is
now a showcase exhibit
of History San Jose.
Opposite page: Pao Wah
Temple on McKee Road
is a newly dedicated
center of the Chinese
Mahayana tradition,
supported by the
Buddhist Society
of America.*

This page: Festa do Espiritu Santo, "Feast of the Holy Ghost," is a Portuguese festival held on Pentecost, the seventh Sunday after Easter. Besides feasting, the festivities include musical bands, folkloric dances and a parade. According to legend, the first Queen of the Holy Ghost Feast was Queen Isabel of Portugal, because she relieved the Azores islands of famine. Opposite page: Five Wounds Portuguese National Church is the spiritual center of Little Portugal on East Santa Clara Street.

3

CHAPTER THREE

❧❧

ARTS, EVENTS & RECREATION

By Susan Ditz

Hakone Gardens in Saratoga is one of the oldest and most beautiful Japanese gardens in America, built in 1918 after a similar display at the Pan-Pacific Exhibition of 1915. There's a koi pond, Zen and tea gardens, an outstanding bamboo collection, and a completely authentic nineteenth century Kyoto Tea Merchant's home and shop.

Henry Coe State Park is home to majestic oaks and host to weekend hikers.

Playtime is as much a part of a Silicon Valley lifestyle as hard work. Wonderful weather and rich natural resources offer an excellent backdrop for exploring an enormous range of opportunities to unwind, especially outdoors.

Getaways are as close as any one of dozens of local parks. Anglers can practice catch-and-release fishing at Almaden or Vasona Lake Park or along Coyote Creek. Windsurfing, water skiing, and sailing are possible on local reservoirs. Wooded hillsides, redwood forests, spectacular wildflower meadows, and deep canyons await discovery by hikers, mountain bikers, and people on horseback who have hundreds of miles of trails to roam. Playfields, expansive lawns, and barbecues beckon families who picnic while watching soccer, volleyball, and softball that seem to go on non-stop every weekend. And Raging Waters, the aquatic theme park out at Lake

Cunningham Regional Park will take you on a wet and wild ride into a giant pool.

Sports and Silicon valley seem to go hand-in-hand. One of the most dramatic changes in the valley took place with the advent of the Compaq Center, originally opened in 1993 as the San Jose Arena. The excitement of Shark-mania has taken the city by storm since the National Hockey League franchise won their first home game on arena ice against the New York Islanders, September 30, 1993. Spring through summer, the SaberCats play the new sport of arena football.

Municipal Stadium has been home to a number of minor league baseball franchises. The San Jose Giants, hometown favorites since 1988, draw crowds of several thousand to the stadium through the summer and fall for California League play.

SharkByte is one of San Jose's largest outdoor art exhibits. The six-foot long fiberglass sharks designed by local, regional, and national artists were displayed for three months before being sold at auction with proceeds benefiting local charities.

Major League Soccer intends to be America's fifth major sport. The San Jose Earthquakes made their debut at San Jose State's Spartan Stadium in 1996, and the Bay Area CyberRays inaugurated women's professional soccer at Spartan Stadium during the 2000 season.

The Silicon Valley Football Classic also debuted at Spartan Stadium the same year.

However, one of the best spectator sports takes place on 120 acres out on Berryessa Road, Wednesday through Sunday. Part international food extravaganza, part mini world's fair, part wholesale produce center, part rummage sale, part street theatre, part foreign marketplace, the Flea Market—considered the largest in the United States—is probably the best place for people-watching anywhere.

Landmarks and Attractions

Just a few minutes from downtown at Kelley Park, San Jose History Park has a complex of restored and replica buildings that give visitors a hands-on experience of nineteenth century Americana.

On the west side of downtown, the Municipal Rose Garden displays 3,500 trees and shrubs, representing 189 varieties of roses. The quiet Rose Garden neighborhood is also home to the Rosicrucian Egyptian Museum, one of the largest collections of ancient art, mummies, and artifacts on the West Coast. Nearby, the Winchester Mystery House is an elaborate but puzzling Victorian mansion built by Sarah Winchester over the course of thirty-eight years, evolving from her strange belief that she was appeasing the spirits of those killed by Winchester rifles. Magnificent carved stairways go nowhere in particular, and there are secret passageways and Tiffany stained glass windows in bizarre designs.

The oldest part of the city, San Pedro Square, has become a magnet for interesting new upscale restaurants, bistros, and sidewalk cafes with a mix of international cuisine—the kind one might find on the boulevards of Paris.

San Jose Museum of Art anchors the downtown cultural scene, with San Jose Museum of Quilts and Textiles offering extraordinary decorative arts collections close by. A short walk away, the Tech Museum of Innovation, hundreds of interactive exhibits, labs, and workshops, tells how Silicon Valley evolved from pastoral apricot orchards, flower farms, and pruneyards after the fruits of people's imagination changed the course of the world with a multi-billion dollar technological harvest. Here at the avante-garde looking mango and eggplant colored Tech, you can watch how a computer chip is made, "fly" with a jet pack simulator, or put on a mask and gloves to conduct a genetics experiment.

Nearby on Woz Way—named for Apple Computer co-founder and museum benefactor Steve Wozniak—is a lavender-colored structure with dramatic angles that is especially popular with families. At the Children's Discovery Museum, young minds can study the themes of community, connections, and creativity while, for example, finding out how electricity is generated, experimenting with water or exploring the artistic possibilities of recycled materials.

In Santa Clara, Paramount's Great America is a family favorite.

Other Diversions

The biggest names in the entertainment industry have found their way to San Jose. American Musical Theater of San Jose, the Bay Area's largest professional musical theater company, is here, as well as Opera San Jose, a professional regional opera company, and the brilliant Ballet San Jose of Silicon Valley. The new San Jose Repertory Theatre has added a fresh dimension to the entertainment scene and also will be home base for the San Jose Japanese Taiko drumming ensemble.

Day or evening, the ambiance of San Jose invites a closer look. Steadfast civic leadership driving a robust urban renaissance is in part responsible for San Jose being designated one of the safest cities in the country for five consecutive years. Adding to the appeal, warm days and cool nights most of the year are especially conducive to a California-casual dress code that's always acceptable. ■

University Avenue offers a leisurely promenade past the shops and cafes of downtown Palo Alto.

The cafes and bagel shops of Willow Glen are a favorite neighborhood Sunday morning hangout.

Silicon Valley's biggest names sponsor Downtown Ice, a new winter tradition, in an open-air rink near the Convention Center.

"The board and staff of the Santa Clara Valley Water District are committed to helping provide a healthy, safe, and enhanced quality of life for all who live and work in Santa Clara County. Serving nearly two million residents and commuters, we are conscious of our responsibility to each county resident—from the Silicon Valley CEO to the suburban soccer mom to the South County agricultural worker. Our contribution to this vision is to be practical, cost-effective, and environmentally sensitive in managing the valley's vital water resources."

—*Stanley M. Williams*
  CEO
  Santa Clara Valley Water District

Top: Menlo Park's main drag is Santa Cruz Avenue, the address of many fine restaurants and shops. Right: South First Billiards is an alternative attraction in a neighborhood of nightclubs and bars. Far right: The Agenda is one of a growing cluster of hot spots in SoFA, the South First Area, downtown San Jose's popular arts and entertainment district.

University Avenue drives straight through the middle of downtown Palo Alto, up to the gates of the Stanford University campus.

The wondrous exhibits of the Tech Museum of Innovation are perennially popular with locals and tourists alike. The museum was designed to promote technology through education and experience, and to inspire young minds to become leaders in the advancement of future technology. Behind the azure rotunda is the city's IMAX® Dome Theater.

Winchester Mystery House is a labyrinth of twisting hallways, a maze of rooms with false doors, and stairways that lead nowhere. It is said that Sarah Winchester never spent a consecutive night in the same room. Winchester Mystery House is open to the public for tours daily.

Left: Every exhibit at the Children's Discovery Museum can be climbed on or clambered over. The museum offers in excess of 150 interactive exhibits ranging from science and technology to arts and humanities. Opposite page: Designed for creative play, McEnery Park is a reprieve for workers, parents, and children in downtown San Jose. While the dragonflies linger above the river, visitors can picnic and play in green grass or refreshing water.

The Children's Bridge leads to Discovery Meadow, a park adjacent to the Children's Discovery Museum. The Meadow is the site of many summer festivals as it winds along the Guadalupe River.

Right: Carson House is former home of the New Almaden Quicksilver Mining Museum, historical monument to the oldest mines in California.

Bottom left, right, and opposite page: San Jose History Park is open for self-guided tours every day except Monday. Docents are stationed throughout the park, where visitors can ride a vintage trolley, tour a working print shop, eat at an old-fashioned ice cream parlor, and visit an antique fire station, gas station, and Chinese temple.

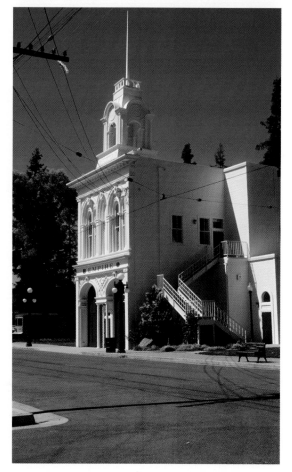

Roaring Camp in Felton is where the historic past of lumberjacks and gold prospectors still lives, along with America's last regular steam-powered passenger train service, Roaring Camp & Big Trees Narrow-Gauge Railroad.

*Happy Hollow Park
and Zoo™ in
Kelley Park has rides,
amusements and,
of course, a petting
zoo, as well as a
Puppet Theater.*

Left and bottom right: San Jose Repertory Theatre routinely draws crowds for major stage productions and touring acts through its professional premieres and comedies that have captivated European and U.S. audiences, alike. The organization offers outreach programs year-round for members of the community from children to adults, allowing others to discover the thrill of live theater for themselves. Bottom left: Towne 3, one of four Camera Cinemas and queen of the Alameda, boasts an eclectic marquee for a discerning audience. Featuring award-winning movies, first-run premieres, and restored classics, among others, these theaters are very popular in the valley. Opposite page: Statues guard the entrance of Rosicrucian Egyptian Museum, which houses the largest collection of ancient African artifacts in the western United States. The museum itself was inspired architecturally by the Temple of Amon at Karnak, and is surrounded by Rosicrucian Park, papyrus-lined paths along walls carved with hieroglyphs, clustered lotus columns, elaborate fountains, and colossal statues.

Opera San Jose, performing Elixir of Love *by Dorizetti, is a unique professional opera company. The Resident Company of Performing Artists specializes in showcasing the best young professional singers in the nation, and performs in the historic Montgomery Theater, one of the most intimate opera houses outside of Europe.*

Conductor Leonid Grin just celebrated ten years of leading the San Jose Symphony.

San Jose Stage Company is a professional theater company producing works of contemporary playwrights in "off-Broadway" fashion including The Colored Museum *by George C. Wolfe, but they also perform classics and adaptations such as* Of Mice and Men *by John Steinbeck.*

Masked merriment on stage in a Northside Theatre Company (NTC) production. A non-profit organization, NTC has been entertaining audiences for more than twenty years, receiving national attention for the development of new plays. The company is committed to promoting the integrity and importance of small theater organizations within the local arts community.

The furious action of lacrosse tramples the Stanford polo grounds.

Over recent years, the sport of golf has gained popularity throughout the country, and the Silicon Valley offers beautifully landscaped courses, including the San Jose Municipal Golf Course, for those who are regular players and those just starting the sport.

Top and opposite page bottom: San Jose's Major League Soccer team, the Earthquakes, play at Spartan Stadium. The team supports the community through endeavors such as the Earthquakes' Ball Kids, allowing underprivileged children interested in soccer, the opportunity to participate in the sport.

*Left: The San Jose Giants
are one of baseball's most
successful triple-A
franchises. Local fans
cherish the small-town
atmosphere, and are
led by Krazy George,
team mascot and
professional cheerleader.*

Silicon Valley's professional hockey team, the Sharks, defends the ice at the Compaq Center, formerly the San Jose Arena, also known as the "Shark Tank."

This page: Hellyer Park, renowned for its first-class dog park and velodrome bicycle racetrack facility, is still a family favorite for picnics, volleyball, and fishing.
Opposite page: Henry Coe State Park is one of many areas of open space that offer the pleasures of walking and hiking.

California's first civilian settlement and third largest city, the City of San José boasts an excellent quality of life and the nation's best public safety record of any metropolitan area. Encompassing 177 square miles with a population of almost one million people, the median household income is $71,000, and the climate averages 50 degrees in winter and 70 degrees in summer. San José also was the site of the state's first capital.

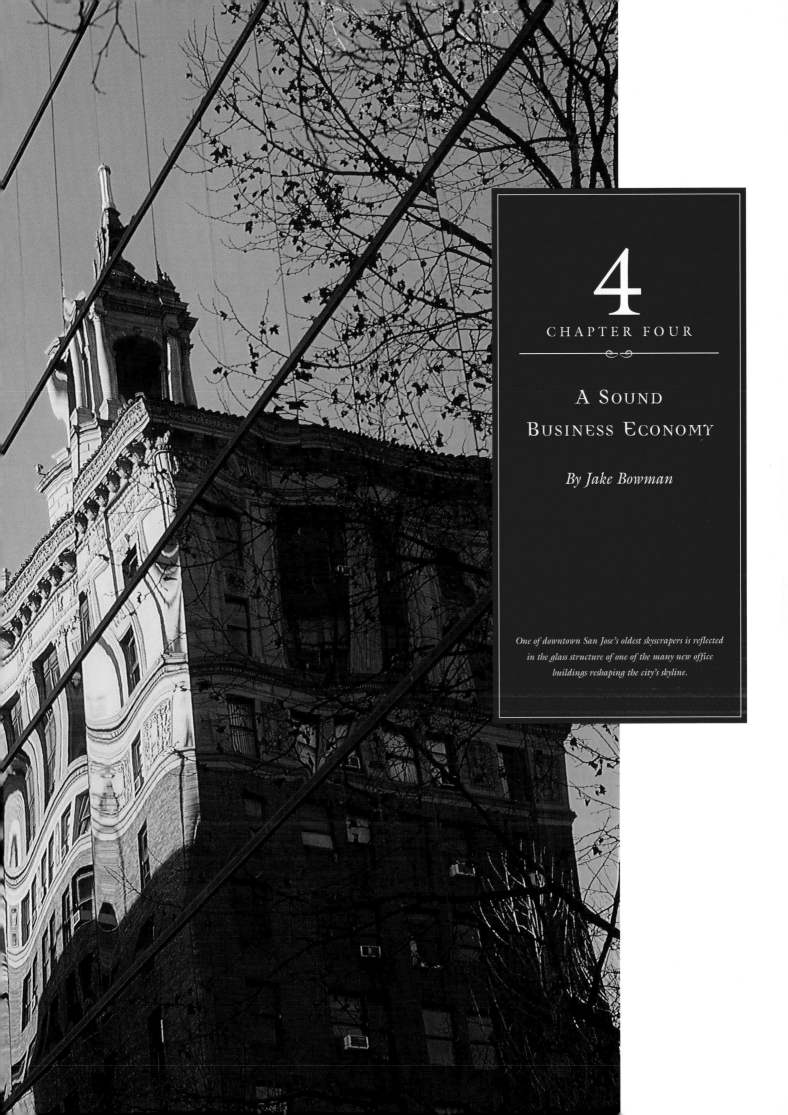

4

CHAPTER FOUR

A SOUND
BUSINESS ECONOMY

By Jake Bowman

One of downtown San Jose's oldest skyscrapers is reflected in the glass structure of one of the many new office buildings reshaping the city's skyline.

There is a foundation to business in the valley that lies far deeper than silicon. The secret to the Silicon Valley economy is less material than that common element. When most people think about the creation of wealth, they imagine the towers of Wall Street, the public markets where profitable enterprise becomes everybody's business. But the financial wizards of the West Coast inhabit a wider avenue. Sand Hill Road is the private market of the venture capitalists, where risky ideas are transmuted into profitable enterprise.

Venture capitalism is the institution of successful entrepreneurs supporting the risks of other entrepreneurs, based on the Western tradition of taking a chance on wide-open territory. After all, only a few generations passed between the settlement of the Old West and the opening of the new information technology frontier.

With all the news and noise surrounding high-tech hype, what's missing is an appreciation of the innovative culture in which all the valley's businesses are steeped. More than a century ago, as an example, the Mirassou brothers used "genetic engineering" to adapt French grape varieties to Santa Clara Valley soil, beginning California's climb to the top of the tradition-bound winemaking business. Venture capitalism is a revolution in an industry as ancient and artful as viticulture: financial services. It's the invention managing the money behind the inventors. In Silicon Valley, even the bankers are innovators.

The Business of Building New Economies

The local investment community took fortunes made in various ways—fruit canning, lumber, railroads, real estate, aerospace—and placed their bets on the technological talents coming out of local universities. Since then, there have been a Biotech Boom or two, the Personal Computer Revolution, a run on data storage, "browser wars," and the "dot-com" explosion that made venture capitalists a household acronym: "VCs."

The real Sand Hill Road is more than just an exclusive address for the offices of technology financiers. The growth planned here creates the wealth underlying the whole business community. Everyone, from construction worker to grocery clerk, benefits greatly from this powerful economic engine. More money was made in real estate here, for example, than in all the dot-com stock boom.

Venture capitalism isn't about technology, it's about taking risks on people with new ways of doing things. It's a whole philosophy about the way the valley does business.

Historic Trolley Car #2001 was built in 1928 by Officine Mechaniche Lodigiane in Lodi, Italy. Donated to the San Jose Trolley Corporation by the Italian government, the streetcar ran on the Milan tramway system until the mid-1980s. From the late 1880s to the late 1930s, electric trolleys operated in San Jose, Santa Clara, and throughout the County on nearly 130 miles of track at the peak of the era. The downtown historic streetcars are a celebration of the retro-fashionable technology of a bygone era.

San Pedro Square is now home to the downtown Farmers Market, which is a huge hit with executives looking for a fresh snack on their lunch break.

The Way of Venture Capitalism

Sand Hill Road begins where it intersects El Camino Real, the main boulevard running from San Jose through the heart of the valley, where it joins the leafy suburbs of Palo Alto and Menlo Park. El Camino is a descendant of the Royal Road of the Spanish Empire, which Padre Junipero Serra walked barefooted from Mexico City through California to consecrate the foundations of the Catholic missions. And, like El Camino, the legend of Sand Hill Road also begins with a journey into the unknown, a bold expedition into a new world led by believers on a mission to build outposts of knowledge.

All along the modern El Camino Real, every type of daily business from huge retailers to small independents is represented: antique shops and cinemas to vacuum parts and wrought iron dealers to dance schools and a chocolate factory. This entire community owes much of its thriving growth to the economic bounty brought forth from imagination into reality on Sand Hill.

From El Camino, the Sand Hill trail enters the oaks of the Stanford campus. The University is the prototype of the institution that supplies VCs with their most crucial resource: believers in technological dreams, like Jerry Yang, the student who programmed a guide to the early Internet with the indefatigable name of Yahoo! A few blocks away is the garage where Mr. Hewlett and Mr. Packard manufactured their first prototype.

As Sand Hill Road climbs toward the Santa Cruz Mountains, it is lined with the offices of VC institutions.

Running parallel to the road is the Stanford Linear Accelerator, which emphasizes the critical symbiosis of public investment in science and private investment in technology. The concentration of university, government, and private laboratories in these hills forms a nexus of the valley's innovation culture. None is more famous than Xerox Parc, "the Park," just off the road, where the mouse and "point 'n' click" graphical user interface were born.

At the top of the hill is the 280 Freeway, six fast lanes to boundless opportunity in both directions, connecting Silicon Valley with San Francisco through the oak-studded splendor of the Stanford Hills.

Driving Global Growth

While popular enthusiasm for everything "dot-com" has adjusted to more realistic proportions, the tireless machine of venture capitalism keeps on chugging. It ceaselessly assembles business plans for the next industrial revolutions, from the biotech frontiers of biocomputation, functional genomics, and proteomics, to the next generations of wireless networking, datacommunications, embedded processing, and the future wonders of nanotechnology.

The bottom line of this ongoing investment in the future is this: a sound foundation for everyday business in the Santa Clara Valley. This unique financial services industry, conceived in the lee of Sand Hill, is the never-finished craft of taking risks on new ideas. Its raw material—imagination—is the most boundless economic resource of all. ■

Right: Avalon on the Alameda is a new urbanist development with shopping on the streetfront and apartments above. Opposite page: The third-story pool deck of the Fairmont Hotel overlooks Cesar Chavez Park. Not only does the Fairmont have a reputation of elegance and excellence, but the hotel is known for its contributions to the community through fund-raisers and charitable events.

" S an Jose is an economic powerhouse supported by first class universities, a highly educated and skilled workforce and home to a concentrated and diverse range of businesses and industries—making it an ideal location for a financial institution like Heritage. We provide financial services to some of the most involved people in the area, and by investing in them, we invest in the future of this unique and innovative community."

—*Brad L. Smith*
Chairman & CEO
Heritage Commerce Corp

Right: The Los Gatos Brewing Company is one of the institutions of this town's dining scene. Microbreweries, such as Gordon Biersch in San Jose, are a palate-cleansing foundation of valley cuisine, with the house beer selection rivaling the wine list in significance on many fine menus. Opposite page: The most mouth-watering appetizer in Los Gatos is a stroll down the street, with stops to read all the menus. Entertaining the taste buds is big business in all the valley's civic centers.

San Pedro Square is downtown's arts and entertainment district, with restaurants, bistros, cafes, and a microbrewery offering European-style patio dining, all within walking distance of theaters, hotels, and performance venues.

"Working in Silicon Valley is an exciting proposition. Technology itself so rapidly evolves and changes, and the economies of the area change along with it. What remains the same for Heuristics is the continual challenging task of finding highly qualified software specialists that guarantee the success of our valley clients. We have the privilege of increasing a company's major asset—its people."

—Elizabeth Patrick
CEO
Heuristics Search, Inc.

This page: Ongoing revitalization of Cupertino City Center will add residential units and a hotel to the offices and retail space, rounding out the urban character of this complex. Opposite page: The restored art deco Civic Auditorium is part of San Jose's downtown convention and cultural complex.

"Our business culture includes a commitment to Total Quality, which is driven by three fundamental principles: continuous improvement, employee empowerment, and satisfying customer needs.

"Continuous improvement means never being satisfied with our performance. Employee empowerment ensures that the knowledge and skills of our workers are brought to bear on our customers' behalf. In the end, satisfying our customers is the ultimate measure of our success."

—*Patrick Edsell*
President and CEO
Spectra-Physics

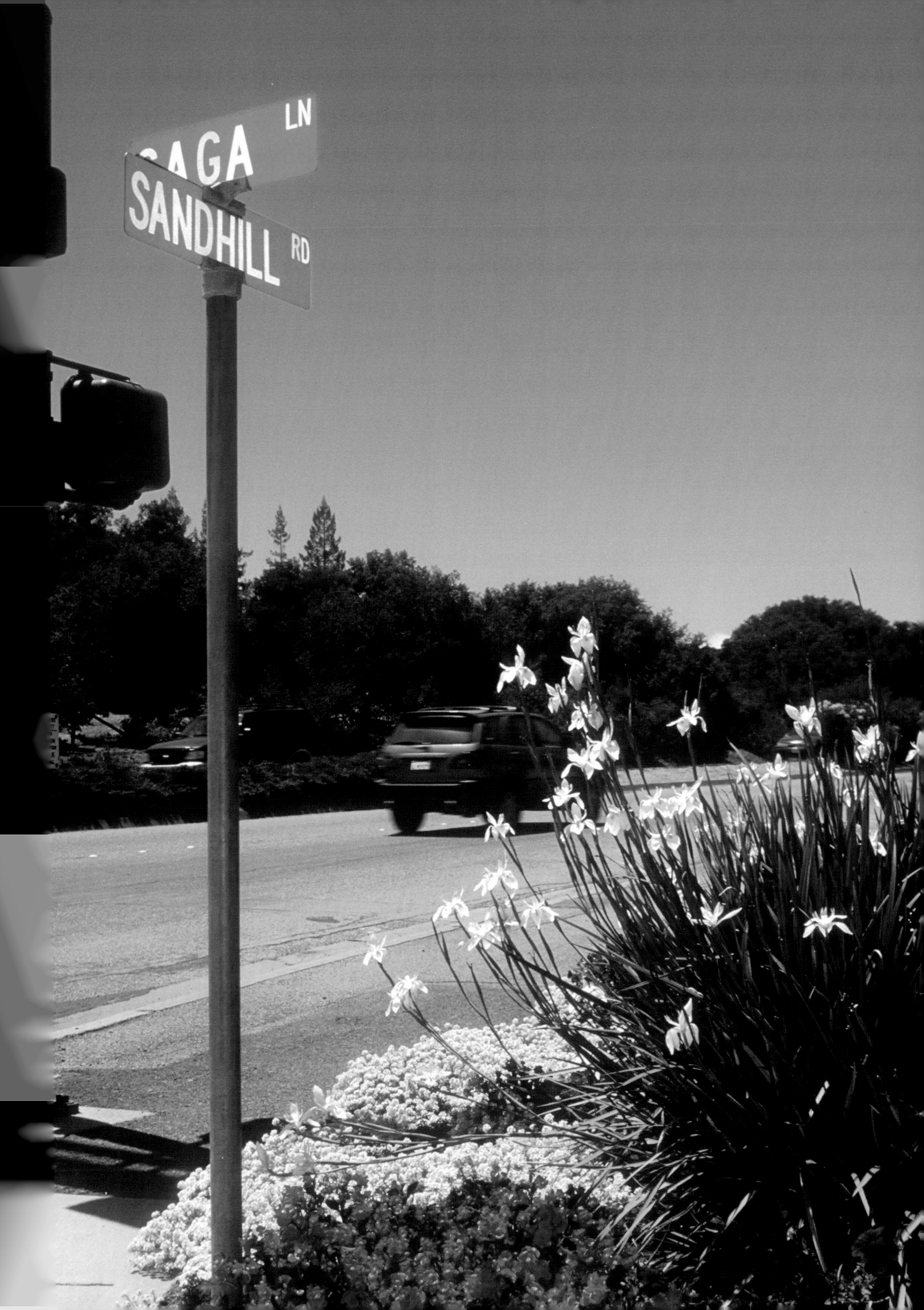
LN
SANDHILL RD

West San Carlos Street
near I-880 is the oldest
center of the Korean
business community
in the valley.
Opposite page: Sand
Hill Road, the West
Coast version of Wall
Street, far removed
from the ordinary
Financial District of
San Francisco, it is the
exclusive address of
venture capitalism.

Left: Hicklebee's
bookstore is a favorite
of Willow Glen's
children and a pillar
of the Lincoln Street
business community.
Far left: Lion Shopping
Center is really the
institution of Mr. Henry
Tran, an entrepreneur
who built his fortune on
Lion Supermarkets,
providing quality Asian
and American foods
for the valley's ethnic
melting pot.

Stanford "satellite dish" is not just the goal of a Cardinal collegiate athlete's grueling uphill jog. The Stanford Radio Telescope Antenna stands as a reminder of the university and public sector's commitment to investing in world-class research facilities, which give birth to the next great ideas.

Although the
number of orchards in
the valley has been
reduced as the area
has been opened to
technological
advancements,
pomology and
viticulture, the
sciences of fruit trees
and vines, have
managed to benefit
with the development
of more effective and
environmentally
safe pesticides.

The Wine Tanks at
Mirassou Vineyards are
enormous vats at the
heart of the winery
business. Santa Clara
County once harvested
more than 12,000 acres
of vineyards, and
though the number has
been reduced over the
decades by prohibition
and, later, by other
industries that have
taken root in the valley,
some of the oldest wine-
making families in
America still carry on
the tradition through
years of dedication
and perseverance.

Right: Andy's Pets is a landmark of the Alameda, a historic boulevard running from San Jose to Santa Clara. Bottom: Gelato shops and cafés line the side-walks of Castro Street in downtown Mountain View, which has come a long way from being a Naval base town of Moffett Field. Opposite page: The giant pineapple in the median at Mercado Santa Clara is the Hawaiian symbol for welcome.

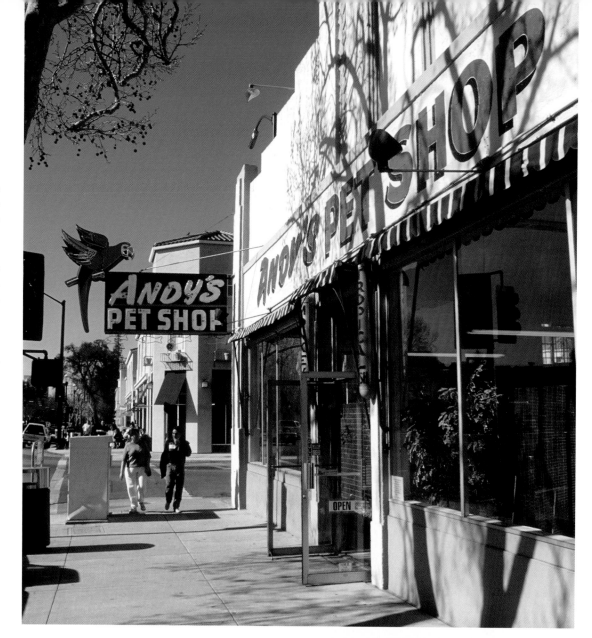

Historic downtown Campbell boasts new urbanist developments with everything from Stacks' eatery to the Unity Bookstore on the ground floor.

Right: Ainsley House on the Orchard City Green is a historical museum located in a historic Roaring Twenties era home. Opposite page: Pruneyard, the commercial center of Campbell, was once known for it abundance of dried plums.

The Dumbarton Bridge spans the southern tip of San Francisco Bay, connecting Stanford and Palo Alto with Hayward on the other side, while Hoover Tower gazes across the water at Mount Diablo.

Top: Traffic is fast and free on 280 in the late afternoon. The "most beautiful freeway in the world" is Silicon Valley's most coveted commute, linking the financial center of Sand Hill Road to San Francisco and San Jose. Left: San Jose International Airport serves Paris, the Americas, and Pacific Rim, linking the valley to technology centers from Japan to Taiwan, including the "nerd bird" flight to Austin, Texas.

Top: The Alviso Slough is a scenic byway of the South Bay's precious wetland wildlife habitat, but in the late 1800s, it served a more vital purpose when the Guadalupe River was realigned with it to create greater access from the south bay to the Port of Alviso.

Right: Passing through Alviso station, the Amtrak Capitol route links Silicon Valley to Oakland and the state capital, Sacramento.

Originally incorporated by San Jose to give the city a port on San Francisco Bay, Alviso has retained its small-town atmosphere and open spaces.

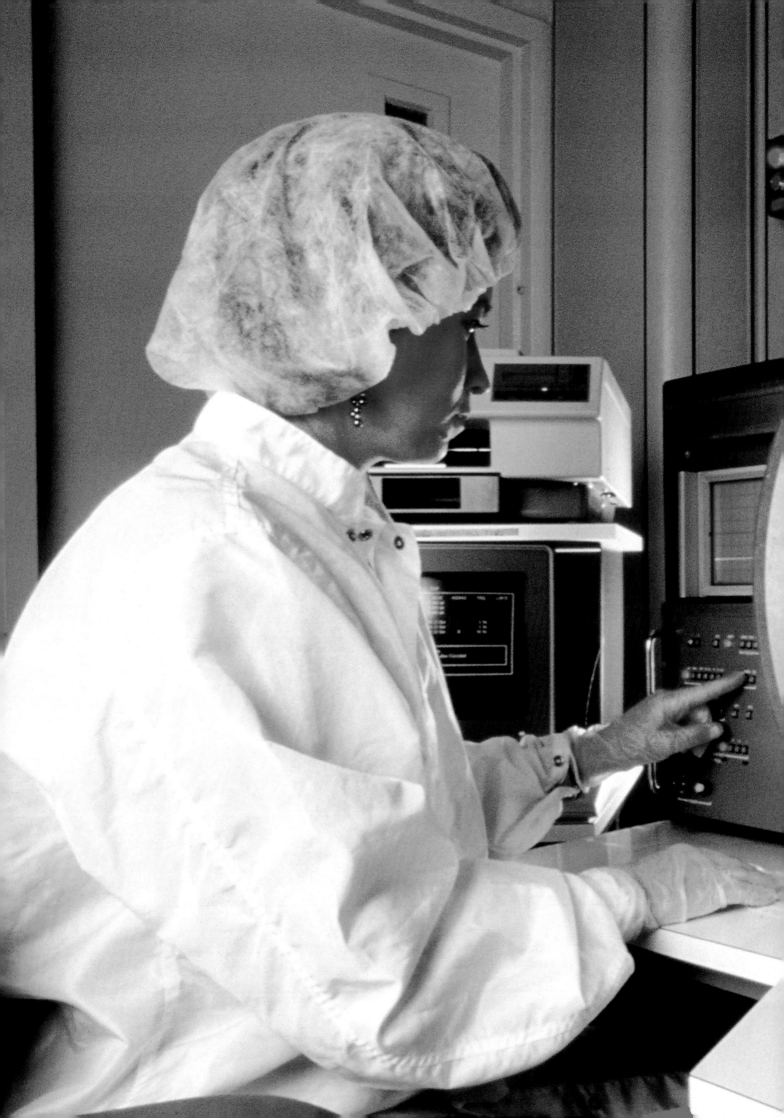

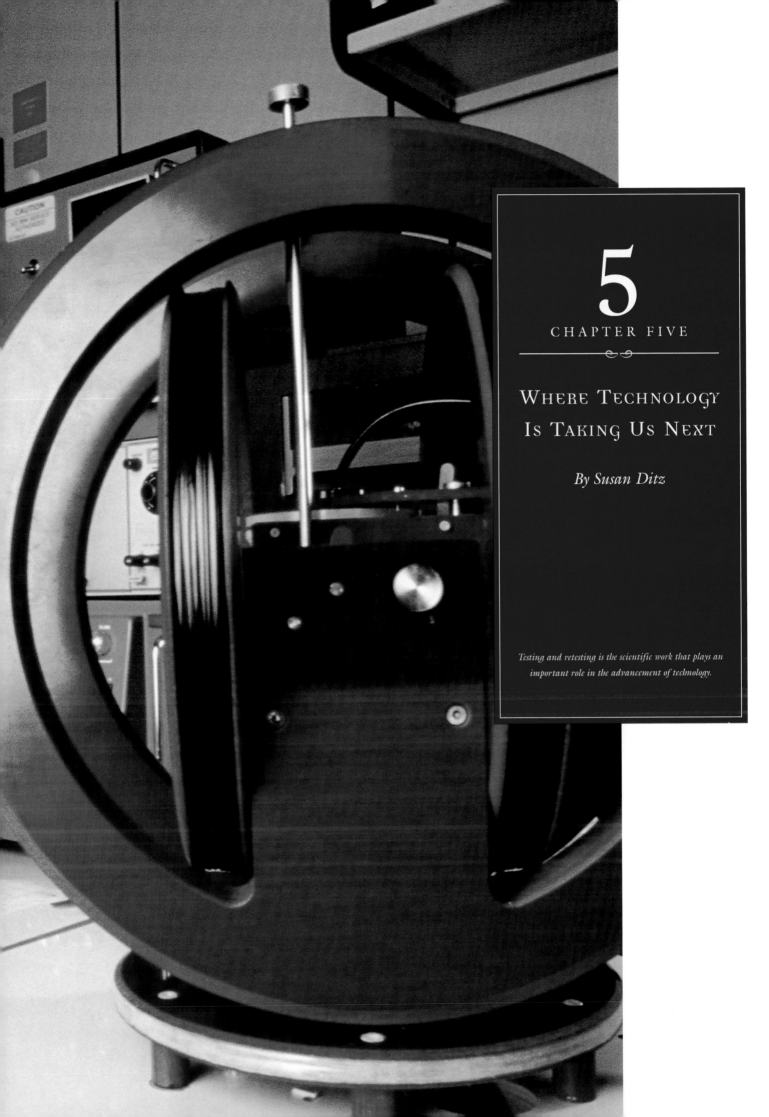

5

WHERE TECHNOLOGY
IS TAKING US NEXT

By Susan Ditz

*Testing and retesting is the scientific work that plays an
important role in the advancement of technology.*

Right: Children discover the Intel Qx3 Microscope in the Intel Museum Learning Lab during the Kid to Work Day class sponsored by Intel Corporation.

The mobile communications industry is undergoing a global growth surge, changing not only how business is conducted worldwide, but also significantly altering the way people live. Apple, 3Com, Palm, Lucent Technologies, and many other Silicon Valley companies are at the forefront of this wireless revolution, regularly making news with exciting advances.

The mobile device market is expected to exceed $18 billion in revenues by 2004, a jump of more than 500 percent in just four years.

The foundation of this emerging technology, named Bluetooth after an ancient Danish king, developed as a result of an alliance between Intel, Ericsson, Nokia, IBM, and Toshiba. It enables numbers of devices to talk to each other using a secure radio frequency so that, for example, a person in Boston can sit in on a meeting in San Jose and transmit images from a camera to a printer in the San Jose conference room. Bluetooth is expected to have a crucial impact on cellular phones, facilitating truly hands-free use.

Using radio waves for transmitting data is a technology that's been around awhile, but the original standard was slow and cumbersome for many applications. Another enabler of the recent boom is the approval of a much higher transmission rate to 11Mbps (megabytes per second). Although the primary focus in the near term is likely to be on improving the quality of messaging, directories, and games, mobile multimedia is not far off, especially as companies improve the Wireless Application Protocol (WAP) to develop better ways for people to access Internet pages through cell phones or other wireless devices.

Bottom: This ubiquitous communications tower transmits microwave signals to cell phones, laptops, and pocket organizers throughout the valley.

Mobile Technology for a Mobile Workforce

Until recently, the primary business consumers of wireless technology were manufacturing facilities, warehouses, and retail operations. Companies have grown accustomed to receiving packages from courier services who use devices to track delivery. Now our global workforce is increasingly spread around the world, with the pressing need for easy access to a network of information regardless of where they are and what time it may be.

3Com spin-off Palm pioneered with the development of its line of Palm Pilot PDAs (personal digital assistants) already a key business tool, now streamlining the work of health-care providers. Life-saving information can be obtained almost instantly in an ambulance, at the office, or the patient's bedside. Doctors and nurses can use a PDA for rapid access to crucial drug information, diagnostic tools, lab tests, or patient records, reducing the chance of error and helping patients take a more proactive role in their care.

The impact of mobile computing on home health care is equally promising. Where once a Type I diabetic would have to regularly go to a doctor's office for blood work and monitoring, this can now be done from home via a PDA, saving money, time and reducing patient loads. Also, using the new generation of wireless devices, visiting nurses can more effectively manage hospice patients at home, improving the quality of life for the terminally ill and their families.

Wireless Goes To School

Opportunities to learn are vastly widened with the Internet. Yet, hard wiring limits how learning takes place in a classroom. The advent of wireless technology means that students can move a computer around rather than be restricted by the location of a phone jack for a modem.

Apple Computer and Lucent Technologies have teamed up to launch AirPort, which lets up to ten users access the Internet at the same time on one line from a base unit less than 150 feet away. A class can move outside on a warm day. Students can work more collaboratively, and they no longer have to wait to get on the computer lab schedule. Laptops can be loaded on to a cart to bring the power of the Internet to students in a lecture hall, the library, or a classroom.

At home, at work, or in school, wireless technology offers the promise of much more to come. Researchers at Hewlett Packard Labs have created their vision of the future called "CoolTown" where "people, places, and things are all first class citizens of the Web". Here anyone can see how smart appliances will eventually recognize us by our voices or other personalized "fingerprints" and be affordable enough to allow everyone to be connected to the Web.

Home appliances likely will be networked via a central management system, a concept pioneered by Sun Microsystems in the last decade. The oven, for example, may be turned on remotely by cell phone so that dinner is ready when a family returns from a busy day.

New vehicles already are equipped to be wireless mobile appliances, and technology is contributing to increased safety options. Right now, top-of-the-line cars are equipped to signal the immediate dispatch of emergency services to the vehicle when onboard computers detect the airbags have been deployed.

Silicon Valley companies are developing new wireless and other technological innovations that will play a key role not only in making our lives easier, but safer as well. ■

The clean suit is referred to as the "bunny suit" by those who wear the indispensable uniform, which protects the equipment from contamination.

Scientists continuously experiment with technology, creating new software and applications to generate more efficient products to be used by the business community, educational programs, and individual people.

Adobe is one of the growing number of enterprises that have located its San Jose corporate headquarters downtown.

*Left and bottom:
Sometimes called the
"Birthplace of Silicon
Valley," the Hewlett-
Packard Garage at
367 Addison Avenue is
where William Hewlett
and David Packard
first developed their
product and conducted
business. There is a
plaque marking the site.*

"While the Semiconductor Capital Equipment market—which includes Automatic Test Equipment (ATE)—is a cyclical industry, it is also an expanding industry. Every year more products are conceived or redesigned to incorporate chips. Because we increasingly rely on semiconductors, the issue of their consistent and continual performance is critical. By virtue of being an ATE company that designs and manufactures highly reliable, accurate testers, Advantest ensures that computer-based products in our homes, hospitals, offices, and defense systems work when we need them to work. As semiconductors evolve, Advantest evolves as well to help create the environment of the future."

—*Nick Konidaris*
President and Chief Executive Officer
Advantest America

San Jose McEnery Convention Center plays host to dozens of major technology-oriented trade shows and conferences each year.

"It's a new economy—a revolutionary economy of ubiquitous electronics, driven by escalating consumer demand. Our job is to collaborate with designers of next-generation systems and help them get new products to market faster. Our customers must solve multiple, complex problems and integrate potentially disparate functions into a cohesive system.

"We're fortunate at Cadence in having the opportunity to deliver on the dreams of technologists who really understand what it takes to do this. Our innovative solutions readily adapt to the emerging standards of this revolutionary technology."

—*Ray Bingham*
President and Chief Executive Officer
Cadence Design Systems, Inc.

Some of the world's
largest technology
fairs are hosted by
San Jose McEnery
Convention Center.

This PG&E Substation is an integral part of the energy infrastructure, which allows the digital city to keep beeping and blinking.

"The world is going digital—and it is running on Intel silicon. Intel technology is at the center of this digital world, from the PCs that enhance the value of personal devices and enable flexible business, to the silicon at the heart of personal wireless devices, to servers and networking gear that connect those PCs and devices, to new servers that provide unprecedented performance. Intel's silicon leadership, manufacturing strengths, and skill in enabling industry standards will play key roles in delivering this vision for businesses and consumers: networks everywhere, connecting clients everywhere, to servers everywhere."

—*Craig Barrett*
President and CEO
Intel Corporation

left and opposite page: The most valuable commercial property in the valley is invisible. The land this tower stands on is excellent property on Coleman Avenue, but the electromagnetic waves all around it are sea lanes of the new merchant empires.

Laptops are as common as berets and goatees at Café Matisse on South First Street. Every coffeeshop is a cybercafe when the wireless crowd is sporting cell phones and palmtops.

"Keeping up with rapidly changing technology means staying ahead of it, anticipating it, and continually evolving. In the Silicon Valley, we are surrounded by the technologies that shape the way we do business, communicate, be entertained, and, essentially, live. Sony understands these technologies, and we are constantly seeking ways to transform them into products that bring new lifestyle benefits to our customers. This is the Sony brand promise—one that will continue for years to come."

—Fujio Nishida
President and Chief Operating Officer
Sony Electronics Inc.

Many cafés offer free wireless Internet connectivity, meaning you can check the weather by looking out the window or through Windows. At the Orchard Valley Internet Café, Campbell residents can wake up to the invigorating qualities of fresh java and broadband.

Right: University of California's Lick Observatory overlooks the entire valley from the heights of Mount Hamilton, an ideal spot for astronomical research. When the original 36-inch refractor telescope was completed in 1888, it was the largest of its kind in the world. Opposite page: A glorious future of infinite bandwidth meets the hard reality of pipe and concrete. Downtown San Jose is installing a massive fiber optic conduit to keep pace with the ever-changing technology in the area.

"The solutions necessary to manage this new age of digital information go beyond the conventions of storage management, which are tactically focused on simply "parking" and protecting data. In the digital marketplace, data achieves its maximum strategic value and impact when in motion, allowing it to be rapidly accessed, shared, replicated, and manipulated in critical applications at every level of enterprise. VERITAS Software keeps data in motion by enabling reliable, unfettered delivery across diverse computing environments, from the desktop to the data center."

—*Gary Bloom*
  President and CEO
  VERITAS Software

6
CHAPTER SIX

GIVING BACK,
THE VALLEY WAY

By Susan Ditz

*The Great Carousel at the entrance of Paramount's
Great America is a symbol of the park's commitment to
childhood and innocence, exemplified by the annual
Carousel to Coaster charity event. Little ones win medals
and earn ribbons in the annual 5k run and walk, which
benefits the Friends of Santa Clara Parks & Recreation.*

*The Center for the
Performing Arts is a
hub of artistic and
cultural events,
especially theater,
concert music, ballet,
and opera. Many of
its participants, such as
the San Jose Symphony,
are supported by
corporate sponsorship.*

Young Silicon Valley entrepreneurs who became wealthy in the wake of successful Internet IPOs are driving the evolution of the latest innovation in charitable giving. Inspired by the examples of William Hewlett, David Packard, Andy Grove, and Bill Gates, this new generation of technology pioneers is building on the venture philanthropy concept, investing both financial and intellectual resources to effect change in the community.

Silicon Valley is remarkably generous. Research shows 83 percent of households in the region give to charity versus just 69 percent nationally. Among high net worth households the figure is 94 percent. A prime example is seen in the way individuals such as Gib Myers of the Mayfield Fund, eBay Vice President Jeff Skoll, and others stepped up to the plate in 1999, donating $14 million to bail out the ailing United Way and ensure that more than

100 local member agencies depending on funding received it. The crisis sparked renewed participation in the United Way among Silicon Valley executives, and now the agency, under dynamic new leadership, is back on track.

However, a 1999 study commissioned by the Community Foundation Silicon Valley revealed that many people in their 20s, 30s, 40s, and 50s in the area have money and talent to contribute, yet often lack the time or the experience to evaluate charitable causes and make informed investments in them.

Seeing an obvious opportunity, venture capitalist Kevin Fong, Infoseek founder Steve Kirsh, and Laura Arrillaga, whose family's foundation has been a major contributor to Stanford University, agreed to spearhead a new fund for young donors called SV2 (Silicon Valley Social Venture Fund). The trio of friends uses informal social gatherings and

a lot of networking to focus on involving young "partners" directly in the philanthropy process by educating and informing them about existing needs, encouraging them to use their skills in mentoring non-profits, and pooling expertise to support collaborative solutions to social challenges.

The strategy is to make being charitable reasonably painless for first-time givers, and the concept is clearly gaining momentum. There are now over 100 members and the fund has raised more than $1 million in just over a year.

The SV2 grants are targeted toward high-impact, high-social return, local charitable causes, and projects with education a priority—but not the only one. SV2 gave its first grant of $225,00 last year to Project HELP, a year-round early academic intervention program designed to provide quality supplemental academic instruction to low-income, under-performing public elementary school students. The group also awarded $225,000 over three years to Child Advocates of Santa Clara and San Mateo Counties, an organization that trains volunteers to act as court-appointed advocates for children of the Juvenile Dependency Court so they don't "fall through the cracks." Individual SV2 donors also have announced they are pooling financial resources to fund $153,000 in grants to two other educational agencies this year, East Side College Prep in East Palo Alto and Downtown College in San Jose.

Internet Enables More Inclusive Philanthropy

The explosion of the World Wide Web and e-commerce has created extraordinary new opportunities for people to give money in support of worthwhile causes. Silicon Valley has its share of visionaries who have seen the potential for Internet good works.

Father of two and a former teacher, Rea Callender, CEO of SchoolPop, may be one of the valley's most popular parents. He could see the possibilities for rescuing financially strapped U.S. schools as he watched people embrace the Amazon.com concept.

As a result, two years ago he bootstrapped SchoolPop, currently one of the most successful online fundraising vehicles for K-12 schools nationwide and a standard-bearer for online cause-related marketing. He says the company was built on "support shopping," which ensures that every e-commerce transaction executed provides some financial benefit to a favored cause.

SchoolPop shoppers visit hundreds of merchants such as Amazon.com, Tower Records, JCPenney, and Lands' End and have up to 20 percent of the purchase contributed to the school of their choice. Schools also generate revenue from other sources on the site including search engines, long distance telephone services, financial services, and credit cards.

Meanwhile everyone is winning. Last quarter they generated an extra $2.5 million for schools across the country.

Along with events like the Silicon Valley Charity Ball that put a local twist on more traditional fund-raising organizations, Silicon Valley continues to be a region where finding "out of the box" creative solutions to social problems is part of the rhythm of life. ■

Across Market Street from the gurgling fountains of Cesar Chavez Park, stands The Tech Museum of Innovation. The plaques commemorating the donors who made the museum possible read like a who's who of Silicon Valley movers and shakers.

"California's Historic Estate for the Arts," Villa Montalvo, is now home to Montalvo, a multidisciplinary nonprofit organization formed by the citizens of Saratoga to hold the trusteeship of these public buildings. The century-old, Mediterranean-style former mansion of James Phelan, three times mayor of San Francisco and the state's first popularly-elected Senator, sits on 175 acres of the Saratoga foothills, most of which is now a County Park. Senator Phelan bequeathed his house in his will to the public as a school for art, music, literature, and architecture.

"It is an amazing feeling to be able to help so many charitable causes, and it truly reflects the diversified culture and solid values of the people who have helped make Adaptec the success story that it has become. I am proud that here at Adaptec we have some of the most giving and caring people that you'll find in any organization and for us to be able to help the community through various programs and contributions is something that brings a great deal of self-worth back to each one of our employees."

—Linda Thompson
   Director of Human Resource Development and
   the Corporate Contributions Programs
   Adaptec

"Air Systems Foundation, Inc., passionately supports numerous programs and charities throughout Silicon Valley and Santa Clara County with the ultimate mission of 'building our children's future.' We raise the funds to achieve this goal primarily through the Air Systems Car Show & Family FunFest and scheduled appearances by our mascot— the Messenger II Starship. In doing so, we consistently honor our fundamental belief that the most positive, powerful, and enduring influences in children's lives result from the direct participation of families and the entire community."

—*Christine Davis*
President
Air Systems Foundation, Inc.

This page: Townsend Park, located on San Jose's north side, is now one of many children's playgrounds downtown. The generous donation of several major corporate citizens made the revitalization of this neighborhood possible. Opposite page: Renowned local sculptor John Battenburg's work decorates Murphy Street, downtown Sunnyvale. Corporate and public patronage supports a thriving local art scene.

Right: United Way Silicon Valley enjoys the support of a wide business community, including the San Francisco 49ers football club.

Bottom: Local corporations such as IBM are dedicated to public education. Area businesses realize that this community contribution is like an investment in the future labor market of high-tech workers.

"Education is everyone's business. At IBM in Silicon Valley our Reinventing Education grant with San Jose Unified School District improves teacher preparation. IBM is working to assure that all children receive a quality education and that the educational system itself continually improves. By focusing our student's education on a curriculum based on world-class standards, on data-driven assessments of both the system and the students to drive continual improvement, and on accountability of all to meet established goals when resources have been provided, we expect that students will be prepared for challenging careers and lifelong learning in our community."

—*Dr. Ted Olsson*

Manager for Corporate Community Relations for the Western U.S.

IBM

The Silicon Valley
Charity Ball (SCVB)
was organized in 1986
by a small group of
business people and
friends who recognized
the needs of those less
fortunate in the area,
and were aware of the
community's desire to
give back. The SCVB
Board of Directors and
Committee members
consist entirely of vol-
unteers whose hard
work is celebrated each
year by the annual
charity ball, which is
not just another
fundraising event for
local nonprofit organi-
zations, but the height
of the social season.

Santa Clara native Michael Bonfante sold his successful grocery store chain, Nob Hill Foods, to realize his dream of creating a socially and environmentally sound amusement park. The Bonfante Gardens is a community charity funding public works in natural preservation, environmental stewardship, and ecological education.

Strange and wondrous figures of the Circus Trees grow in Bonfante Gardens. These natural sculptures of sycamore were rescued from a forgotten plot in Santa Cruz and the obscurity of their visionary creator, a farmer named Axel Erlandson.

Left: The Cherub Fountain decorates the gardens of Winchester Mystery House. Coins tossed into the fountain are donated to Books Aloud, a charity that records books on tape for the blind and others who are unable to enjoy the pleasure of reading directly.

Bottom: One of the most popular and successful forms of corporate contribution to the community is in the form of human resources. Intel employees visit Oak Grove High School to share high-tech and real-world experience as part of the Innovation in Education Program.

"Therma, Corp., takes 'giving' very seriously. The corporate logo includes the image of an outstretched hand designed into the Capital 'T.' We have been very fortunate over the years, and we feel it is essential that we give back. Our expectation is that by giving to those who are less advantaged, they in turn will help someone else along the way."

—Joe and Nicki Parisi,
Co-founders
Therma, Corp.

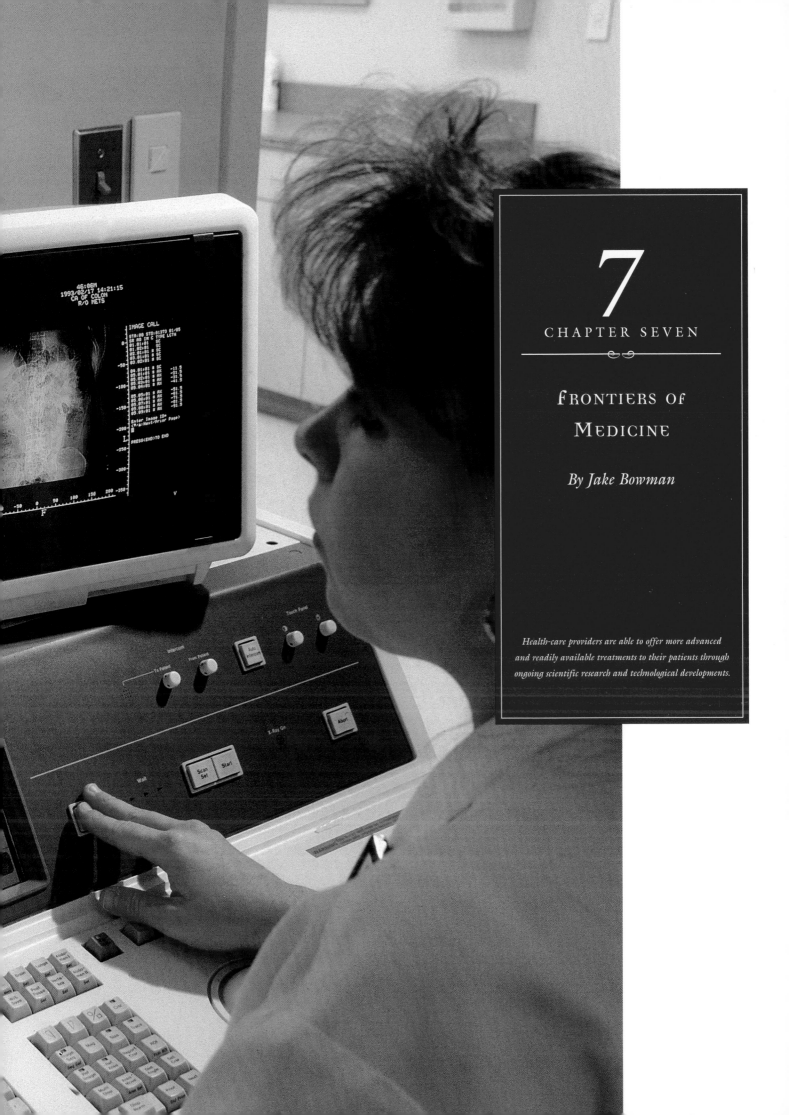

7
CHAPTER SEVEN

FRONTIERS OF MEDICINE

By Jake Bowman

Health-care providers are able to offer more advanced and readily available treatments to their patients through ongoing scientific research and technological developments.

When the twentieth century began, the Santa Clara Valley was a rural area on the frontier of Western medicine. San Jose's first doctor, Benjamin Cory, started up the area's first health-care facility, County Hospital, in 1876. The Santa Clara County Medical Association was founded the same year. These early pioneers laid the foundation for a century of innovation, transforming a Western frontier town into a metropolis on the frontier of medical science and practice.

From children to adults, from preventive medicine to advanced procedures valley residents can be assured of receiving quality health care through a number of facilities located in the area.

The valley's health-care system is on the foremost edge of research and community service, exemplified by such leading institutions as San Jose Medical Center, which opened in 1923. Nowadays, the facility houses a rehabilitation center, a specialized staff for sleep disorders, the county's designated trauma center, and a leading cancer care institute. The rehabilitation center, for example, is a cutting edge simulation of real life challenges posed for patients relearning how to perform everyday tasks, while the trauma center features helipads to fly in challenging trauma cases from surrounding counties. Beyond the merely technological advancements, San Jose is a leader in humanizing the health-care experience and educating the community about the hospital.

The focus on education began early, when the first training program, a nursing school with three students, was established in 1903, and the first

internship began in 1908. In 1959, a residency program affiliated with Stanford University was introduced, the beginning of a long and fruitful relationship. A decade later, the Surgery Department was integrated with Stanford and the Institute for Medical Research formed the following year. In the 1970s, the Department of Medicine became formally affiliated with Stanford, leading to internships, joint recruiting, and Integrated Medicine fellowships.

A Pediatric and Maternity Unit was added in 1939 and 1940 to what would eventually become known as the Santa Clara Valley Medical Center. In 1952, the Valley Medical Center was one of the first hospitals in the nation to be accredited by the Joint Commission for the Accreditation of Hospitals. The original County Hospital building was demolished in 1968 and the construction of modern facilities continues: the Rehabilitation Center was completed in 1970, the West Wing with the new Intensive and Transitional Care Units in 1990, and the new Main Hospital building opened in 1999.

The valley's other medical institutions, lasting until the present day, also were founded near the turn of the century. In 1889, Judge Myles P. O'Connor opened a sanitarium, known as a nursing home today, which would become O'Connor Hospital. The Daughters of Charity of St. Vincent de Paul have historically provided the nursing backbone of this institution. It was the valley's first private hospital and the setting for the area's first nursing school, which was created in 1903.

The end of the World War I ushered in a modern medical emergency of catastrophic proportions that transformed the nascent local health-care industry. During the influenza pandemic that killed half a million U.S. citizens in twelve months, temporary facilities were set up in numerous public buildings. The San Jose Normal School, now San José

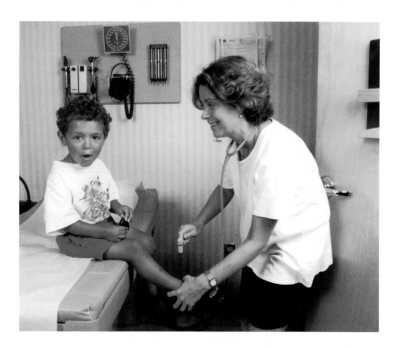

The San Jose Fire Department is the designated First Responder to incidents reported in fire response areas, but other emergency medical services are provided by American Medical Response (AMR).

State University, was turned into a makeshift hospital, where students and faculty were drafted to cook meals and assist with nursing duties. To reduce the spread of the disease, people wore masks when they went out in public.

In 1924, the roots were planted for what was to become a world-renowned model of group practice: the Palo Alto Medical Clinic. Later, it would become known as the Palo Alto Medical Foundation. The clinic's growth was based on the concept that each partner's vote carried equal weight. That policy, which was extended to every new partner, became a cornerstone of the clinic's health-care model, which remains in effect today. Oakland-based Kaiser Permanente actually pioneered the concept of pre-payment in 1933, when it contracted to care for workers on the Los Angeles Aqueduct project, but it was the Palo Alto Clinic that introduced the idea in the Santa Clara Valley in 1946, by contracting with Stanford University to take care of all of its students for $5 a semester each.

Today, the effort to extend the benefits of breakthrough medical research and biotechnology to all the valley's inhabitants enjoys broad support in municipal government. Santa Clara County has expressed the political will to make universal healthcare coverage happen for every citizen, following on the success of several innovative programs for children, the elderly, and the disadvantaged. With a majority of San Francisco residents voting for universal municipal health care recently, the Silicon Valley may have started a regional trend. Another century of firsts on the frontiers of medicine has begun. ■

This page: San Jose Medical Center, along with other local facilities, is a fine example of the top-notch health-care services available in a general acute-care hospital. Opposite page: Palo Alto Medical Foundation is now part of Sutter Health, a northern California network of physicians based in Sacramento.

Part of the Stanford University Medical Center health-care system, Stanford Hospital applies the latest in biomedical research to the health-care challenges of a booming region.

O'Connor Hospital in Santa Clara is one of the many endowments of the Honorable J.P. O'Connor, an Irishman who came to America in 1838 to study law. He made his fortune in mining, settled in San Jose, and was elected to the State Assembly and Senate. It's now a part of the Catholic Healthcare West system.

First-class obstetrics
and gynecology facilities
include the finest in
pre- and post-natal
care. Columbia Good
Samaritan has a Level
III rated Neonatal
Intensive Care Unit,
providing the best
available care for
high-risk newborns and
premature births.

San Jose City College is a leading member of the vocational and occupational educational system, which supports the technical job market, including health care.

Physical therapy and rehabilitation services are offered by local health-care systems such as San Jose Medical Center, Santa Clara Valley Medical Center, and Kaiser Permanente, and include a range of specialists such as physical and occupational therapists, speech-language pathologists, social workers, and psychologists.

From the time she was a student at Stanford in the 1930s, Lucile Salter volunteered at what was then the Stanford Home for Convalescent Children. Now Lucile Salter Packard Children's Hospital is an integral part of the Stanford University Healthcare system.

8

CHAPTER EIGHT

EDUCATIONAL
OPPORTUNITIES
ABOUND

By Connie Young Yu

*Tower Hall's ivy-covered tower commands the quad of
San José State University.*

With education as its lifeblood, San Jose has the extraordinary distinction of having the highest percentage of college graduates of any city in the United States. While Silicon Valley has attracted well-educated professionals from all over the world, many of the graduates are from colleges in Santa Clara Valley. Outstanding educational opportunities are available in and around San Jose, and graduates of local colleges remain here to live and work.

San Jose's excellent public school districts are among California's best, and certainly some of the most diverse and innovative. Highly-rated elementary and middle schools offer something for every K-12 child, with a number of magnet programs at the elementary level feeding into focused high school programs. San Jose High School, for example, San Jose's first and for nearly a century its only public high school, continues a tradition of excellence with its highly acclaimed International Baccalaureate college preparatory program. In other K-12 schools throughout the area, there are visual and performing arts programs, science and technology programs, and imaginative events such as a Silicon Valley Robotics Competition that started locally and now attracts high school teams from all over the country. Partnerships with business and industry include high school internships such as a NASA summer work-study opportunity.

San Jose school administrators use the term "scaffolding" to describe curriculum development that focuses on supporting K-12 students from the beginning until their educational goals are met.

Santa Clara University Was First

From the beginning, the Valley of the Heart's Delight was a joy for the mind, as well, and amid the orchards and fields, three great institutions of higher learning put down their roots. Begun by a Jesuit order in 1851, Santa Clara College was California's first college. It became Santa Clara University in 1912 with a graduate school of engineering and law. Featuring a beautiful campus and an outstanding faculty, it offers top tier programs in arts and sciences.

San José State Set The Public Standard

San José State University (SJSU) began in 1857 as Minn's Evening Normal School, and became the State Normal School in 1862. In 1870, the legislature chose Washington Square in San Jose as the permanent location of California's first public university, the foundation of a state college system that remains a model for state-funded higher education systems worldwide. In 1921, it was named San Jose Teachers College, and, in 1974, renamed San José State University with majors in the arts, sciences, and engineering. Located in the heart of downtown San Jose, the university has a dynamic environment, yet is bounded by historic buildings and picturesque courtyards. SJSU is the largest source of engineering, science, and business graduates for Silicon Valley, with 80 percent of its graduates remaining local.

Santa Clara County is divided into two public school districts, including San Jose Unified and East Side. The county also contains a full complement of private and parochial school options, representing many different disciplines and denominations.

Leland and Jane Stanford's Legacy

Fifteen miles north of downtown San Jose, Leland Stanford Jr. University first opened its doors in 1891, established by Senator Leland Stanford and his wife, Jane, in memory of their son. One of the "Big Four" who built the Transcontinental Railroad, Stanford believed that a liberal arts education combined with technical training was the best preparation for life.

Stanford is among the finest universities in the world, its graduate schools in business and engineering ranked at the top. Stanford Medical School is a leading center for genomic research and transplant therapy.

Electronics pioneers David Packard and William Hewlett were students of Stanford engineering professor Frederick Terman, who championed campus-based research and development. What emerged from this concept is a continuous stream of innovations and discoveries in technology that have changed our way of life.

A Community of Colleges

The seven excellent community colleges in Silicon Valley focus on preparing students for life and work here. They are the valley's most affordable educational resources. De Anza College in Cupertino, consistently ranked among the top community colleges in the nation, is used by the technology industry for recruiting, training, and teaching contract courses. Foothill College in Los Altos Hills, another outstanding two-year college, serves northern Santa Clara Valley with career and exploration courses. The West Valley-Mission Community College District, with West Valley College in Saratoga and Mission College in Santa Clara offers career training programs and leisure courses, as well.

The San Jose City/Evergreen Community College District serves more than 700,000 residents within its 303-square-mile boundaries. Residents who are high school graduates or at least 18 years of age may attend either college. San Jose City College is near downtown, and Evergreen Valley College is located on a 175-acre site in the eastern foothills of San Jose. Both colleges offer associate degrees in the arts or sciences and prepare students for transfer to State University, the University of California system, and other four-year colleges. They feature industry-directed programs that prepare students for high-skill, high-wage jobs in growth occupations such as multimedia, computer networking and administration, laser technology, and high-tech manufacturing.

San Jose attracts students to its higher learning opportunities, not just for the goal of lucrative employment, but also for the excitement and fulfillment of learning right where things are happening. While new graduates continue to reinvent the future at the frontiers of technology, they also are confronting issues raised by a high-tech society such as the energy crisis and environmental emergencies.

Perhaps nowhere in the world is there as much access, for as many, to an almost incredible wealth of educational opportunities. ■

De Anza College is a major player in technical training for Silicon Valley workers.

Right and bottom right: San Jose Unified School District is a leader in specialized educational services for children of every ethnic and cultural background. Bottom left: Silicon Valley public schools have been ground zero for the deployment of technology in the classrooms.

The Head Start program run by the Santa Clara County Office of Education has served low-income children and their families for over thirty-five years.

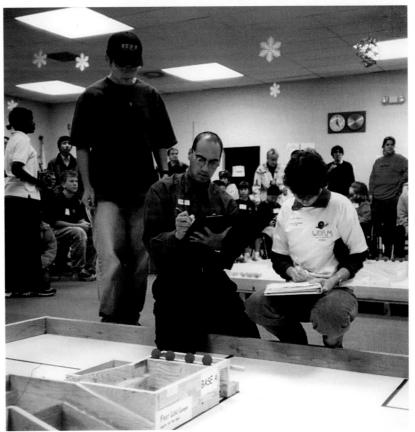

Local school programs are enthusiastically supported by San José State University, which has proudly hosted the FIRST Robotics Competition. FIRST, For Inspiration and Recognition of Science and Technology, provides high school students the opportunity to work with local businessmen and universities as they explore the world of engineering.

The best technical education includes the finest technique: the Fine Arts Quad at San Jose City College offers a place to gather and reflect.

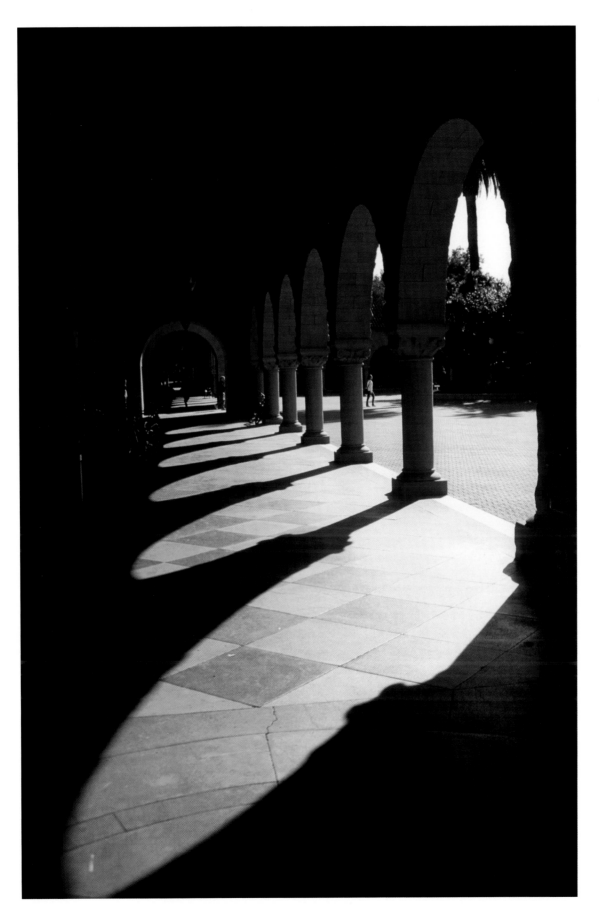

Stanford campus life was enlivened by attendance of the world's best students, from all over the globe, including the former President's daughter, Chelsea Clinton.

San Jose City College
forms part of the
backbone of technical
education in the valley,
which keeps the Silicon
Valley workforce
educated and
up-to-date.

Santa Clara University is the region's oldest Jesuit institution, having been founded in 1851 and become a university in 1855.

Top: In the best community curriculum, such as this outdoor art class, people learn about where they are. Opposite page: Hoover Tower is the familiar icon of Stanford University, known more for its intellectual campus life. Arched corridors line the Stanford University quad. It's come a long way from being Rancho San Francisquito, Governor Leland Stanford's stock farm for breeding horses.

Left and opposite page: Flint Center for the Performing Arts at De Anza College brings top tier entertainment to the Silicon Valley community, including nationally touring acts.

Bottom: Resources for students are available at Evergreen Valley College Learning Resource Center.

San José State University graduates go on to form the backbone of the Silicon Valley executive and engineering workforce.

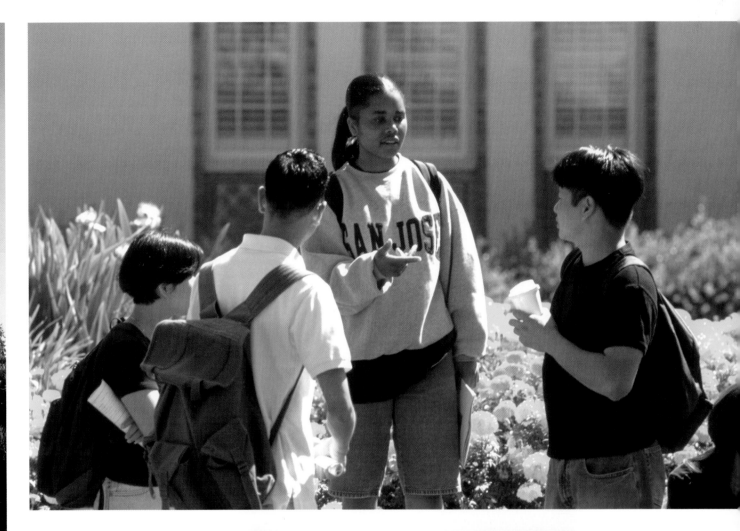

San José State University College of Business is the backbone of the Silicon Valley business education community. The "spinal cord" of the valley has to be San José State's Mathematics and Computer Science department, exemplified by professor-cum-science-fiction-legend, Rudy Rucker, who holds a special place among the cyberpunk stars of postmodern literature.

San Jose Museum of Art is one of the last remaining sandstone Romanesque buildings in Northern California. Built in 1892 as a U.S. Post Office, the sandstone was quarried from New Almaden. Then, in 1971, it was transformed from a public library into the museum, and a 45,000-square-foot wing was added in 1991. The newly expanded facility offers art classes and educational programs to the whole community.

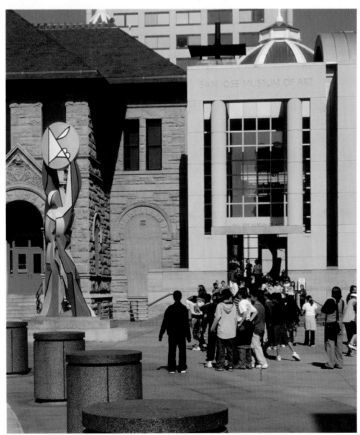

The latest addition to the San Jose skyline is The Tech Museum of Innovation. With its azure dome and mango walls, it is a unique architectural contribution designed by the famous Mexico City architect, Ricardo Legorreta. Underneath the azure dome is the cutting edge in educational technology programs for school-children and adults, where dozens of interactive exhibits inspire innovative thinking and encourage young and old to explore the world.

9
CHAPTER NINE

INNOVATIVE GROWTH MANAGEMENT

By Jake Bowman

Soon the Great Mall in Milpitas will be linked by Light Rail to the rest of the valley.

As we move into the next century, the very quality that drew so many to this area, wide-open space, has been threatened by the crush of people who came here to take advantage of it. Civic and community leaders consider growth management to be the key issue in maintaining a livable metropolis.

The Bay Area is fortunate in that many still living can remember when there was more open space here than people knew what to do with. New arrivals also are very conscious of the fact that precious open space is one of main attractions of living here. There is a broad consensus that the remainder, from the wetlands to the foothills, must be preserved, and open space initiatives enjoy wide political support.

Hiking, biking, and equestrian trails crisscross the foothills of the Santa Cruz and Diablo Mountains ringing the valley, and extend along the edges of the South Bay marshes. This mixed use is not just a feature of the parks, however, and bicycles and pedestrians are making a comeback on the streets, as well. Municipal planning is re-engineering for alternative transport: bike lanes line the roads, bike racks have sprouted on buses and trains and in stations, and greenways wind their way through recently redeveloped downtowns.

Pedal power and shoe leather are hardly the commuter's only options. Light rail transit is expanding, with the Mountain View Light Rail route just inaugurated and new routes serving both east and west sectors of the valley.

Controlling Sprawl

The region's civic government is a leader in progressive measures to preserve open space and control sprawl. The San Jose Greenline Initiative solidified the city's commitment to discouraging encroachment by establishing an Urban Growth Boundary. One unintended benefit of this thoughtful policy has been improved collaboration between San Jose and the County of Santa Clara, as these environmental amendments to their respective General Plans require a coordinated approach. This program has been so successful that the area's other municipalities, such as Milpitas and Morgan Hill, have adopted Urban Growth Boundaries as well.

One priority of all the sprawl limitation efforts has been to preserve the natural beauty of the hills, which surround and define the valley. The West Valley Hillside Preservation joins Cupertino, Los Gatos, Saratoga, and Monte Sereno

The newly-extended Light Rail whisks passengers through downtown San Jose.

However, the largest improvement so far is the Altamont Commuter Express (ACE), which is modern transit from the Tri-Valley to the Silicon Valley. Train lines begin in Stockton and Tracy, traversing the Altamont Pass much faster than traffic on the 680 Sunol grade. The program has been such a success that new routes are planned from as far away as Manteca.

New routes are just the beginning of a whole new approach to mass transit. The concept of "transit villages" implied a total redesign of town centers around train and bus stations. Several municipalities have either changed zoning laws or allowed exceptions for the construction of higher-density housing near transit hubs. San Jose has taken the lead within Silicon Valley in promoting transit-oriented development.

In 1991, San Jose identified seventy sites along existing transit corridors where the construction of higher-density housing would be encouraged. To foster development in these sites, the city offered a number of incentives, including zoning changes and, in some cases, public financing. The result is the creation of convenient, high-value housing for urban professionals, where the car-obsessed, future-focused West Coast gives way to more traditional European-style urban livability.

A New Urban Philosophy

Outward growth is being replaced with inward development. The trendsetter was the pioneering San Jose downtown redevelopment, which is a combination of many strategies. Historical sites such as the Hotel St. Claire, De Anza Hotel, and San Pedro Square were restored. New development was encouraged, including the Adobe and AboveNet corporate headquarters. The Guadalupe River has made a spectacular recovery; the San Jose Arena, now the Compaq Center, was constructed to attract professional hockey; and a thousand other improvements were made to transform the center of Silicon Valley into a world-class metropolis.

Those towns that hadn't maintained their downtowns as scrupulously as Palo Alto and Los Gatos have now seized the chance to rival their neighbors with ambitious urban planning. Sunnyvale is transforming a mall parking lot into a pedestrian garden connecting the redesigned mall to a redeveloped city center. Meanwhile, Mountain View has already captured headlines with a revitalized downtown hailed as a triumph of New Urbanist architecture, designed by Peter Calthorpe. The task of containing the demand for more housing and better cities is being embraced as an opportunity to achieve beautiful solutions. ■

Fifth and sixth generations of the Mirassou family own and operate the Mirassou Vineyards in San Jose, whose wines have ranked among the nation's most highly awarded wineries for ten consecutive years. Ancient industries such as these coexist with the growing metropolitan area of San Jose. Commercial construction and real estate development, though necessary, are controlled by the Urban Growth Boundary.

together in developing zoning development policies for the Santa Cruz Mountains' unincorporated foothills.

Environmentalism is not just aesthetics, however. Controlling the city's sprawl is a deeper commitment to mitigating our impact on the entire ecosystem. The scenic Lower South San Francisco Bay was designated an impaired water body by the Federal Clean Water Act, leading to the Santa Clara Basin Watershed Management Initiative. This coordinated effort among the Federal, State, and local authorities is aimed at protecting the water supply for the entire natural ecology, from people to the protected wetlands.

The Silicon Valley is Charted to Become a Regional Rail Hub for Northern California

Bay Area Rapid Transit (BART) is being extended to link San Jose and Santa Clara with the older urban centers of San Francisco and Oakland. Caltrain, the railroad that travels up the center of the San Mateo Peninsula, also is undergoing renovation to hasten the commute. Amtrak has just expanded Capitol service, increasing the frequency of trains between San Jose and Sacramento, the state capital.

Compaq Center hosts the San Jose hockey team, along with arena football, figure skating, and many other entertainment events.

"As the valley grew, so did the sophistication of Air Systems, Inc.'s client base. Over the last 10 years, managing and controlling energy consumption with an automated energy management system (EMS) has been the primary requirement of our clients, and has been particularly effective in high-tech, biotech, and other large building complexes.

"Our forward thinking led us to form an EMS unit, which is focused on providing that capability to our clients. Air Systems has consistently been one of the top producers for Automated Logic and its energy management system, earning the top sales award in the world for calendar year 2000."

—*John Davis*
  President and Chief Executive Officer
  Air Systems, Inc., an Encompass Company

Commercial construction in San Jose is ongoing, with the latest in a long line of technology companies building its corporate headquarters downtown.

Left: Old sits next to
new, where everyday
decisions are made to
preserve historic treasures
along with planning for
future development.
These Victorians are
being relocated to
provide housing for yet
another generation

"Wireless telephony and data have become crucial business tools, allowing employees to stay in touch and exchange information while on the move. With Globalstar, people can be connected around the world and even in remote areas, as nearly half of the U.S. and over 85 percent of the world is outside the range of cellular coverage.

"Globalstar also provides, through its fixed applications, communications to places around the world where telecommunications are only now becoming available. Globalstar can serve these communities without the expense of laying costly landlines. For developing countries, this can mean the difference between being connected or not."

—Gloria Everett
Executive Vice President of Sales and Marketing
Globalstar LP

Left: Construction
proceeds apace at the
Fairmont Hotel,
keeping up with the
economic development
in downtown.
Opposite page:
The Gold Building is
home to Federal offices
as well as MAE-West,
the primary node of
the Internet on the
West Coast.
Next page: The
Caltrain line runs from
Gilroy to San Francisco.
Caltrain is a popular
option for urban
commuters up and
down the Peninsula.

Right: Light Rail is often the first option for a commuter who lives close to a station, and is just one form of public transportation available in the growing area.

Bottom: Construction booms with every expansion of the local economy. Whether technology-related, or not, businesses locate in San Jose because of the economic opportunities found here.

Left: The Fairmont Towers are capped with the Knight Ridder sign, a familiar icon on the Silicon Valley skyline. Information technology giants like Knight Ridder choose San Jose for their corporate headquarters for good reason—it's the capital of Silicon Valley. Next page: The Caltrain line runs from Gilroy to San Francisco. Caltrain is a popular option for urban commuters up and down the Peninsula.

The Caltrain line
linking San Jose and
San Francisco was
originally planned in
1851. In 1863, rail
service went as far as
Mayfair, now called
California Avenue,
just one stop beyond the
historic Palo Alto
Train Station. From
there, riders needed to
take a stagecoach to
reach San Jose.

Santa Clara Train Station is just one stop of Caltrain, which is a popular way to get to Pacific Bell Park for San Francisco Giants games, but the train recorded its highest ridership, some 170,000 sports fans, during the 1994 World Cup soccer games at Stanford.

Suburban sprawl is now restricted by the Urban Growth Boundary (UGB). Established by the City of San José along with the County of Santa Clara in 1996, UGB, also referred to as the Greenline Initiative, preserves open spaces and conserves municipal resources.

Top: Coyote Valley is a
prime example of the
compromises that enable
necessary developments—
housing and industry—
to exist side by side with
a green belt area that
preserves the beauty
of the valley.

Left: Palo Alto
Baylands, a wetland
preserve, is one region
that has been able to
retain its natural
beauty alongside
economic development.

San Jose International Airport is undergoing a $2 billion improvement program that will modernize passenger terminals, expand air cargo facilities, improve airport ground access and expand corporate aircraft services.

A jetliner preparing to land at San Jose International Airport soars above the River Park Towers. The only airport in Santa Clara County, SJC averages more than 800 daily commercial and general aviation flights.

PART TWO

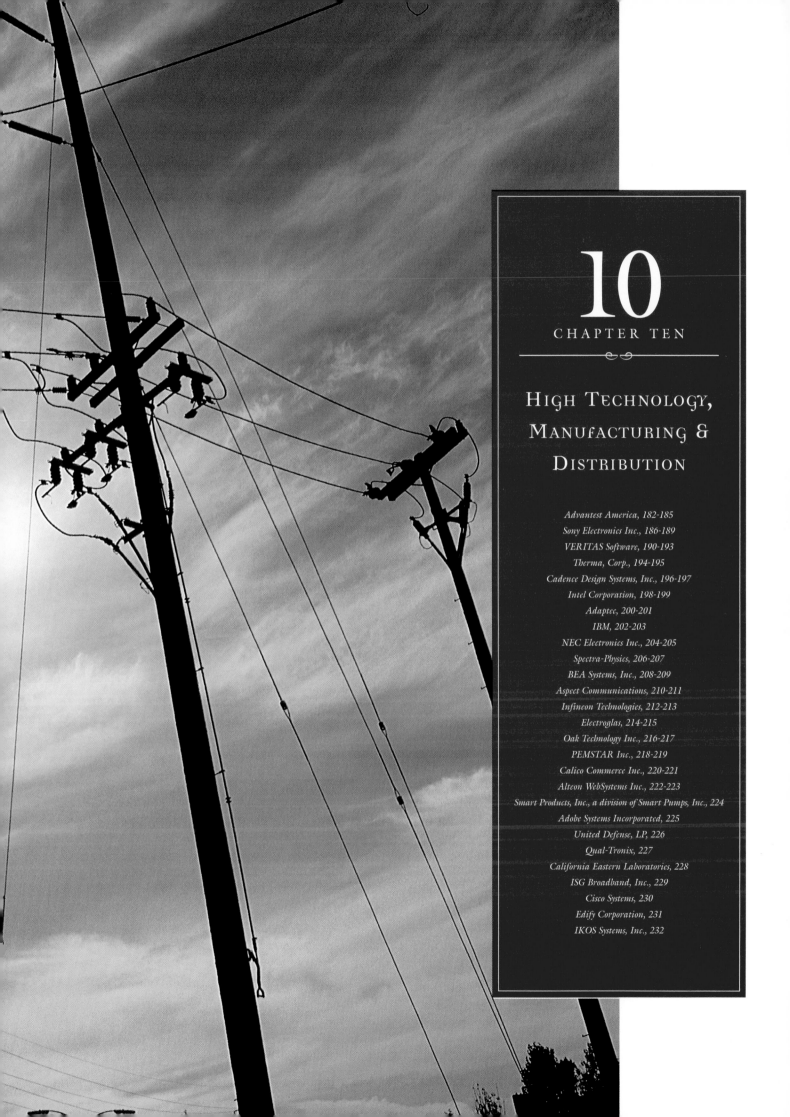

10
CHAPTER TEN

HIGH TECHNOLOGY,
MANUFACTURING &
DISTRIBUTION

*Nick Konidaris,
president and CEO,
Advantest America, Inc.*

"You can test. Or you can Advantest," says Advantest, the world's leading automatic test equipment (ATE) supplier to the semiconductor industry.

Throughout its history, Advantest has prided itself on its test systems' accuracy, reliability, and speed—bringing added value to the whole ATE process. With a reputation for superior quality and comprehensive service, the company is regarded as the "pacesetter" of the ATE industry.

"No matter how you evaluate Advantest systems—cost effectiveness, productivity, mean time between failures, accuracy, reliability, speed, functionality," says Nick Konidaris, president and CEO of Advantest America, "you'll find they set the standard in the industry."

For 12 consecutive years, Advantest has been ranked by VLSI Research as one of the Top Ten Best semiconductor equipment companies, based upon customer satisfaction.

Advantest has stood apart as the only ATE company to offer one-stop shopping with a full-line of testers, handlers, and interface products, which it designs and manufactures. While other companies now market a similar product line-up, they have either acquired outside companies or partnered with third-party vendors to provide the package. "Advantest is still the only company that manufactures the total test solution from the ground up," stated Paul Patton, Advantest America's director of product engineering, "and that difference strengthens signal integrity between products and ensures greater accuracy and reliability to the device under test."

In addition, Advantest offers the best mean time between failures (MTBF) in the industry. This translates to the best "up time" for the company's customers. This is critical for the semiconductor industry, since time to market is a key competitive advantage.

*Management group in
lobby of Advantest's
Santa Clara
headquarters.*

More than 13,000 Advantest systems are installed worldwide in world-class semiconductor design, fabrication, and production facilities. These are complex systems—themselves sophisticated computers—that test the circuitry and electromechanical functionality of semiconductors. Many of these installed systems include Advantest handlers, which actually bring the chips to the test head, so that the data on the chip can be read and verified. While testing is normally done at the end of the process used to manufacture the semiconductor chips, more and more Advantest products are being used in the front-end, or characterization phase, of the chip design process to ensure the testability and functionality of the final product.

Also behind the slogan "You can test. Or you can Advantest," is the fact that the company prides itself not only on keeping pace with the semiconductor industry, but on looking ahead to future needs—meeting the test challenges of new generations of integrated circuits. Advantest accomplishes this by working with manufacturing companies during their "design-in" process to design testers that meet new evolving chip standards that are getting faster and more intricate all the time.

"With an investment of more than 10 percent of annual sales into R&D, we are able to consistently bring new products to market and keep pace with the design curve for new devices," stated Patton. Research and development is conducted in the U.S., Japan, and Europe. Advantest America's R&D Center, based in Santa Clara, is dedicated to the development of future generations of test systems, incorporating state-of-the-art methodologies and solutions for microprocessor test and design.

*Nick Konidaris
with Torben Gronning,
director of operations,
and Greg Perkins,
vice president of sales.*

The semiconductor industry can be broken down into three main sub-markets: memory, SoC (System on Chip), and mixed signal. As the semiconductor market continues to expand—with demand continuing to escalate for "smart" consumer, telecommunications, business and medical products, and computers—the worldwide ATE market is also expected to increase.

Advantest is clearly the industry leader in memory. According to recent data, Advantest has approximately 63 percent of the world memory test market. Its T5500 memory test family is designed to test mass production of DRAM and other complex devices, including RIMM module devices, SSRAM, cache, and networking RAMS. In addition, in the area of flash memory testing, Advantest has the dominant system for back-end flash testing.

While memory testers have been the staple of Advantest business, the company is also a significant player in the logic tester market, holding over an 18 percent share; it offers the broadest variety of SOC test solutions especially with its new T6000 family, which serves both low- and high-volume needs. Advantest also has the largest share of the robotic pick-and-place handler market, at 29 percent.

Advantest America is the North American subsidiary of Tokyo-based Advantest Corporation, a $2.6 billion (FY2000 est.) Japanese company established in 1954 as a leading producer of electronic and optoelectronic instruments and systems. Since then, the semiconductor ATE equipment has become the dominant portion of Advantest's worldwide business.

The corporation employs over 4,700 people globally in Europe, North America, and Asia Pacific, and is listed on the Tokyo stock exchange. In a recent *Business Week* survey of the world's largest corporations, measured by market capitalization, Advantest was ranked 250th. Most Fortune 500 semiconductor manufacturers are Advantest's customers.

*Engineers at work on
Advantest's high-speed
digital production
test system.*

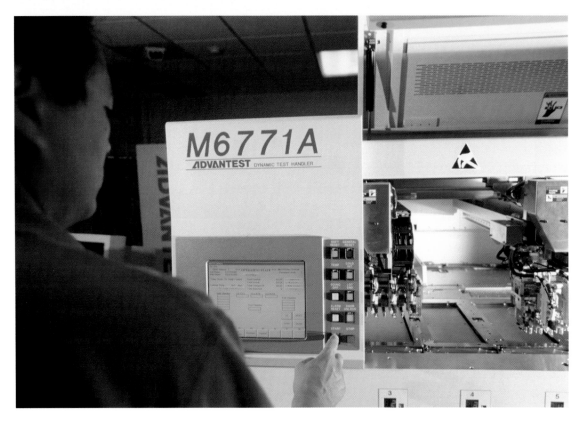

Programming the sophisticated pick-and-place device handler.

In the area of sales, 85 percent of Advantest's revenues come from the automatic test equipment market with the remainder from fiber-optic and wireless measuring instruments. And in fiscal year 1999, for the first time in the history of the corporation, export sales surpassed its own domestic Japanese revenues, with over 60 percent coming from the worldwide market. The ratio is somewhat higher in fiscal 2000.

Trade shows are an excellent forum for Advantest to reach its customers.

Advantest America has been an important part of the mother corporation ever since it first opened in the U.S. in 1982, with its headquarters on the East Coast designed to service a growing semiconductor market and an expanding customer base. The company soon found itself at the right place at the right time, able to catch the dawn of the personal computer revolution.

In 1985, Advantest America moved its headquarters to a major production facility outside of Chicago in the Buffalo Grove suburb. In 1998, the company relocated to its current Santa Clara site in the heart of Silicon Valley. Since that time, Advantest America has grown from its original handful of employees to over 250 with 12 offices across the country in Boise, Burlington, Folsom, Austin, and other customer locales. Manufacturing, equipment service, application engineering, new software architecture development, and interactive customer training are managed at the U.S. facilities.

"The move to Santa Clara made sense for Advantest, placing us in the center of the U.S. semiconductor industry where we could forge even stronger relationships with customers," stated Advantest America's president, Kondaris, who spearheaded the strategic move. Lending a truly global vision to Advantest's international business, Kondaris, a Greek-American, received his electrical and mechanical engineering degree from the National Technical University of Athens, and an MBA from the Massachusetts Institute of Technology.

Although the semiconductor industry is growing, a rising tide doesn't necessarily lift all boats. If an ATE company has not planned properly, they will not grow with the market.

Instead, the market grows away from them. That's not the case with Advantest. Advantest is riding high on the tide of demand because it prepared itself strategically to take advantage of changing market conditions.

"In 1984, Advantest opened its state-of-the-art manufacturing facility in Gunma, Japan," stated Kondaris, "which incorporates a highly flexible production system." It developed new products to maintain the corporation's lead in the memory market and renew its commitment to logic sales. He continued, "And now, Advantest has an unbeatable line-up of innovative test solutions."

"We quickly realized that to grow, we had to sell to every maker of devices," Kondaris stated. "Among our customers are IDMs, test houses, fabless device makers—whatever the industry wants to call itself, in whatever hybrid form it morphs into, Advantest calls them all 'customer.'"

And finally, Advantest has built a strong management team. Under the leadership of Hiroshi Oura, who has been director and president of Advantest Corporation in Japan for the past 11 years, the company has attained the position of a world-class organization.

To better serve its worldwide customers with faster product and on-target solutions, Advantest is working to speed up its business processes and global support system. In 2000, Advantest started revamping its company-wide Enterprise Resource Management (ERM) Systems and is expanding this activity on a global basis. When completed, this is expected to shorten the production process by an entire month and accelerate inventory turnover by as much as 30 percent.

"In order for us to be successful on a global level, we not only have to strengthen our technological might, but our brand name as well," stated Oura. In the near future, Advantest Corporation plans to spread its "blue chip" Japanese reputation to America as the corporation seeks listing on the New York Stock Exchange by the fall of 2001. It's a bold move, considering there are only 13 Japanese companies currently listed on the NYSE.

So far, Advantest's strategies and forecasts have been right on target, but stated Oura, "No matter how accurate our market forecasts may be, our future success rests on the assumption that we remain dedicated to satisfying our customers." The corporation bears in mind the fact that Advantest's success is intimately intertwined with the success of its customers.

What lies behind the company's slogan, "You can test. Or your can Advantest," is a solid global corporation and first-class American subsidiary, which is committed to customer satisfaction, cutting-edge technologies, worldwide facilities, and superior integrated test products. ■

At the International Test Conference each fall on the East Coast.

SONY ELECTRONICS INC.

Each year, members of Sony's staffing department participate in various job fairs throughout the region and country to recruit talented employees.

A World Leader Through Innovation

For most Americans, Sony is a household name. Virtually all of us, at one time or another, have owned a Sony Trinitron® television, listened to a Sony Walkman® personal stereo, watched a Sony Pictures Entertainment movie, talked on a Sony cordless telephone, listened to a Sony Music Entertainment artist, or played along with popular Sony-produced television game shows.

At any given moment, we can be presented with the Sony name countless times, and as a result, Sony is one of the most recognized brand names in the world. As a matter of fact, in an annual "Best Brands" survey conducted by Harris Interactive, Sony has been rated number one in U.S. brand recognition for four out of the last six years. In the seven years Harris has conducted the survey, Sony has not placed lower than third. No other brand comes close to matching this record.

Sony has definitely come a long way since its humble beginnings in post-war Japan in 1946. Founded by Masaru Ibuka and Akio Morita, Sony, originally called Tokyo Tsushin Kogyo (Tokyo Telecommunications Engineering Corporation), set the standard for innovations early on by producing Japan's first magnetic tape recorder (1950) and first transistor radio (1955). In the following decades, Sony went on to produce numerous other "world firsts," such as the first home-use open-reel videotape recorder (1965), first Walkman personal headphone stereo (1979), first Compact Disc player (1982), and first MiniDisc system (1992). Other revolutionary products include the Memory Stick® integrated circuit storage device, PlayStation® game systems, and the Cyber-shot® digital camera.

Sony Electronics Western Region headquarters in San Jose has been a strong presence in the Silicon Valley since its opening in 1993. The 642,500-square-foot facility is a key center for Sony Electronics' research and development and engineering operations.

In a mere 50 years, Sony pushed the envelope in technology to become a world leader in audio, video, communication, and information technology products for both consumer and professional markets. Sony has also made a name for itself in the entertainment industry, with such companies as Sony Music Entertainment, Sony Pictures Entertainment (owner of the Columbia/Tri-Star Motion Picture Group), and Sony Computer Entertainment.

As a total entertainment company, Sony is the name behind such popular recording artists as Tony Bennett, Herbie Hancock, Jennifer Lopez, and Ricky Martin; blockbuster movies like *Crouching Tiger, Hidden Dragon, Men In Black*, and *Stuart Little*; along with the *Jeopardy* and *Wheel of Fortune* TV game shows.

Employees—The Mind and Heart of Sony Electronics

Contributing to Sony's widespread success are thousands of employees from almost every continent and nearly 50 nations, making Sony a truly global company. Sony's largest overseas sales contributor is Sony Electronics Inc. in the U.S, which manufactures and markets consumer and professional audio and video equipment, computer and peripheral products, recording media and energy products, semiconductors, and other electronic components.

Headquartered in Park Ridge, New Jersey, Sony Electronics has approximately 25,000 employees throughout the U.S. and Mexico in various research and development, sales and marketing, and manufacturing and engineering facilities. In California, the company has had a presence in the Silicon Valley since the 1970s, making it among the first technology companies to have roots in what has been called the birthplace of the technological revolution.

To accommodate the company's growing U.S. design and development activities, Sony Electronics opened a 642,500-square-foot facility in San Jose as its Western Region Headquarters in 1993. The magnificent facility is graced by

a black glass exterior that mirrors the numerous palm trees outlining the building. The facility houses business units that formulate corporate strategies, develop new technologies, and pursue strategic business relationships and alliances critical to Sony's success. Additionally, its ideal location in the heart of the Silicon Valley has helped propel Sony Electronics into the digital era. This has also allowed the company to harness the intellectual and technological strength of the area's workforce.

Today, Sony Electronics employs more than 1,300 employees in the Silicon Valley and nearby Bay area. These employees are as diverse in age, race, gender, and culture as the area's population, and they bring innovation and a creative spirit to the Sony culture. In the San Jose facility, it is not uncommon for employees to hear numerous languages spoken and to work with individuals who were born in other countries. This atmosphere of diversity adds to the spirit of Sony. It is embraced and recognized as well through the work of Diversity Volunteers, a committee of employees who share the goal of heightening diversity awareness through specially planned events and lectures.

Recognizing that there is more to an employee's life than a productive workday, Sony Electronics supports a variety of employee activities managed by an Employee Activities Committee. Some of these events include company picnics, ski trips, casino trips, sports leagues, art and book fairs and a variety of other activities aimed at bringing fun to the surroundings. Unstructured events abound as well, and the site provides the perfect setting for impromptu lunchtime sand volleyball tournaments, basketball games, and departmental barbecues.

"There is a strong sense of camaraderie and fun here at Sony," commented Leah Arruda, a Sony Electronics employee. "Of course, there is something to be said about working in such a beautiful location, but regardless, we are all a part of the Sony team and contribute to that team. Being a part of a number one company is surely something special."

A Spirit of Giving

That "something special" translates into a spirit that permeates not only within the company but throughout the community as well. Through the Sony USA Foundation, established in 1972 as the first Japan-based philanthropic foundation in the U.S., Sony Electronics employees volunteer their time, and Sony its resources, to charitable causes in six different areas: education, health and welfare, minority affairs, civics, environmental efforts, and arts and culture.

Recognizing that today's employees value the importance of helping others, Sony Electronics provides two paid days off a year for each employee to volunteer their time to charitable organizations. Many use this time to participate in the company's Global Volunteer Day, an event that mobilizes Sony employees across the world in simultaneous community involvement efforts. Employees and employee-run volunteer committees often conduct food, clothing, toy, and book fair drives, in addition to participating in various outreach events throughout the year.

Sony Electronics employees enjoy an outdoor luncheon barbecue on the first day of summer, one of the many events organized by the Employee Activities Committee.

Sony Electronics employees spend their lunch break playing a friendly game of hoops on company grounds. The region's mild weather and sunny days make for plenty of opportunities for employees to enjoy Sony's outside volleyball and basketball courts and picnic areas.

Right: The impressive four-story atrium area of Sony Electronics' San Jose facility greets employees and visitors with natural light and views of the Silicon Valley through a wall of glass windows.

Bottom: In 1972, Sony became the first Japanese company to establish a private, non-profit philanthropic foundation in the United States. The Sony USA Foundation Inc. supports numerous national and community efforts annually. Locally, Sony Electronics donates time and resources to such causes as the CIC Fundraiser Golf Tournament for the Boys and Girls Club of Silicon Valley.

Sony Electronics' San Jose facility also features a Community Involvement Council (CIC), a committee of employee volunteers who coordinate all corporate contributions and community involvement activities for the site and work closely with the Sony USA Foundation. Each year, the CIC donates at least 50 percent of its budget to local elementary, middle, and high schools. The remaining budget is allocated to non-profit organizations. With the help of Sony Electronics' employees and resources, many of these organizations, such as the Boys and Girls Club, the San Jose Family Shelter, and various educational institutions, can enhance their programs and offerings to the local community.

Reaching to the Future

Enhancing people's lives is central to Sony Electronics' operating principles. Behind the Sony name is a promise… a promise of quality and commitment and a promise of providing customers with the best possible product innovations. Looking ahead, Sony's future lies in the development of broadband entertainment and network connectivity. Through the years, Sony Electronics has evolved with the times, staying ahead of technology and consumer innovations. Today, Sony continues on that path of evolution. Its goal for the future is to heighten the profitability of its electronics-related businesses by enhancing product development and expanding the network connectivity of its electronics devices.

Said Sony President and COO Kunitake Ando, "This will be based on a ubiquitous value network that is always connected, on demand and interactive. It will be a strengthened form of our 'four network gateway strategy,' integrating the electronics, games, and internet/communications service businesses."

Behind this goal is the dedication and commitment of thousands of creative and innovative employees. Nobuyuki Idei, Sony's Chairman and CEO, recognized this when he described Sony employees as "Digital Dream Kids," pointing to the energy and imagination that enables them to create the technologies that captivate the world and make Sony what it is today.

States Idei, "Some call Sony a hardware company, a media company, and even a game company. But what we are, and will be, is a Personal Broadband Network Solutions Company. Sony is an open business platform company. Let's combine our ideas, passion, technologies, software, and creativity. I believe this will achieve greater prosperity for all of us. What we share with you today is the desire to bring greater joy, and greater connection around the world. We are the 'Digital Dream Kids' of the Network."

Do you dream in Sony? Dream On™.

For additional information regarding Sony, visit www.sony.com and www.sonyjobs.com. ∎

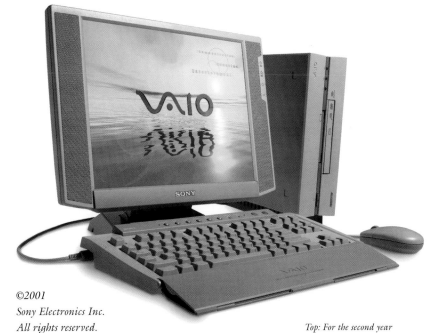

©2001
Sony Electronics Inc.
All rights reserved.
Reproduction in whole or in part
without written permission is prohibited. Sony, Cyber-shot,
Dream On, Memory Stick, Trinitron, VAIO and Walkman
are registered trademarks of Sony. Playstation is a registered
trademark of Sony Computer Entertainment Inc.

Top: For the second year in a row, in 2000, Forbes Magazine recognized Sony as the number one consumer appliance company. Sony's continuous introduction of new products, such as the VAIO personal computer line, emphasizes the company's philosophy of "pushing the envelope" and bringing to the market technologies of the future.

Left: With PlayStation 2, Sony Computer Entertainment has created and developed a new world of computer entertainment for the broadband era through the fusion of games, music, movies, and broadcasting.

The new 425,000-square-foot headquarters for VERITAS Software at 350 Ellis Street in the heart of the historic Middlefield-Ellis-Whisman area of Mountan View reflects the change that is taking place in the Silicon Valley since its beginnings in the mid-1950s. The new VERITAS Software site is on land that hosted Rheem Semiconductors starting in 1958. That building was then purchased and operated by Raytheon from 1961 until it was taken over by Fairchild in 1997.

This area, regarded as the birthplace of the Silicon Valley, will now change its emphasis from silicon to software with the opening of the VERITAS Software headquarters. Considered to be one of the most successful of the area firms and one of the top-five software companies in the world, VERITAS Software is commemorating the history of the location with a display board in the public commons area of the building complete with artifacts of items manufactured on the site.

Gary Bloom, president and CEO of VERITAS Software, took over the leadership role in November 2000 to navigate VERITAS Software to the next level of expansion and growth.

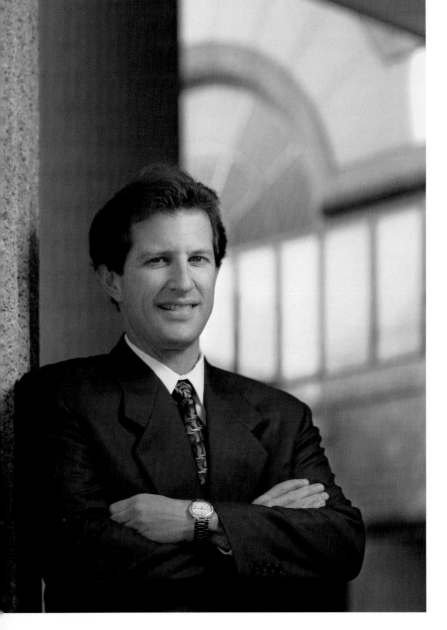

VERITAS Software was founded in 1989 and has become a leading provider of storage software solutions that enable its customers to protect and access their business-critical data. With the growing complexity of data in today's new economy and the networked environments that are so necessary, VERITAS Software is dedicated to providing products that ensure "Business Without Interruption." With more than 5,500 employees in 25 countries and more than 100 offices worldwide, VERITAS Software has become the market's leading innovator of storage software and is the de facto standard for solutions with more than 85 of the world's leading servers and operating systems integrating its software.

In today's world, even a few minutes without being able to access data can have a profound effect on a company's revenue and efficiency. E-commerce sites can lose millions of dollars if they are down for even a few minutes while ATM customers, if unable to access their accounts at one machine, will not wait but go to another bank. That represents revenue lost. In addition, the inability of a health-care facility to access the increasing amount of medical information that is now online (even if only very briefly) can have a significant impact on the safety of patients.

The amount of data stored electronically is rapidly growing and VERITAS Software is providing a full range of systems and solutions to ensure that its customers have the ability to always protect and access that data. With a projected investment of $4 billion over the next five years for software research and development, VERITAS Software solutions are at the forefront of storage management software technology that span all operating platforms.

The VERITAS Backup Exec is the world's number one Windows NT and Windows 2000 backup solution and the first certified by Microsoft for Windows 2000. VERITAS File System and VERITAS Volume Manager provide continuous access to critical information and applications. They also provide protection from storage device failure through automated fault management, journaling for faster recovery from system failures, and online reconfiguration tools for uninterrupted access to online storage.

VERITAS Cluster Server is the most comprehensive cascading service-level failover solution for HP-UX, Solaris, and Windows NT. VERITAS ClusterX is the first configuration and management tool for multiple Windows NT and Windows 2000 clusters. VERITAS Volume Replicator, Storage Replicator, and File Replicator are often used as part of highly effective disaster-recovery strategy. VERITAS Software has also optimized its data availability solutions to enable crucial storage area network (SAN) applications such as online SAN virtualization, heterogeneous clustering, LAN free backup, and hierarchical storage management. This results in reduced cost and complexity

for the management of expanding SAN environments and provides for the new levels of performance and availability necessary to support Internet-based business operations.

In addition, VERITAS Software offers a range of application-focused solutions called VERITAS Editions. These combine key VERITAS Software solutions that are optimized and integrated into leading applications including Oracle, Sybase, SAP, Web, and file servers. For the consumer and small home office business as well as corporate environments that require protection and management of valuable data residing on desktops and mobile devices, VERITAS Software ensures individual data availability through powerful and easy-to-use storage management solutions.

VERITAS Software solutions can be found in a very diverse range of companies. In Japan for example, Sony Music relies on VERITAS Software to assure real-time response to customers buying music through its revolutionary Internet music distribution system. In the UK, Charles Schwab Europe is being assisted in its move to e-business by VERITAS Software, while the US Census Bureau relies on VERITAS Software to provide access and protection solutions for critical data residing on multiple platforms throughout the more than 500 field offices around the country.

All of these solutions are delivered to customers worldwide through a mix of five sales channels including a direct sales force, value added resellers, an international two-tier distribution infrastructure, OEM partners, and online. VERITAS Software has also developed strategic partnerships with all major industry leaders in order to ensure "out-of-the-box integration" for its data availability solutions. The OEM and strategic partnership list includes more than 85 firms from the device level to the high-end Windows NT and UNIX vendors. The goal of this strategic partnership is to enable customers to enjoy integrated, scalable data availability solutions that will grow with any expansion effort.

Top: VERITAS Software's new 425,000-square-foot global headquarters campus.

Left: VERITAS Software products such as NetBackup Storage Migrator allow the user to store archived data while allowing space for new data.

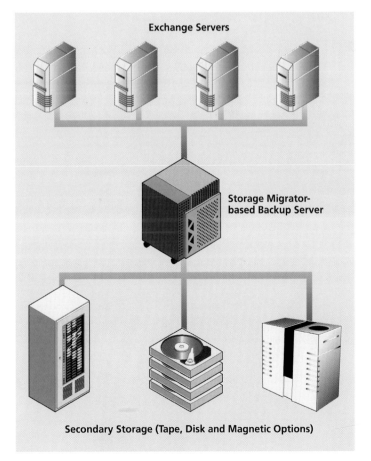

Exchange Servers

Storage Migrator-based Backup Server

Secondary Storage (Tape, Disk and Magnetic Options)

Crucial for any customer is service and support and VERITAS Software's focus on increased communication and customer partnership has resulted in technical service and support solutions that are second to none. Called VERITAS Vsupport, customers are provided with personalized care to shorten the time to problem resolution, help to proactively avoid issues, and help to increase the effectiveness of the customers' investment in VERITAS Software technology.

VERITAS Software has become a trusted supplier and one that its customers can rely upon because of its corporate values. These values are based on mutual integrity, trust, and openness. The company encourages these values by entrusting employees with critical information and promoting open communication to employees, customers, partners, and stockholders. As a result, the company's customers have high praise for the service they receive.

Tim Wilson, the Chief Marketing Officer for Digital Island, a wholly owned subsidiary of Cable & Wireless, stated that "with VERITAS Software solutions we have a data availability platform that delivers failover reliability and guarantees restoration of critical customer data." According to Chuck Henning, vice president, MIS, for Precision Steel, "the productivity gains achieved with VERITAS Software solutions are most visible when full-blown outages occur. You can never completely eliminate the vulnerabilities inherent to the IT

infrastructure that result in outages. However, VERITAS Software data protection solutions make major outages seem like momentary pauses. Service is easily restored, and our data is once again accessible. VERITAS Software truly delivers business without interruption."

Under the leadership of its founder, Mark Leslie who served from 1990 to 2000, VERITAS Software grew to a company with revenues of $1 billion. VERITAS Software was added to the NASDAQ-100 index in January 1999 and the S&P 500 Index in March 2000. On October 2000, the company received a market capitalization of $59.6 billion. Having achieved the $1 billion goal, Leslie has moved on to become chairman of the board and has left the goal of reaching the $5 to $10 billion mark to the new CEO and President Gary Bloom.

Bloom was appointed to these positions in November 2000 from Oracle where he was executive vice-president. Gary was in charge of Oracle's core database business and led the execution of its internet and e-business vision as well as many other activities such as mergers and acquisitions. At VERITAS Software, he is responsible for all corporate functions and for the formulation of current and long-range plans and objectives.

In June 2000 VERITAS Software Corporation created the VERITAS Software Foundation. The Foundation was established because the company wished to share its successes with the communities where it has offices. Contributions to the foundation are made both corporately and by individual employees, and the current focus is on supporting education.

In January 2001, VERITAS Software made its first grant to the NEA Foundation for the Improvement of Education for an initiative to incorporate high-quality professional development into the lives of teachers. VERITAS Software employees expressed an interest in supporting programs that will help to improve education for students. After reviewing several nonprofit

organizations, they realized that one of the best ways to improve student education is to help teachers develop professionally and to gain new teaching skills. As a result, the foundation's very first grant went to the NEA because VERITAS Software believes that by helping teachers you will help the students.

The VERITAS Software Charitable Foundation was initially provided with $1 million when it was set up, but in early 2001, the company was able to add an additional $2 million to that funding. ■

Left: VERITAS Software Foundation, established in June 2000 to support community programs that improve and promote education.

Far left: VERITAS Software offers a wide array of data protection and storage software products

THERMA, CORP.

Therma Corporation was founded in 1967. The company focus has been mechanical contracting for industrial, commercial, and biomedical users. The needs of these users are multifaceted, i.e., heating; ventilation and air conditioning; clean rooms; special exhaust systems; process piping; plumbing; refrigeration; acid neutralization; energy conservation; environmental and process controls; extended service and specialty manufacturing of skids; processing piping assemblies; gas sticks; and gas cabinets.

Joe Parisi, the company president, and Nicki Parisi, the company CFO and co-founder, have always been innovators in their business dealings. Both Joe and Nicki Parisi support a corporate attitude of working smart for a better future.

Therma has had a significant impact on the innovative growth of the mechanical industry in the Bay Area. Therma's corporate philosophy is "working smart" and the employees' attitude of "we can do," made Therma, Corp., a familiar presence throughout the Silicon Valley and now the greater Bay Area.

Therma was born out of a kind of a synergy between Joe and Nicki. Joe had a curiosity for the business having majored in engineering at San Jose State University. And Nicki was born into it with three generations of her family in the business—her grandfather was a plumbing contractor and her father owned a large mechanical contracting firm in San Jose. As a young girl, Nicki visited job sites and eventually worked in the office of her father's company where she picked up skills that came in handy later.

"In the beginning, Nicki set up the books, and there was myself and one other plumber," recalled Joe Parisi thinking about the early days. From then on Therma grew and grew to over 1,500 employees today, including more than 1,000 craftsmen from the Pipefitters, Plumbers, and Sheetmetal unions. It is currently the largest union construction employer in the Bay Area.

In the early years of the semi conductor industry growth, delivery of clean air supply hoods became restricted. In response to this situation, Therma founded a company and mass produced them. When hoods became inefficient, Therma consolidated them. When individual hoods became architecturally unacceptable, Therma custom built cabinetry.

Top: Installation of large diameter exhaust duct within high rise enclosure.
Right: Clean room fan deck area.

When temperature control became critical to manufacturing, Therma designed and installed control systems to straight line at one tenth of a degree Fahrenheit 24/7. Therma pioneered many items now used or integrated into the industry's vernacular.

"We were at the right place, at the right time," stated Parisi, referring to the fact that Therma got started when the semiconductor industry was just blossoming in the valley. Therma performed the original mechanical work in fab areas of many founding semiconductor companies when they were startups like IBM, Fairchild, Memorex, and AMD. "In fact, we've had an on-site crew at IBM, Intel, and National Semiconductor as long they've been in business," commented Parisi.

Establishing relations that have spanned decades with global leaders, Therma's high-tech clients also include Varian, Texas Instruments, and Hewlett-Packard—where Therma has been a major contractor for the past 20 years. And in the early-'90s, Therma started working with biotech companies building pharmaceutical manufacturing and R&D facilities. Among the biotech, bio-pharmaceutical clients are Chiron, Genentech, Abgenix, Bayer, and Alza.

But the latest chapter in Therma's history is really its new 247,000-square-foot headquarters facility on Las Plumas in South San Jose. This complex has the most modern duct fabrication and pipe prefab facility in Northern California. The sheetmetal department manufacturers spiral, rectangular, and welded duct and fittings to the most stringent SMACNA standards. The sheetmetal shop sits alongside the class 100,000 piping prefab with several clean mini environments. Therma's new facility also houses a 60,000-square-foot, ASME-certified, large pipe and plumbing fabrication shop utilizing a multi-ton bridge crane for moving the heavy pipe around the prefab area.

The Therma shops are supported by the latest computerized documentation, CAD, and design systems available. The Therma library includes Auto-Cad, Pipe Designer 3D, CAD duct, and Profile Master (PM2000).

Therma also maintains branches offices for the convenience of its customers, including several South San Jose locations, offices in South San Francisco, Oakland, Vacaville, and Sacramento, and the company oversees the largest Service Group in the Bay Area.

On May 1, 1998, Therma was selected for special recognition when President Clinton visited its fabrication facility and held a roundtable with employees to learn more about the company's long history of success.

"If you stand back and think about it," commented Parisi, "Therma has for the past 34 years built and maintained the equipment that keeps Silicon Valley companies running." Therma has also advanced the mechanical contracting industry and mechanized its own business to keep pace with the challenges of the commercial industrial market and their ever-expanding client base. ■

Custom skids for Biotech and Semiconductor applications.

Custom-made cell pot for pharmaceutical manufacturing application.

CADENCE DESIGN SYSTEMS, INC.

Entrance to the Cadence campus, San Jose, California.

*C*adence Design Systems' President and CEO Ray Bingham offers his personal insight into the nature and importance of the electronics industry to today's world economy and beyond. This is an industry to which his company is a vital part, as a leading full-service provider of electronic design automation solutions and services. The partnerships Cadence has with the top companies in the industry help facilitate the introduction of new products to market—better and faster.

If the economy is not growing fast enough, we are not innovating enough.

The electronics industry has proven beyond any doubt that innovation—the fruits of well-designed, creative, forward-thinking research and development—has the power to drive the entire economy. Electronic design innovation has not only changed Silicon Valley; it has changed the world.

Now it's time to do it again.

Ray Bingham, President and CEO of Cadence Design Systems, Inc.

The electronics industry has built a profitable $1.1 trillion industry by converting the dreams of incredibly smart engineers and designers into reality. But that's no reason to stop. The electronics revolution is still in its infancy.

Microsoft chairman Bill Gates had it right in May 2001 when he said that the coming decade can bring even greater growth for the technology sector than we have already seen. This is why R&D is more important than ever. Electronic design companies have to continuously anticipate the future and innovate towards it. The industry has to be rigorous in its pursuit of the highest standards and its encouragement of the very best thinking.

The hard reality is that electronic design companies remain hard-pressed to solve all the technical challenges brought on by the deep submicron, system-on-chip era. However, the pace of design innovation is accelerating all the time. One only needs to look at some of the leading-edge design methodologies that are in place at the world's top electronics companies. Approaches such as true system-level design, placement-knowledgeable synthesis, and real concurrent design (that combines hardware and software, digital and analog, chip and board) were just thoughts on a white board five years ago. Today, these methodologies are being delivered by the electronic design industry and are a major factor in the impressive expansion of the electronics industry. Now computing, communications, and multi-media are converging in a single product. This is the wave of the future.

The tools that are required to drive this—and fuel economic engines—include more than just money. Innovation requires brainpower, creativity, passion, and trust:

• Brainpower means ensuring that schools are teaching children about math and science and history and so much more. It means making advanced learning about technology possible for more than just a few talented students.

• Passion means the drive to explore the unknown, to investigate new ideas, to find out how and why things work the way they do—and how to make them work better.

Passion means the energy to wake up in the middle of the night to record a dream about the way something new can be accomplished, and then to actually do it. And it means the passion to deliver results to customers, to never compromise about meeting or exceeding their needs, and to think ahead of customers so that the industry delivers solutions even before new challenges develop.

• Creativity means allowing people to think freely, to explore ideas, to experiment until they are proven right or wrong. It means investing in talented employees and recognizing that many of the best products emerge after years of research, at times with an uncertain result.

• Trust means giving smart, creative people the opportunity to develop careers, feed and shelter their families, and live well when their thinking leads to innovative new products. It means creating an environment where intellectual property is treated with the same respect as any other property, where engineers can be comfortable to brainstorm and share ideas knowing that their property will not be taken without compensation.

Without these essential elements, innovation cannot be sustained and Silicon Valley companies can't keep up with product life cycles running as short as six months. The innovation seen in past years has been truly remarkable, but there is no reason to think that innovation is slowing down. The integrated circuit may be the steam engine of the

20th century, but the hard work, creativity, and engineering occurring now is on track to produce the next steam engine that will power a new period of economic growth. In short, innovation is the only way to create new value for customers and success for those who provide it.

—Ray Bingham, President and CEO
Cadence Design Systems, Inc. ■

Creativity means allowing people to think freely, to explore ideas, to experiment until they are proven right or wrong.

Innovation requires brainpower, creativity, passion, and trust.

Chip making in the 1970s—an early Intel manufacturing line.

"Don't be encumbered by history," said Intel co-founder Robert Noyce in 1970. "Go off and do something wonderful." That's exactly what Intel's handful of founding employees did more than three decades ago. Along the way they inspired thousands of people inside Intel and across Silicon Valley.

While times have changed and the company is now hurdling ahead into the Internet Age, that forward-thinking mindset continues to thrive at the world's largest chip maker. "The Internet is the growth engine of the future," stated President and Chief Executive Officer Craig Barrett. Intel continues to invest in the future by going beyond the core microprocessor business and pushing into new networking and communications businesses.

At the Intel Developers Forum in San Jose in February 2001, Barrett pointed out that, "Intel's four architectures are designed to provide the technology foundation upon which the industry can capture growth opportunities created by the Internet. Intel is focused on providing customers with the basic architectural building blocks for client devices, networking equipment, and servers that will allow greater innovation, faster time to market, and lower costs."

It would have been hard to imagine the Intel of today when the company was started in July 1968 by Gordon Moore, Robert Noyce, and Andy Grove, who all dreamed of building a successful company. But as of 2000, Intel's revenues had surpassed $33 billion, it employed over 85,000 people, and the company was selling 80 percent of the world's microprocessors.

Intel's culture is at the core of its phenomenal success. Rejecting the status-oriented bureaucracy of traditional corporations, the founders laid the groundwork for a more egalitarian, merit-oriented company. The idea was an open, accessible management style, a no-frills attitude, with a high value on employees. That attitude has continued to grow as new managers have taken the helm: Andy Grove in the 1980s and much of the 1990s, and now Craig R. Barrett, who was named the company's fourth president in 1997, and chief executive officer in 1998.

A regular on the list of "100 Best Companies to Work for in America," Intel was, for example, the first Silicon Valley company to offer its employees sabbaticals—eight weeks of paid leave every seven years—in addition to their regular vacations. The company rewards employees through generous yearly bonuses and profit-sharing programs; in 1997, all Intel employees worldwide became eligible for stock options.

Intel's history is one of continuing innovation. The integrated circuit, co-invented by Noyce in the mid-1960s, enabled the miniaturization of electronic circuitry on a single silicon chip, starting a trend that continues to this day.

Chip making in the 1990s—bunny-suited manufacturing technicians in a fab clean room.

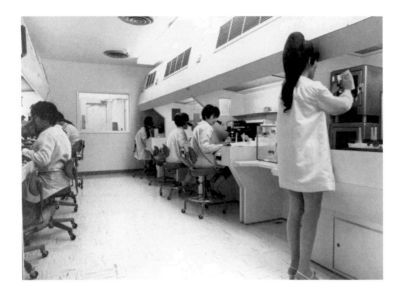

to 1.5 GHz. The Pentium 4 processor (42 million transistors), with a new architecture, delivers a new generation of performance for processing video and audio, exploiting modern Internet technologies, and displaying 3-D graphics.

Intel's ability to keep rolling out new technologies comes at a price. Intel will spend over $4 billion on research and development this year. And when many companies were cutting back on new expansion, Intel announced it would spend $7.5 billion on new manufacturing capacity, an increase of 12 percent.

Even as you read this, Intel is working on new microprocessor-driven technologies that will pave the way for new uses of the computer, some you can only dream about. If history is any guide, technology will continue to advance, changing the way we live and do business. And you can bet Intel will be right at the heart of the movement. As Moore once said, "This is a phenomenal industry in which the only rule is change." ∎

High-tech bunny suits, not mini skirts, are the required garb in today's chip manufacturing line.

Intel's founders set out to make semiconductor memory practical. In 1970, two years after the company's founding, Intel introduced the 1103 dynamic random access memory (DRAM), the world's first merchant-market large-scale integrated DRAM, which was smaller, more powerful, and more energy efficient than magnetic core memory.

In 1971, Intel unveiled an alterable storage medium—erasable programmable read-only memory (EPROM)—that gave computer manufacturers a flexible, low-cost way to store microprocessor programs.

That same year, Intel introduced the world's first commercial microprocessor, the 4004. Smaller than a thumbnail, it was packed with 2,300 transistors. Intel's new chip executed 60,000 operations in one second, as much computing power as Eniac, the first electronic computer, which required 18,000 vacuum tubes in a 3,000-cubic-foot-room. By the time Intel introduced the 8088 in 1979, which became the "brain" of IBM's original PC, the pattern was clear: more power, more speed, more performance.

Over the years, Intel has continued to announce dramatic increases in chip performance and speed at a record-breaking pace. The latest generation of processors were launched in 1993, when Intel introduced the Pentium® processor. The chip contained 3.2 million transistors and ran at 100 million instructions per second (MIPS), better than 1,500 times the speed of 4004. The Pentium® III processor, announced in 1999, has 9.5 million transistors and runs at a whopping 1 "Gigahertz" (1 billion instructions per second).

Today, the beat goes on with the rollout of the Pentium® 4. In November 2000, Intel's newest microprocessor designed for high-performance computers was introduced, operating at up

Intel's 106 employees in front of the Mountain View plant in 1968. Included here are Robert Noyce and Gordon Moore (front row, left to right) and Andy Grove (second row, far right). Next to Mr. Grove is Marcian E. "Ted" Hoff (with glasses), one of the inventors of the microprocessor.

One of Adaptec's first controllers.

In the 20 years that Adaptec Inc. (NASDAQ: ADPT) has been in business, the company has evolved from a storage company to one that is now transforming storage access technologies so that they become more available to broader markets. For that reason, Adaptec of Milpitas is pioneering IP Storage, a technology that enables customers to have access to storage networking technology through use of their existing Ethernet investments.

Shortly after the company's founding in 1981, Adaptec began manufacturing SCSI adapters or Small Computer System Interfaces. These adapters allow computer users to connect various internal and external devices such as hard disk drives, scanners, and laser printers to a computer or a server thus making the transfer of data possible. However, as the computer industry continues to rapidly evolve, Adaptec has repositioned itself as the company that brings complex storage access technologies to broader markets.

Adaptec's products.

The firm no longer just provides SCSI connectivity, but a wide variety of I/O interfaces, including iSCSI, Fibre Channel, ATA, USB2.0, and FireWire (1394), that improve data performance and access on servers, desktops, and networks. Combined with its broad array of RAID and external storage products, Adaptec offers a wide variety of solutions that enable companies to move, manage, and protect data and digital content for e-business and Internet applications.

Information is a valuable commodity that people and companies require. Adaptec's role is to ensure that data is readily accessible when people need it, and that it is well protected.

Adaptec is targeting three market spaces: servers, networks, and desktops—all of which are growing. In the desktop area, the sale of new PC units may be slowing but the existing base of 400 million PCs requires input/output upgrades. The FireWire (1394) adapter made by Adaptec is now the leading SKU with major retailers and is among the top-selling SKUs in catalogues. The FireWire market is approximately $100 million per year in size today, and growing at a rate of 20 percent annually.

Adaptec is also the leading supplier in the transition from USB to USB2.0. The industry's first USB2.0 adapter was shipped by Adaptec in early 2001, and the company expects to have them on 3,000 retail shelves within a short period of time. This is another $100 million market with a compound annual growth rate of about 40 percent projected over the next three years.

Adaptec's storage access solutions.

The second market Adaptec participates in is the server market. As data continues to grow in volume and importance, data protection is becoming a mainstream requirement. As a result, Adaptec is extending its SCSI franchise to the RAID (Redundant Array of Inexpensive or Independent Disks) market where the company is the acknowledged leader. RAID boosts computer performance and protects data stored on disk drives. Adaptec's RAID products are designed into servers made by such leading manufacturers as Dell, Hewlett-Packard, Fujitsu Siemens, Gateway, and IBM. They are also critical components in high-performance networks, servers, and workstations.

Adaptec's RAID Everywhere is an aggressive initiative aimed at making RAID data protection more accessible to a broader market. The initiative includes the development of several new form factor RAID products that set new price/performance standards, reseller campaigns, a training and certification program, and a bold open systems initiative. The company's success with RAID is the foundation upon which Adaptec is moving ahead into the external storage

market. This is rapidly developing into a large market that is growing at the rate of 65 percent per year.

The third market Adaptec participates in is storage networking, where the company is aggressively moving with its innovative iSCSI products. As one of the early innovators of IP Storage, the company is well positioned to win a major share of this new market. Robert N. Stephens, CEO and president of the company, believes that Adaptec will continue to be "at the forefront of change" as storage becomes an increasingly critical element in people's business and personal lives.

Of course, the needs of very large companies are different than those for the smaller ones. For large Fortune 100 firms, cost and complexity are not an issue. They are for smaller businesses and Adaptec is not ignoring those needs. Adaptec is taking the large advanced storage technologies previously only available to the large firms and adapting them so that they are accessible to a broader market. By focusing on issues like price, interoperability, availability, scalability, and ease-of-use, Adaptec is making intelligent storage available to all. ■

IBM

In **Silicon Valley**

IBM has deep roots in Silicon Valley that reach back over half a century. In fact, a critical part of the computer revolution was brought about because of the work of a small team of local IBM engineers, and the history of IBM in San Jose is essentially the history of the computer information storage industry.

IBM set up shop in the Santa Clara Valley in the 1940s, and in 1952 Reynold Johnson and his team developed a new way for computers to store and process information. Until that time, mainframe computers used cards, magnetic tapes, or drums to store information, which could only be accessed sequentially. Many users were storing data on as many as 16 billion punch cards that had to be hand sorted and stored in huge bins.

IBM, Silicon Valley Laboratories.

Johnson and his team created a random access disk drive. It was still a cumbersome system that originally required 50 two-foot diameter disks that could store an amazing five megabytes of data. But it could access information in milliseconds. They later refined the system to require only 12 platters that could store eight megabytes.

Even their production techniques were crude by today's standards. They fashioned the first disks with a home workshop router. To create the magnetic coating, they strained, through nylon stockings onto the disk, a mixture of magnetic oxide particles and a base similar to that used to paint the Golden Gate Bridge. In 1956 the San Jose facility introduced the IBM 305 RAMAC (Random Access Method for Accounting and Control), the world's first hard-disk drive product. It is Rey Johnson who also later developed the world's first floppy disk, making the personal computer possible. Today the disk drive technologies developed by IBM are the heart of the information industry, providing fast reliable access to billions of pieces of data for corporate giants, small business owners, students, governments, schools systems, and universities. Data can now be stored 10 million times more densely than on the original RAMAC at about one millionth the cost—about a penny a megabyte.

IBM's first one-gigabyte disk drive, introduced in 1980, was the size of a refrigerator and weighed 550 pounds. It cost a mere $40,000. Last year, IBM introduced the one-gigabyte Microdrive, a device the size of a half dollar that can hold a thousand 200-page novels, 1,000 digitized photos, or close to 18 hours of digital music—for a cost of about $500.

IBM, Almaden Research Center.

It is this revolutionary IBM technology that provides affordable, high-capacity storage for a wide variety of handheld electronic products, including digital cameras, video cameras, PDAs, and portable Internet music players.

Through IBM storage technology, scientists and engineers have transformed disk drives from the huge, expensive behemoths of the '70s and '80s to featherweight devices that can fit into a shirt pocket. Possible future applications are endless, including storing electronic books and music, electronic wallets, maps and directions from Global Positioning Satellites, and information from wearable personal computers.

In December 2000, President Clinton awarded IBM the National Medal of Technology for its decades of innovation. IBM has also received the most patents worldwide for eight straight years, more than all Silicon Valley high-tech firms combined.

All of this means that IBM is and will continue to be an industry leader. From being the world's largest computer company as well as the largest services company in the world, IBM has now evolved into the most successful computing utility for e-businesses, offering the most complete range of computer services online.

A Major Valley Employer

With about 7,000 employees in its three principal San Jose locations, IBM is a major contributor to the valley economy. IBM and its employees have significant impact on local sales taxes, employee taxes, and real estate taxes that help support the valley's municipalities, as well as the state and federal government.

At 1GB, IBM's newly hatched MicroDrive platter is smaller than a quarter. For half a century of leadership in storage technology, in 2000 President Clinton awarded IBM the National Medal of Technology.

IBM's three main sites here are divided according to function. The 5,000-employee San Jose plant produces its technical marvels. When it opened in 1977 Silicon Valley Laboratory (SVL) was called the Santa Teresa Laboratory. It was one of the first labs built specifically for program-mers. Today the 1,500-member team develops products for a wide range of applications, with an emphasis on database development, a critical element of the Internet economy. The lab is also a software development house and a server farm.

One of the crown jewels of IBM is the 500-person Almaden Research Center, one of IBM's eight labs worldwide that do theoretical and practical research. Since 1983, nestled in the bowl of a pastoral hill separating two valleys, IBM's 630-acre lab houses the scientists creating tomorrow's technology and the fundamental science that distin-guishes the future. And what a future it will be! ■

IBM, Storage Technology Division plant.

Right: NEC's 64-bit MIPS RISC high-performance processor offers exceptional scalability and flexibility. Committed to meeting customers' cost, performance, and time-to-market requirements, the company offers solutions ranging from standard products to system-on-a-chip (SOC) solutions, as well as customized products for next-generation designs.

Bottom: NEC Electronics Inc., headquartered in Santa Clara, California, is one of the leading developers, manufacturers, and suppliers of semiconductor products in the United States.

NEC Electronics Inc. of Santa Clara is part of the worldwide NEC Corporation, which has provided cutting-edge technology in a number of fields since 1899 and is now emerging as a leading provider of global Internet solutions. In 2000, NEC Corporation set up three separate market-specific in-house companies to focus on the Internet solutions business. This restructuring came about as a response to the specific needs of NEC customers and their markets.

NEC is now better able to offer exceptional service, market insight, and strategic business partnerships through each of its new companies. NEC Solutions will offer Internet solutions directly to commercial and individual users, NEC Networks will provide Internet solutions primarily to the network operator market, and NEC Electron Devices will focus on the broadband market and provide semiconductors and electronic components to equipment manufacturers. Each area is important for the future of the Internet and NEC will be able to focus its strengths in each to offer customers new solutions and greater business opportunities.

NEC Electronics Inc., a subsidiary of NEC Electron Devices, one of the three new entities in the newly structured corporation, has been a leading supplier, designer, and manufacturer of innovative semiconductor technologies in the United States since 1981. In addition to its headquarters office in Santa Clara and its 709,000-square-foot manufacturing facility in Roseville, California, NEC Electronics has

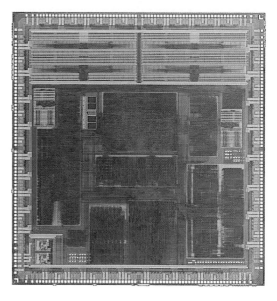

an extensive network of sales offices, representative offices, and distributors throughout the United States. Thanks to its technology, design expertise, manufacturing ability, and extensive resources, NEC Electronics is able to offer total systems solutions for its rapidly evolving target markets.

NEC Electronics provides a highly diverse line of products in a number of different areas. ASICs include CMOS and BiCMOS technologies, embedded arrays,

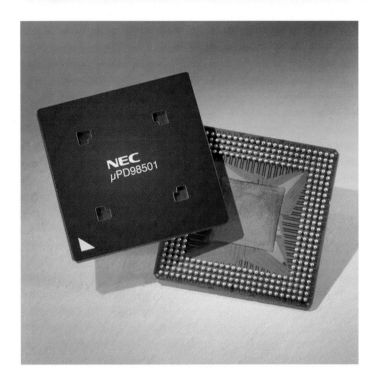

Company engineers work closely with customers in California and at seven additional design centers across the U.S. to provide hands-on support ranging from design evaluation to final testing. NEC engineers are skilled in all levels of system design and in developing solutions tailored to customer cost, performance, and time-to-market needs.

For over 15 years, NEC Electronics has been manufacturing a vast array of products from its Roseville plant and shipping to customers throughout the country. Offshore companies have difficulty matching these manufacturing facilities or the expertise of the NEC staff. A high-caliber facility like the one in Roseville is able to provide better access, faster problem resolution, and quicker time to market than other plants located outside the country. Plans are presently being formulated to expand manufacturing operations with a $1.4 billion 600,000-square-foot addition scheduled for completion within the next few years, depending on market conditions.

standard-cell CPU and PC peripheral cores, multimedia and consumer cores, and interface macros, to mention just a few. Other products include rechargeable lithium-ion batteries and standard and custom battery packs; communication devices such as Ethernet MAC and PHY cores; flat panel displays such as plasma display panels; microcontrollers; microprocessors; memory products; and consumer devices such as home networking 1394 PHYs and JPEG and HDTV cores.

All of this local design, production, and technical support is backed by the global resources of the international parent company. NEC has offices in 161 countries, 55 plants, and over 150,000 employees worldwide. This global manufacturing capability and the extensive system-level expertise of an international network translates into shorter design cycles, better access, securer supplies, and faster time to market for NEC customers in the U.S. ∎

NEC's innovative uPD98501 Network Controller provides communications technology to develop turnkey reference designs, which shorten product development time and help OEMs bring new products to market faster. NEC's chip, middleware, and reference design offerings allow you to rapidly develop tomorrow's solutions.

NEC Electronics' semiconductor manufacturing facility in Roseville, California, provides manufacturing close to its customers.

SPECTRA-PHYSICS

Spectra-Physics'
world headquarters
located at 1335
Terra Bella Avenue
in Mountain View,
California.

Spectra-Physics—the world's first commercial laser company and one of the oldest companies in the Silicon Valley—turned 40 years old in 2001. It was founded less than a year after the invention of the laser, and its history tracks the evolution of what is today a $4.6-billion industry.

Headquartered since inception in Mountain View, California, Spectra-Physics pioneered the laser industry through a succession of firsts: the first gas laser, the first ion laser, the next generation of argon ion lasers, and high-power helium neon (HeNe) lasers. Throughout the 1960s and '70s, the market for laser applications was largely scientific. The first industrial applications, powered by Spectra-Physics lasers, consisted of bar-code scanning and high-speed, non-contact printing. The company's launch of the first fiber-coupled semiconductor-based lasers in the 1980s led to the growth of the direct-to-press thermal imaging market in the '90s. For the last 10 years, Spectra-Physics' continued firsts have driven the laser industry's transition from conventional to semiconductor-based technology, culminating in the photonics paradigm of the 21st century.

SP lasers are used in
numerous computer
and micro-electronics
manufacturing processes
including wafer
repair, disk texturing,
via-hole drilling, and
PC board imaging.

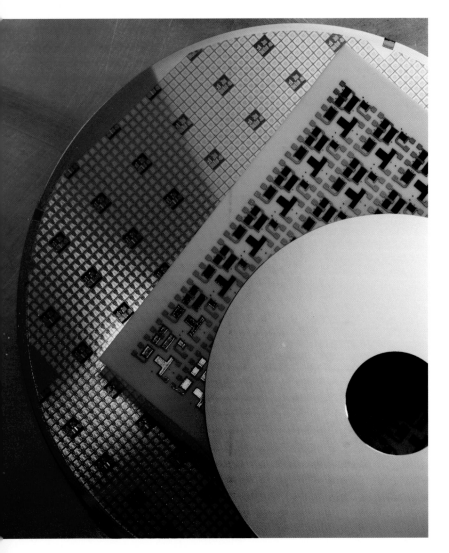

Photonics is the use of light to move data, process materials, and make measurements, among other applications. As the electronics industry evolved from vacuum tubes to transistors to integrated circuits over a 40-year period, so the photonics industry has evolved from gas and flash lamp-pumped lasers to high-power diode and diode-pumped solid-state lasers. Progressive generations of semiconductor-based lasers have reduced operating costs and physical size, while increasing efficiency and reliability, by orders of magnitude. The result of these economies is a proliferation of photonics applications in a wide range of markets.

The photonics opportunity for Spectra-Physics consists of six strategic markets. In addition to the original market from the 1960s—scientific research—and the first industrial market from the 1980s—image recording—the company's core markets today include computer and microelectronics manufacturing, industrial manufacturing, and medical diagnostics and treatment.

Spectra-Physics provides pump and seed lasers for research laser and amplifier systems, and high-power semiconductor lasers for commercial printing and graphics systems. Manufacturing applications range from the fabrication, inspection, and repair of semiconductors and computer displays to the prototyping and processing of industrial materials. Medical applications include confocal microscopy systems for cell research and a wide range of therapeutic and cosmetic procedures, from heart surgery to hair removal.

Spectra-Physics' newest and fastest growing market— and one at the center of the photonics revolution—is telecommunications, where the Internet explosion has fueled the build-out of fiber-optic networks and the resulting demand for dense wavelength division multiplexing (DWDM) applications.

As an industry leader in semiconductor-based laser and optical technologies, Spectra-Physics holds more than 140 patents, with a pipeline of applications pending. The company's operations are vertically integrated to

Multi-kilowatt direct semiconductor laser sources are the next step in the evolution of industrial material precessing systems.

support in-house design and fabrication of all strategic components—from semiconductor wafers to complete end-user systems. Manufacturing operations are based in Mountain View and Oroville, California; Tucson, Arizona; and Stahnsdorf, Germany.

As one of the largest global manufacturers of lasers and optics, Spectra-Physics has more than 800 industrial OEM customers and 1,200 research customers, with nearly half of its annual net sales sourced from outside the United States. Direct sales, service, and support offices are located in North America, Europe, and Japan. The company also has a network of more than 30 international distributors covering all major geographic markets. Spectra-Physics' total work force exceeds 1,150 employees worldwide.

Spectra-Physics originally went public on the New York Stock Exchange in 1967. The company was acquired first by Ciba-Geigy of Switzerland in 1986 and then by Pharos of Sweden in 1990. The current entity completed an initial public offering in 1997, and its common stock is traded on the Nasdaq National Market System under the symbol, "SPLI."

Spectra-Physics' business strategy consists of four key points: 1) to focus research and development on high-growth revenue opportunities in telecommunications, solid-state ultraviolet lasers, and other selected markets; 2) to continue expanding its manufacturing capacity and capabilities; 3) to leverage its vertically integrated manufacturing processes; and 4) to pursue strategic investments in the acquisition of businesses and technologies.

Looking to the future, Spectra-Physics expects continued growth in the telecommunications market, as well as in its five core markets. To the photonics opportunity of the 21st century, Spectra-Physics brings more than 17 years of experience in semiconductor-based lasers and 40 years in high-power optics for laser applications. At multiple levels, the company is a Silicon Valley original. ■

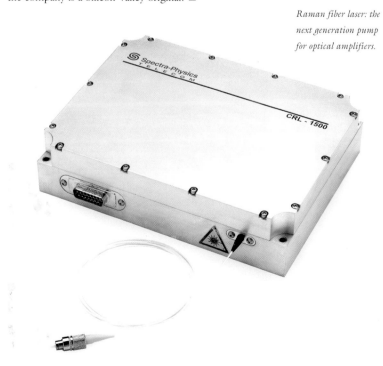

Raman fiber laser: the next generation pump for optical amplifiers.

BEA SYSTEMS, INC.

Bill Coleman, founder, chairman, and CEO (left) and Alfred Chuang, founder, president, and COO (right) of BEA Systems, Inc.

Founded in January 1995 by computer industry veterans Bill Coleman, Ed Scott, and Alfred Chuang, BEA Systems, Inc., has risen in only six years to become a world leader in the e-business software industry. With 3,200 employees, 10,000 customers, and 92 offices in 32 countries around the globe, and a $1 billion annual revenue run rate in early 2001, BEA provides the infrastructure that enables its customers to succeed in the challenging and ever-evolving environment of e-business.

San Jose was the optimum location for the development of such a company as BEA. Being in the "platform business, we're able to thrive in this unique culture," says Kevin Faulkner, vice president of investor relations. A location in the heart of Silicon Valley ensures that BEA has quick access to the best software and database developers, hardware companies, application companies, and other professionals devoted to the growth and continued success of the computer industry and the companies that depend on it.

The foundation of BEA's success has always been to anticipate and quickly respond to challenges faced by its customers in conducting their business operations. In the beginning, BEA's founders responded to the need for an operating system for the new client server networks that began to emerge in the mid-1990s. BEA's foundation product, Tuxedo®, provides the enterprise middleware solution for application servers. It quickly became a proven operating system for networks. BEA's Tuxedo handles many transactions—including inventory updates, billing, shipping, and recording transactions in financial records—as a single business event, greatly simplifying the complicated transactions that e-business requires.

The next wave of computer evolution was the development and growth of the Internet. BEA responded to that wave in the same successful manner, with the BEA WebLogic® E-Business Platform, a comprehensive infrastructure for developing and deploying reliable, scalable business applications. BEA WebLogic, which includes BEA's Tuxedo, has become the infrastructure of choice for the New Economy. BEA WebLogic "allows a single, central

BEA's headquarters in San Jose, California.

system to control business-to-business, business-to-customer, and core operations," explains Faulkner. It "future-proofs" e-business by enabling companies to respond rapidly, supporting growth, providing built-in agility, and protecting existing investments in enterprise systems. Today, BEA WebLogic is the de facto standard used by more than 1,900 systems integrators, independent software vendors (ISVs), and application service providers (ASPs).

Unlike its competitors' similar products, BEA software is not fashioned to optimize only BEA solutions. Instead, BEA products provide an open system independent of hardware, operating systems, databases, tools, and so on. BEA's Tuxedo and BEA WebLogic, which account for more than 80 percent of BEA's license revenue, can be installed on any existing system its customers may already use. Faulkner says this is one reason why BEA products "exceed what anyone else is able to do."

Rather than target one industry, BEA products operate in a variety of businesses. BEA has won the trust—and the business—of many large corporations, including E-Trade, Charles Schwab, United Airlines, British Airways, Citibank, Enterprise Rent-A-Car, Amazon.com, and FedEx. In fact, 91 percent of the *Fortune* Global 500 telecommunications companies, computer/office equipment companies, and financial securities and diversified financial companies all use BEA products. BEA also counts a majority of the *Fortune* Global 500 pharmaceutical, health-care, airline and delivery service, and commercial banking companies among its customers.

The metrics of success for BEA are many:
• BEA was the fastest software company in history to reach the $1 billion annual revenue run rate.
• BEA logged 22 straight quarters of record revenue, as of the first quarter 2001.
• The BEA WebLogic server is the world's number one Java application server.
• BEA has more than 1,900 partners, growing by 100 a month.
• *BusinessWeek* named BEA the Number One Technology Company with the highest shareholder return: 884 percent (June 2000).
• BEA WebLogic Server won eight "best of category" awards in 2000 alone.
• BEA has more than 100,000 developers, growing by more than 50 percent a quarter.

"It's a continuing challenge from a technology standpoint," says Faulkner. "We always want to be at the leading edge of the revolution. It's all about the adoption of technology. We are constantly diversifying and expanding within the realm of infrastructure, and those markets are constantly changing and redefining themselves. We've moved from the client server era to the Internet era and now to the wireless era, where access to the Web will expand immensely and the infrastructure will also have to expand to meet the need."

BEA's goal is to be in the forefront of these changes, just as it always has, enabling its customers to successfully ride the next wave of the Information Age. ■

Headquartered in San Jose, Aspect employs 2,600 people worldwide, with sales offices in more than 20 countries.

No one knows better than Aspect how important the word "relationship" is. "The economy of today and tomorrow is a relationship economy. Successful businesses have to manage a complex web of relationships with customers, suppliers, partners, and employees," stated Beatriz Infante, president and chief executive officer of Aspect Communications. "And Aspect supplies the software solutions that make customer relationships work."

Aspect is a leading provider of customer relationship management (CRM) software, which enables companies to effectively manage the different media—phone, fax, e-mail, or Web—that customers use to contact their businesses. This multichannel contact center enables companies to blend customer interactions, streamline operations, reduce costs, increase revenues, build their brands, and promote customer loyalty. As a matter of fact, over 80 percent of the *Fortune 50* companies use Aspect solutions to provide better service more efficiently.

Saks Incorporated is a perfect example of an Aspect customer who uses the software to their advantage. When people hear the name "Saks," they automatically think of the well-known New York store that has a reputation for customer service and quality products. With customers expecting premium, personalized service no matter how they contact the company, Saks turned to Aspect to help them exceed customer expectations and build customer loyalty.

Beatriz Infante led Aspect's transition from a call center hardware vendor to a provider of enterprise solutions for companies wanting to manage voice, e-mail, and Web contacts seamlessly. Aspect is now the leader in multichannel contact centers.

Through the use of Aspect CRM solutions, Saks has been able to reduce its average speed to answer from 45 seconds to eight seconds and ensured that its gold customers experience only a one-second wait. Aspect has not only enhanced the customer experience and the company's reputation, it has also saved Saks over $1 million a year in payroll costs alone and increased productivity by 40 percent.

Aspects' package of advanced software products has other uses, too. It allows companies to automatically route each customer to the most appropriate person to help them with their request. It also provides employees with access to customer histories, account, and credit information instantly at the moment of contact, so they can give their customers personalized service.

"We not only help companies manage real-time contacts," stated David Puglia, Aspect's senior vice president, Global Marketing, "we also help them forecast their contact center staffing requirements to ensure that they are delivering a consistent level of customer service at all times." Aspect's eWorkforce Management software takes the guesswork out of staffing by capturing historical data to predict future needs—such as a particular time of day, season, or peak period.

"If you don't have enough people in the call center, obviously customers are not going to stay on hold forever," stated Puglia, "and if you have too many, the company is losing money." The challenge, then, is for businesses to optimize their resources while building long-term purchasing relationships through personalized care.

the complex dynamics of customer care and voice-based customer interactions. With the advent of the Internet we have extended that knowledge into other media, including e-mail and Web."

Aspect continues to innovate and help its customers prepare to leverage new technologies such as IP (Internet Protocol). In 2000 and 2001, Aspect introduced three new IP-based contact center products.

Aspect has also extended its reach into the community. "As a socially responsible company, we've always seen the communities around us as stakeholders in our corporate success," says Infante. In 2000, the company set aside over three-quarters of a million dollars of their profits in the U.S. to invest in programs like San Jose's Orchard Elementary School. A school partner since 1996, Aspect's commitment has progressed over the years from employees visiting classrooms and sharing insights about the working world to now funding an Extended Learning Program. Since Aspect began their involvement at Orchard, the school's test scores have improved 85 points, which is pretty remarkable considering 25 percent of the students are speaking English for the first time.

Whether assisting companies to build strong relationships with their customers or building strong relationships in the communities where Aspect operates, one thing is for sure: Aspect is a progressive company that stays one step ahead of the rest. ■

The trend to converged voice-data networks brings new challenges to businesses. Aspect solutions help companies apply the same business rules they use for managing their telephone calls from customers to managing contacts in the wireless world, including those via Web-enabled cell phones and handheld devices.

What sets Aspect apart from its competitors is 17 years of experience in the CRM industry; a global presence that includes 2,500 employees in 28 offices in the United States, Europe, Australia, and Asia-Pacific; and knowledge and expertise gained from over 7,600 implementations world-wide. "A complete CRM solution consists of a variety of technologies. Aspect provides a foundation server that ties these technologies and others together, and manages large numbers of customer interactions smoothly," stated David Puglia. "Coming from the call center industry, we understand

Aspect's leading-edge technology solutions allow contact centers to synchronize all their contact points, whether customers make contact via phone, e-mail, or the Web.

INFINEON TECHNOLOGIES

In the Silicon Valley, especially in San Jose, high technology is ubiquitous. People are talking about technology at the stores, on the radio, and while standing in line. But even outside of San Jose, electronics are everywhere—in computers, mobile phones, PDAs, toys, cars, jet airplanes, heart pacemakers, and automatic teller machines. In fact, the average person encounters chip-powered devices about 60 times a day.

Infineon Technologies designs, produces, and sells the semiconductor chips that make up these intelligent electronics. "We are very well positioned to supply the industry with nearly all of the most important, and most valuable components of smart machines," says Jan du Preez, president of Infineon Technologies North America Corporation. Infineon provides manufacturers with the building blocks to create smart products for today and tomorrow—from the "brain" or microprocessor to the memory where data is stored, through the communications components that allow devices and people to converse with each other electronically.

Infineon Technologies was created in April 1999 when Siemens AG spun-off its semiconductor business operations. The company, which is headquartered in Munich, Germany, and operates in the United States from San Jose, in Asia-Pacific from Singapore, and in Japan from Tokyo, is now one of the top 10 semiconductor manufacturers in the world. It is a leading supplier of integrated circuit (IC) solutions for wireless and mobile communications, automotive and industrial, and security systems and chip card applications. In fact, Infineon's semiconductors are in 7 out of every 10 mobile phones and are in most European-made automobiles.

"Through chip miniaturization and performance optimization, Infineon leads the continual development of new and improved products and systems," stated du Preez. For example, new portable computers and small, feature-rich mobile phones will soon include Bluetooth wireless networking capability, thanks to Infineon's "BlueMoon" chipsets. The company's "Audo" line of microcontrollers is being designed into next generation cars from Detroit and Germany. And Infineon's PAROLI modules and transceivers are helping companies around the world build new broadband communications networks through fiber optic links.

At Infineon's core is a young, dynamic company with a progressive viewpoint to explore the endless possibilities of innovation. As a matter of fact, its name is derived from "infinity" and "eon" (from the ancient Greek for eternity and life). And its 29,000 employees truly practice their corporate motto of "Never Stop Thinking" by developing innovative approaches to designing "systems-on-chip," new processes for manufacturing components such as power diodes (known as Schottky's) made with silicon carbide, and reducing the size of GPS location systems to just two chips. Infineon's inventiveness also shows in its intellectual property portfolio that includes more than 28,000 patents worldwide in almost 100 countries.

"Operating in the high-risk environment of the high-tech industry calls for a pioneering spirit, a healthy portion of entrepreneurial courage, and the ability to adjust rapidly to new challenges," says Dr. Ulrich Schumacher, president and chief executive officer of Infineon Technologies AG. "At Infineon Technologies, we are equipped with years of experience as well as leading-edge technology and manufacturing know-how. This means we are a reliable, credible partner right from the word 'go.'"

With a global presence, Infineon Technologies (headquartered in Munich, Germany) operates in the U.S. from its San Jose location (shown here), in the Asia Pacific region from Singapore, and in Japan from Tokyo.

It also means that Infineon's customers are requiring more comprehensive solutions from their design partner for increasingly complex applications as consumers expect more features in less space in their electronic devices. Thus, Infineon has geared itself as a formidable competitor in the semiconductor arena and is a global market leader in many of its product areas.

In the year 2000, Infineon was one of the top three providers of controller chips for GSM cell phones and electronics in automobiles, and the number one supplier of chips for cordless home phones. Furthermore, the company has been recognized for its manufacturing expertise in the area of DRAM and other memory chips used in computers, communications systems, video displays, and portable devices.

Infineon has also been ranked by researchers at Frost & Sullivan and Gartner Dataquest as the world's number one supplier of security and chip card ICs, the products that make 'Smart Cards' smart.

Global leadership requires global presence, and Infineon has operations worldwide, including top manufacturing facilities on three continents and design centers strategically located in the heart of the industry's "brain concentration centers" such as Sophia-Antipolis in France and in Silicon Valley (San Jose).

"Just as the digital revolution has made electronics a worldwide business, Infineon's core technologies also must be everywhere," says du Preez, "especially in San Jose, where more than half of the nation's largest electronics firms are located. As a global player in the electronics industry, we are proud to be among the many who have established their presence in one of the world's premier digital cities." ■

Top: Peter Bauer, executive vice president sales and marketing, and Dr. Ulrich Schumacher, president and CEO, with San Jose Mayor Ron Gonzales at the open house celebration for Infineon's San Jose location.
Left: Infineon Technologies offers semiconductor and system solutions for applications in the wired and wireless communications markets, for security systems and smartcards, for the automotive and industrial sectors, as well as memory products.

"We don't make the computer chips that run your electronic equipment. We make the manufacturing process for those chips more efficient."

This paraphrase of a popular television ad sums up what Electroglas is about. Its products play a vital part in the making of integrated circuits (ICs) for the global semiconductor industry.

ICs are the brains behind every electronic product, from coffee makers to cutting-edge computers. Within each integrated circuit is an infinitely complex and intricate world of transistors, diodes, capacitors, and other electronic devices. Connected together, these devices allow ICs to perform their intended functions, whether for memory, logic, communications, or microprocessing.

Manufacturing and testing the silicon wafers on which integrated circuits are fabricated is equally intricate and complex. A modern chip fabrication and assembly facility can cost more than $2 billion. As many as 30,000 wafers can be manufactured each month in this facility, and each wafer can contain more than a thousand ICs. Because of the incredibly complex fabrication process, as many as 25 percent of the ICs can be defective. This "yield loss" costs the manufacturer millions of dollars.

Electroglas helps worldwide manufacturers improve their fabrication operations to reduce process variability and improve yields, thereby improving efficiency and profitability for the industry.

One of Silicon Valley's pioneer companies, Electroglas has provided the tools and software to make the semiconductor fabrication process more accurate, more efficient, and more profitable. A resumé of its efforts reads like a history of the semiconductor industry.

• 1959 Arthur Lash starts manufacturing glass capillaries (tiny tubes) for the new semiconductor industry in his garage in Sunnyvale.

• 1964 Electroglas introduces the first commercial prober for testing semiconductor "die" (the finished wafers with their built-in circuits).

• 1973 Electroglas introduces the 1034X wafer prober, considered a milestone in the semiconductor industry.

• 1982 The company introduces the Electroglas 2001X prober, the industry's first fully automated prober. The 2001X earned $85 million in sales in 1984 and became the industry standard.

• 1985 Electroglas brings out the 2010X wafer probing system that utilizes a robotic material handler, processing wafers quickly and safely without operator intervention.

• 1992 The fourth generation of Electroglas wafer probers comes on stream, the automatic 4060X with the new EGCommander system software.

• 1993 Electroglas becomes an independent company, with public stock offering on the NASDAQ (Symbol EGLS).

• 1996 Introduces the Horizon 4090X prober for faster speed, improved accuracy, and broad compatibility for enhanced productivity.

Top: Electroglas' chairman and chief executive officer, Curt Wozniak (second from left), San Jose Mayor Ron Gonzales (right), and members of the San Jose Redevelopment Agency at ribbon-cutting ceremony for Electroglas' new headquarters in south San Jose. Right: Electroglas' new corporate headquarters in south San Jose, California.

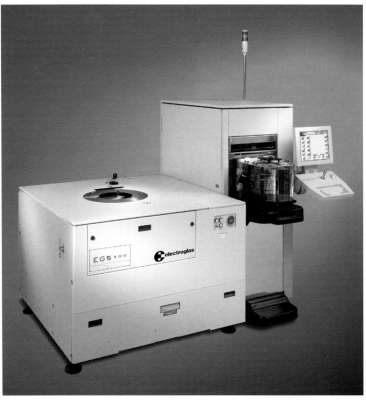

Electroglas' EG5|300, wafer probing system. The EG5|300 prober is designed to meet the demanding probing requirements of 300-mm wafers and offers exceptionally high accuracy and throughput.

More than 4,000 trees and shrubs were planted to restore the natural beauty and countryside appearance of the grounds. Outside, employees can use the sand volleyball court, full-size basketball court, and the bocci ball court set in the middle of an olive grove picnic area. Inside, there is a 1,700-square-foot fitness and exercise facility with locker rooms.

Perhaps even more beneficial to the 650 employees of Electroglas is the fact that its new campus in San Jose's Edenvale Industrial Park allows a "reverse commute" for more than 90 percent its workforce. This has proven to be a major time-saver for Electroglas' employees, to say nothing of the reduced stress level getting to and from work.

According to Curt Wozniak, chairman and chief executive officer: "Electroglas is a friendly, informal type environment where employees can enjoy their work and each other. At the same time, we are a dynamic, growing company that saw net sales increase by 78 percent in 2000. Electroglas has mirrored the growth of the Silicon Valley itself, building our reputation as an industry leader while establishing a firm footing as a company with true roots in this area. Our blend of growth and stability makes Electroglas an excellent place for skilled workers to grow and advance their careers." ■

• 1997 Knights Technology, Inc., joins the Electroglas family, with advanced software products to help manufacturers improve production yields, reduce costs, and shorten time to market.

• 1997 Electroglas brings Techné Systems on board. Renamed the Inspection Products Division, this Electroglas operation supplies high-tech post-fab inspection systems to automate identification, classification, and measurement of wafer defects.

• 1999 Automatic Wafer Probing Systems EG4|200 and EG5|300 are introduced. The EG4|200 can exert the extremely high probe loads required for multiple die and bumped wafer testing. The EG5|300 features new system architecture and advanced automation features for testing 300-mm wafers.

• 2000 Electroglas introduces the Horizon 4090f automatic film-frame probing system for testing die on ultra-thin wafers, the EG5|300 high-throughput, automatic prober for 300-mm wafers, and the QuickSilver automated optical inspection system for identifying defects on gold-bumped wafers.

• 2001 Electroglas adds Statware, Inc., to the family. This operation specializes in software tools that enable real-time analysis and graphical data reporting from test equipment via Web browsers.

Electroglas celebrated the end of the millennium by moving into its new, state-of-the-art corporate campus in south San Jose, California. This 260,000-square-foot facility is set against picturesque foothills and designed for employee comfort.

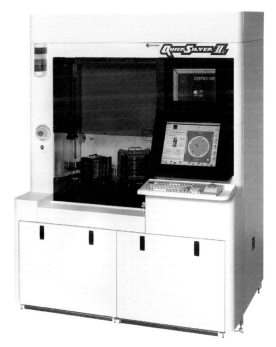

Electroglas Inspection Products' QuickSilver IIe, optical wafer inspection system. The QuickSilver IIe is an automated semiconductor wafer inspection tool that automatically identifies, measures, and classifies defects on processed semiconductor wafers at production rates.

Young Sohn,
Chairman and CEO
Oak Technology, Inc.

The old adage "From little acorns, mighty oaks grow," resonates well in the 21st century, especially when referring to Sunnyvale-headquartered Oak Technology Inc.

From Silicon Chips To System Solutions

Founded by David Tsang in 1987, the acorn that began as a silicon chip manufacturer stands tall at the beginning of the new century. It has evolved into a solutions-oriented company that holds first-place supplier standing for its fully integrated products and technologies. These include high-performance integrated semiconductors, software, and platform solutions supplied to original equipment manufacturers around the world that serve the optical storage and digital imaging markets. Oak's product family includes integrated circuits, system solutions, and supporting software and firmware for storing, manipulating, and distributing all types of digital content. Its mission is to bring easy-to-use and affordable convergence technologies to everyone.

Organizationally, Oak operates in two divisions. The first, the Optical Storage Group headquartered in Sunnyvale, serves the CD-RW and DVD markets. Its sister division, Oak Imaging Group headquartered in Woburn, Massachusetts, provides digital imaging for advanced copiers, printers, faxes, scanners, and MFPs. Key customers include Canon, Hewlett Packard, LG Electronics, Mitsumi, Ricoh, Samsung, Sharp, Toshiba, Xerox, and Yamaha, among others. Its imaging market includes more than 40 original equipment manufacturers that represent about 80 percent of the printing peripheral market.

Worldwide Operations

The company employs about 450 worldwide at research facilities, design centers, and sales offices. About 80 percent of its workforce is in the United States, with about 175 on staff at its Sunnyvale facility. More than half of those are technical and engineering professionals. Besides its Sunnyvale and Woburn, Massachusetts, facilities, Oak Technology operates in Tucson, Arizona; Austin, Texas; and San Diego, California, in the United States. Globally, the company's offices include Dortmund, Germany; Seoul, Korea; Manchester, England; Tokyo, Japan; Taipei, Taiwan; and Guangdon, China.

Acquisitions Spark Growth

Like rings on an oak tree, several milestones mark the company's growth. In 1993, the company pioneered the IDE/ATAPI CD-ROM controller, shipping 2 million by the next year when it also debuted the industry's first MPEG controller specifically for personal computers, allowing PCs to play CDs. A 1995 independent public offering and subsequent trading on the Nasdaq Stock Exchange at OAKT, took the company from the small private sector to the public eye and investments. That same

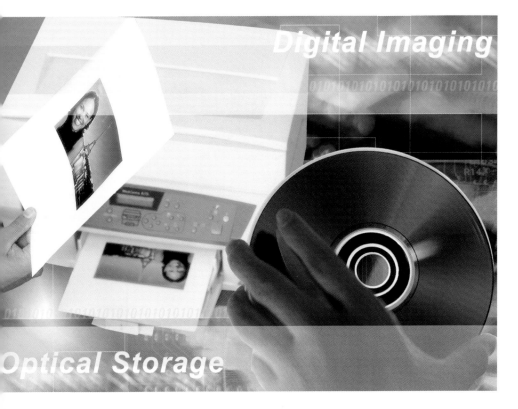

Digital Imaging

Optical Storage

DVD-RW technology and will deliver digital video recording capability to homes beginning in 2002. Driven by increased Internet broadband access, digital photography, improved inkjet quality, and the speed of personal multifunction printers, the trend is toward PC-less printing. And Oak Technology has positioned itself for the new paradigm by leveraging its DSP technology, color imaging algorithm, connectivity software, and XHTML print solution.

Venture Fund Fuels New Developments

Recognizing that its strength depends on continued new technologies, the company established the $25 million Oak Technology Venture Fund in 2000. The fund provides investments focusing on technologies that bring together audio, video, and data content for computing and consumer-electronics applications, such as iAppliances. The fund targets early stage projects that have reached the prototype stage, with business plan and key executives in place. Target portfolio companies must demonstrate a substantial technological and/or market synergy with Oak's core technologies and businesses, which enables the companies to leverage each other's capabilities to exploit market opportunities.

In keeping with the stature of its name and the contributions oak trees make to communities, Oak Technology contributes, too. In Sunnyvale and San Francisco, the company is a sponsor of the San Francisco Symphony, KTEH Public Television, and the Churchill Club, among other philanthropic endeavors. ■

year, Oak acquired Pixel Magic, entering the digital imaging market. The next year brought the launch of the first CD-R/CD-RW controller, so end users could now record and listen from the same device.

In 1999, retaining his post as board chair, founder David Tsang turned the presidential and CEO reigns over to Young Sohn. That year, the company introduced the first single-chip controller for CD-RW devices. The year 2000 brought another acquisition—Xionics Document Technologies, and its embedded software for digital offices; expansion of the Imaging Group to Woburn, Massachusetts; introduction of its highly integrated combo CD-RW/DVD controller; and announcement of its SimpliCD CD recording software. By early in the 21st century, Oak had sold more than 130 million optical storage controllers.

Today, an experienced management team, proven long-term partnerships with leading customers, and a debt-free, strong balance sheet make Oak Technology well-positioned for enabling the new digital world to capture, store, and distribute data effectively at light speed.

With an eye to the future, the company is poised to continue its penetration of the CD-RW drive market because of the demand for after-market attachments, with more than 500 million personal computer users seeking attachable drives in 2001. The company is also investing in

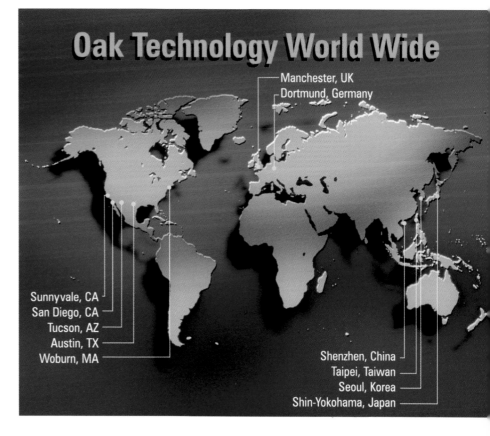

Oak Technology World Wide

Manchester, UK
Dortmund, Germany

Sunnyvale, CA
San Diego, CA
Tucson, AZ
Austin, TX
Woburn, MA

Shenzhen, China
Taipei, Taiwan
Seoul, Korea
Shin-Yokohama, Japan

PEMSTAR INC.

Got an idea for an electronic product? PEMSTAR can design and manufacture the product, and ship it directly to your customers. The company provides expertise to handle the full continuum of engineering, manufacturing, and fulfillment services—from concept to customer. PEMSTAR's customers enjoy faster time to market, improved product quality, and increased profitability.

Top: PEMSTAR's ProCenter facility at 1877 Senter Road. Right: PEMSTAR employees use the latest technology to perform opto-electrical alignment.

Silicon Valley makes the perfect location for two PEMSTAR facilities that together employ over 600 of the company's 4,000 workers. Both located in San Jose, one site is the company's product realization and optimization center, or ProCenter, located at 1877 Senter Street. It opened in August 2000 and employs about 200. The other PEMSTAR facility, two blocks away at 2020 South 10th Street, is a technologically advanced electronics manufacturing plant that PEMSTAR acquired in 1999.

ProCenter

One of five such centers that PEMSTAR operates worldwide, the San Jose ProCenter provides full new product introduction capabilities to customers, specializing in products for the optical and wireless telecommunications industries. The center's wide range of activities includes design engineering, prototype production, low volume production runs, and testing. Its unique development process, which is ISO 9001 certified, synchronizes prototyping with manufacturing and testing. PEMSTAR's ProCenter facility reduces development time, manages potential technical risks, and provides a smooth transition from the engineering phase to the manufacturing stage. The ProCenter's engineering services include industrial design; mechanical and electrical hardware; firmware and software; and integration skills, such as electro-mechanical, system level, manufacturing process, testing, and technology integration. Services also include

core engineering, program and product management, manufacturing readiness reviews, product assessments, supplier selection, and management. Company-designed roadmaps for each of PEMSTAR's customers outline the best component choices, facility where it should be built, and material and delivery management.

In addition to new product introduction services, the ProCenter also provides product optimization services. Utilizing continuous improvement processes, engineers continually refine and enhance customers' products.

These turnkey engineering and product management services differentiate PEMSTAR from others in the electronic manufacturing services industry, providing a more comprehensive set of services and a competitive edge.

Electronics Manufacturing

A workforce of about 400 at the 10th Street facility produces electronics components and systems for the communications, computer, data storage, and industrial equipment industries. The company's contract engineering, manufacturing, and fulfillment services supply a mix of industry leaders as well as emerging companies.

Products made in San Jose include components for Western Multiplex's point-to-point radios, SANCastle's Global Fabric telecommunications switch, and ONI Systems fiber-optic communications products, among others.

PEMSTAR's manufacturing facilities can accommodate monthly product volumes that range from just a few systems each month to several thousand each day. Manufacturing services utilize the cell method and a cross-functional team,

PEMSTAR *has the technology and the expertise to manufacture a wide range of electronic products on a worldwide basis.*

and include optical component, module and systems manufacturing, fiber handling, splicing and connectorization, flex cable and printed circuit board assembly, and systems assembly. Extensive testing ensures that products are fully functional before shipment. The company-developed build-to-order process incorporates customer-specified configurations. PEMSTAR also warehouses customers' products, providing global distribution services as well as aftermarket warranty and repair.

As a specialist in technically demanding, precision electro-mechanical assembly, the company takes pride in its entry-level high-tech workforce at its San Jose manufacturing facility. There, workers enjoy opportunities to expand their skills, excel, and be vital contributors to the technologically advanced marketplace while reaping attractive benefits. These include tangibles, such as stock options and profit sharing, and a company culture that values production workers as key to the company's success.

International Reach

Founded in 1994 by eight IBM executives, and head-quartered in Rochester, Minnesota, PEMSTAR began the new millennium with 15 facilities at 13 global sites. Its manufacturing facilities and engineering centers encompass more than one million square feet, with locations in the United States, Asia, Mexico, Europe, and South America.

PEMSTAR's chairman and chief executive officer, since the company's founding, Allen J. Berning, received the 1999 national Ernst & Young Entrepreneur of the Year Award.

The company, too, has been widely recognized. In October 2000, PEMSTAR was named one of the 500 fastest-growing private companies in the country by *Inc. Magazine*, based on results through 1999. PEMSTAR's rapid climb also earned it high billing in the 2000 Deloitte & Touche's Technology Fast 500, a ranking of North America's fastest-growing technology companies, and it ranked fourth on Deloitte & Touche's list of Minnesota Technology Fast 50 companies. PEMSTAR completed an initial public offering in August 2000 and a secondary offering in June 2001 and is listed on the NASDAQ exchange at PMTR. ∎

PEMSTAR's *receiving and transmitting optical subassembly program incorporates the latest in fiber-optic technology and optical engineering capabilities to build components for IBM's Optical Interconnect Devices.*

Shopping is easy and great for those who know just the product they need. And thanks to Calico Commerce Inc.'s pioneering technology for selling, it can be convenient and effective even for those who don't know precisely what they want.

Take the shopper visiting the Staples Web site looking for a computer, for example. "Home or business?" the interactive site asks. Then, "High performance, cutting edge, or affordable?" and "Desktop or notebook?" With each answer, the Staples site gives recommendations on the best buys for the purchaser's needs. And the guru behind that recommendation is Calico Commerce Inc., founded in San Jose, California, in 1994.

Interactive Selling

The Staples' site illustrates the needs analysis, recommendation, configuration, price, and quote capabilities of Calico Commerce's products that help businesses successfully sell through all their channels. The benefits prove particularly effective for those selling complex products, such as computers, with fluctuating pricing.

During the needs analysis, the Calico system first works to understand the customer's requirements and quickly narrows down the options. Calico dubs this "understanding the buyer." Using Calico's guided-buying process, the system then recommends the best product or configuration, presenting alternative solutions to meet the customer's needs. This intelligent assessment of the customer's needs presents the user with only the information vital to the current shopping experience, rather than broad catalog-based selling. In the configuration stage, customers can trade off options and compare alternatives while ensuring the product they ultimately choose delivers what they need. Finally, the system delivers a quote for the purchase.

In addition to delivering compelling selling experiences to customers, Calico's products ensure that quotes and orders are complete and accurate, making sure every customer receives exactly what he wants, the first time around.

Recommending Products To Shoppers

Together, these products and services have put Calico on the map as a source for advanced technology in configuring and recommending products and systems in the high-tech, industrial, telecommunications, financial services, and retail sectors. Besides Staples, other companies who have put Calico products to work for them include Best Buy, GE

CEO Alan Nauman is dedicated to growing Calico into the leading interactive selling solution provider.

Capital, Honeywell, Kodak, UUNET, Mitsubishi, Sharp Microelectronics, and numerous more. For each customer, Calico delivers a flexible product that can be tailored to individual needs, provides training, implementation services, and post-implementation maintenance and consultation.

Calico also has a strong alliance program that offers a full range of enterprise solutions to help customers sell more effectively, deploy applications quickly, and realize rapid return on investment.

Continuing to develop highly interactive web-based recommendation and configuration applications that lead the industry in scalability and performance is on the agenda for Calico's future.

A California Company

While the name "Calico" might imply a purring kitten or a snuggly quilt, its origin is pure Silicon Valley. While studying at the Massachusetts Institute of Technology, the company's founder told his classmates he was headed to California to start a company. He created the name as an abbreviation for "California Company."

Traded on the Nasdaq exchange at CLIC, Calico Commerce became a public company in October 1999. In addition to its San Jose office in the River Park Towers, the company operates sales offices at several U.S. locations—Atlanta, Boston, Chicago, and New York. Outside the U.S., it has offices in Japan and Europe.

Calico customer service representatives are always happy to support valued customers.

Among Calico's breakthrough developments was the March 2000 launch of Advisor, the first 100 percent Java standards-based configuration and recommendation application. It was the first company to achieve such a milestone with artificial intelligence technology.

In November 2000, Calico was ranked 63rd on the Deloitte & Touche Technology Fast 500, a ranking of the five hundred fastest-growing technology companies in North America. It achieved this rank for its revenue growth from 1995 to 1999, when the company boosted sales by 6,500 percent. Calico was also named 14th in Deloitte & Touche's Fast 50 Silicon Valley listing.

While its business focus is on high technology leadership, Calico's community focus is firmly planted on the ground. Among other community activities, the company supports Habitat for Humanity and was a founding member of the Entrepreneur's Foundation. ■

Calico employees share a joke at the weekly beer bash.

Top: Dominic Orr, president and chief executive, Alteon WebSystems. Dr. Orr has over 20 years of experience in the computer and high-speed networking industries. Most recently, Dr. Orr was a senior vice president at Bay Networks, leading its LAN switching, hub, and network management business. Prior to this, Dr. Orr spent 12 years at Hewlett Packard directing the company's Asia Pacific operations. Prior to HP, Dr. Orr was with Hughes Aircraft where he led the design and implementation of the first large-scale local area networks for the Radar Systems Group. Dr. Orr received his PhD in physics from the California Institute of Technology. Bottom: Selina Lo, vice president of marketing, Alteon WebSystems. Known as the "Dragon Lady" of Silicon Valley, Ms. Lo's "take-no-prisoners" management style was a big factor in Alteon's success. Prior to Alteon, Ms. Lo was a co-founder and vice president at Centillion Networks, acquired by Bay Networks in May of 1996.

Hate to wait? So do Web users. Capitalizing on that impatience, Alteon WebSystems Inc. achieved a quick and skyrocketing climb to success with its pioneering Internet switch that finds the best—and fastest—way to serve content to users through the network, eliminating that dreaded "Web wait."

Quick Climb To The Top

While many companies grow slowly over decades, Alteon's growth came as close to overnight as you can get. Founders John Hayes, Wayne Hathaway, and Ted Schroeder began working on high-speed interface cards for servers in May 1996. In less than five years, the company had launched a breakthrough product, brought in millions, gone public, and sold for nearly $8 billion to Nortel Networks Corp.

Besides its products, Alteon's key to success was its people. Originally, the three founders intended to operate an egalitarian, we're-all-in-this-together kind of a company. Within months, they realized that wasn't going to take them to the top, and they needed some cohorts with better business sense. Dominic Orr was their man and Selina Lo their woman. Both came on board in 1996, Orr as president and chief executive officer and Lo as vice president of marketing and products.

Alteon shipped its first product—a Layer 4 through 7 Web Network Interface Card—in February 1997, and as is said, "The rest is history."

IPO, Then Acquisition

Ready for the next level by 1999, Alteon generated $76 million in an independent public offering. Then in January 2000, the company sold another five million shares in a follow-on public offering. In October 2000, Alteon sealed a deal with Nortel Networks Corp., (traded on the Toronto and New York Stock Exchange as NT). Alteon is now part of Nortel's Intelligent Internet Group. The merger brings a new level of intelligence and personalization to the Internet, the companies believe, with the high-performance Internet able to prioritize and speed information to its destination by looking beyond the IP address and into the request sent by users and the content resident in server farms.

Alteon's products are primarily geared for service providers, enterprises, and e-commerce and content publishing sites. Its products include modular and stackable Web switches, integrated traffic management software, and a line of service delivery products. Its systems are used in Internet data centers around the world by customers such as UUNet, Yahoo!, TicketMaster Online, GTE Internet, DLJdirect, DIGEX, WebTV Networks, Global Crossing, Cable & Wireless, NTT, and many more.

From humble beginnings as Alteon Networks, the company saw a meteoric rise in business after the highly successful IPO. To differentiate itself in the marketplace, Alteon coined the term "web switching" and changed its name to Alteon WebSystems.

Awards and Achievements

As would be expected of a company enjoying such dramatic success, its accolades and awards are numerous. Deloitte & Touche named it one of Silicon Valley's Fast 50 Rising Star companies for its growth from 1997 through 1999, when revenues increased more than 14,000 percent. *PC Magazine* named the Alteon 180e Web switch as its Editors' Choice in March 2000. And two products were named Product of the Year in 2001, first by *Network Magazine*: the ACEdirector 4 Web switch in the Content Aware Switch/Traffic Manager category, and second in *Network Computing* for the company's SSL Accelerator.

Orr, who now serves as president of Nortel Networks Intelligent Internet WebSystems, attributes the young company's quick success to three obvious factors. One, Alteon was the first to market, giving it the lead. Two, the unique technology embedded in the switch classifies and routes traffic quickly and intelligently. And, three, the company created a culture of listening closely to its customers and quickly responding to their needs. That created a loyal customer base, Orr says.

Less obvious but equally critical to the success of Alteon was Orr's desire to keep the workforce energized and motivated. "Work hard, make an impact, and have fun," was Orr's mantra. When competition heated up and market forces demanded more strenuous motivation,

Orr served up the flipside refrain, well known by all employees: "The sick are killed, and the wounded are eaten." His message was clear, that without execution in critical areas Alteon would be somebody's lunch.

As Alteon transitions to Nortel, the company is staffed by about 300 employees, most of them engineers and most in San Jose. By August 2002, the company will move into new headquarters, adjacent to its current facility. The new two-building, 300,000-square-foot campus is in the Valley Oak Technology Park.

Not everyone has been able to achieve such success, Alteon employees know. Their willingness to share is perhaps best related via anecdote. One Thanksgiving, Alteon employees decided that families with less than they had should all have turkeys for dinner. Knowing that competition can heat things up, they challenged their top competitor in a fundraising match for a local food bank. When all was said and done, Alteon had raised more than $10,000, half of which came from an impromptu parking lot challenge as employees from both companies began a bidding war to raise the stakes and return some of their good fortune back to the community. ■

Smart Products, Inc., a Divison of Smart Pumps, Inc.

*Doris H. Patterson,
CEO of Smart
Products, Inc.,
a division of Smart
Pumps, Inc.*

The key word at Smart Products is "Quality, Quality, Quality," according to Doris Patterson, owner and CEO. As a longtime broker of "high-end" residential real estate, she adapted the old "Location, Location, Location," slogan when she bought the near-bankrupt Smart Products business in 1985. She expected to turn the company around in six months and sell it.

Patterson quickly realized that Smart Products badly needed two critical skills that she possessed—sound management and effective marketing. Once she implemented these ideals, she made a turnaround and achieved a company sales growth of 1,368 percent. "We have had growth every year in the 'double-digit' range," Patterson stated.

Smart products makes plastic check valves, fittings, and pumps used in things like medical equipment, soap and beverage dispensing machines, water treatment systems, auto emission equipment, including those for high-speed racing cars, ice machines, ink jet printers, car-wash machines, carpet cleaning devices, and many more.

*Smart Products designs,
develops, manufactures,
and markets pumps,
check valves, and fittings
for a broad range of
industries and uses.*

When she recently commissioned a market research study by RTL & Associates, customers' comments such as: "always responsive to special requests and changes," "not the cheapest; however, the quality and life expectancy are worth it," "the quality of their check valves is unmatched in the industry," and "everything about them has been great; they're very easy to deal with" were reported.

Smart Products has a worldwide customer base, and "our largest market is in the medical area," Patterson said. "There are over 16,000 combinations in our check valve line. This allows the engineer to design a custom valve using our shelf stock." Thus none of its orders are filled on an "off-the-shelf" basis. "Everything is customized," she explained. "A customer can tell us their exact requirements, or they can tell how and where the product will be used. We do a lot of engineering consultation with clients to assist them in solving their flow problems."

To avoid product flaws, Patterson insists on "very tight quality control procedures." The company was first certified ISO 9001 in 1999. There are "first article inspections" on every order and hourly production checks.

Furthermore, Patterson has made her company a family business, employing her two sons as directors of production and engineering, as well as her daughter, director of marketing, and her daughter-in-law, director of sales.

Patterson attributes much of her success to the quality that she insists goes into every product and the close relationship she has with her clients from start to finish. It is clear that customer satisfaction is Smart Products' goal, and judging by customer comments, it is one that has been accomplished time and again. ∎

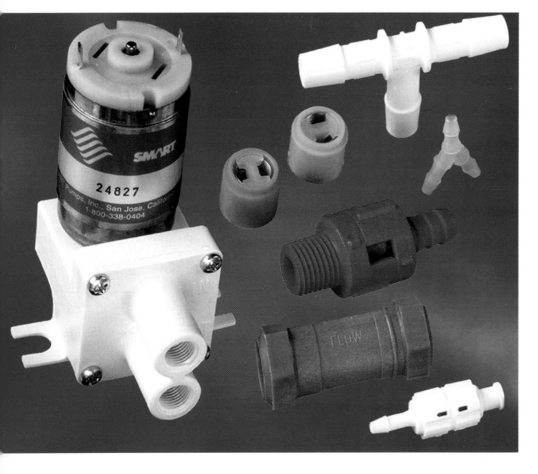

"I'm always taken aback by the fact that Adobe is truly everywhere you look," stated Bruce Chizen, Adobe Systems Incorporated's president and chief operating officer, "anything you can read or view, chances are Adobe touched that content." That's because, as the second largest PC software maker in the United States, Adobe has a full line of products that spans the Web, print media, motion, and e-paper markets.

As veterans of Xerox Corporation's Palo Alto Research Center, Dr. John Warnock and Dr. Charles Geschke founded Adobe back in 1982 with a simple vision—to develop an operating system to be embedded in printers and to eventually grow the company to 50 employees.

Their dream, however, was far exceeded. With the desktop publishing boom of the '80s and the rapid expansion of the Web in the '90s, Adobe was propelled to expand its product line well beyond its original offering. Today, Adobe plays a crucial role in the publishing revolution, helping people communicate more effectively through visually rich content designed with software programs like Adobe® Acrobat®, Adobe Photoshop®, Adobe Illustrator®, and Adobe Premiere®.

Adobe now has over 3,000 employees in offices throughout North America, Europe, the Pacific Rim, Japan, and Latin America and just recently announced plans to expand its downtown San Jose headquarters by adding a third high-rise tower. "We need the space to grow and will continue to hire employees in the Bay Area," stated Chizen.

What Adobe is really gearing up for is the "third wave of publishing." During a press conference at the Tech Museum of Innovation in October 2000, Adobe identified a groundbreaking category called Network Publishing. "The idea behind this new mode is to allow for content to be managed and delivered reliably wherever the user wants,"

explained Chizen, "whether it's a Web page, printer, cell phone, handheld device, PC, or Internet appliance."

In addition to efforts to develop its software for use across multiple platforms, Adobe plans to realize the Network Publishing vision by building strategic partnerships with companies like Hewlett-Packard, Nokia, Real Networks, and Interwoven. For example, a customer will be able to create a compelling Web site with Adobe's GoLive™ software and then they could deliver that same content to the 18.7 million iMode users in Japan who are accessing the Web from cell phones.

Adobe's supportive and innovative working culture recently earned it a ranking of the 30th best company to work at in America by *Fortune* magazine. Adobe is also one of the few companies in the world with the breadth of products to be able to address many aspects of this new Network Publishing era. It's apparent that Adobe has both the core values and innovative software necessary to enable it to remain at the forefront of its industry—touching content anytime, anyplace, and anywhere. ■

Adobe Systems San Jose Headquarters.

Bruce Chizen, Adobe President and CEO.

Right: Much of the engineering work on the hybrid electric drive vehicle was performed at United Defense's Santa Clara facility. Powered by batteries and a small diesel engine, this high-tech vehicle is quiet, consumes less fuel, and provides an onboard source of electricity to operate battlefield lasers, defense shields, and communications equipment. Bottom: United Defense's Santa Clara facility employs more than 900 people and is the principal location for research, development, and engineering programs, with laboratories for software and electronics integration, hybrid electric drive systems, ballistic testing, and composite materials.

In the future, the military will likely look very different to us, with unmanned robotic vehicles communicating with each other, more sophisticated armor protection, and cockpit-controlled manned vehicles operating silently with hybrid electric power, equipped with intelligent munitions.

"United Defense is playing a crucial role in preparing the military with equipment and systems for warfare in the future," said Raj Rajagopal, vice president of research and engineering at United Defense. "We are developing brand new combat systems that are lighter, faster, and more effective for our U.S. and allied customers."

United Defense's Santa Clara facility, which employs about 900 people, is developing new types of vehicles and modernizing the military's existing vehicles like the Bradley Fighting Vehicle and the Vietnam-era M113 Personnel Carrier.

The company is gearing its technology toward building lighter-weight vehicles that use less fuel and take fewer cargo planes to deploy. In keeping with the aim to reduce the weight of the vehicles and still protect soldiers' lives, United Defense is working on "layered defenses." They have designed a stealthy defensive shield to avoid detection, on-board counter measures to knock out in-bound missiles, and a revolutionary lightweight armor skin (comprised of composites, ceramics, and metal laminates). "We also have contracts to develop radio-controlled, unmanned vehicles for front-line reconnaissance and to keep humans out of the most hazardous tasks," added Rajagopal.

The Santa Clara facility is developing an advanced family of hybrid electric drive vehicles—from troop carriers to tanks—that are powered by a hybrid of advanced batteries, electric motors, and a small diesel engine. The hybrid engine has the dual purpose of powering the transport from zero to 20 miles-per-hour in less than three seconds, while storing energy to power on-board systems such as battlefield lasers, defensive shields, or communications equipment.

In addition to supplying military core technologies, the Santa Clara facility includes a Corporate Technology Center (CTC) that houses a world-class materials laboratory and engineering department and provides a wide variety of analytical and technical services to defense, chemical, petrochemical, semiconductor, biomedical, machinery, and industrial equipment customers worldwide.

Also located at United Defense's Santa Clara facility are two state-of-the-art labs—a combat hybrid electric power integration lab and a combat system integration simulation lab.

United Defense is owned by the Carlyle Group, which purchased the company in 1997 from FMC and Harsco. The company operates 12 development, manufacturing, and service sites in 10 states, and has joint ventures in several foreign countries, including Sweden, Saudi Arabia, and Turkey. ∎

Qual-Tronix was founded back in 1966 when Frank Casale, who remains the company's chief executive officer today, and two former partners began the company as a subcontracting business to assist the electronics industry. Today, Qual-Tronix has expanded its repertoire and is a leading provider of engineering prototypes, electro-mechanical assembly, and turnkey systems.

What sets Qual-Tronix apart from its competitors is its experience, superior customer service, flexibility, and reliability. In business since the virtual beginning of Silicon Valley, Qual-Tronix has built its reputation by assisting top companies in meeting the ever-changing demands for electronic products. At the same time, the company has provided exceptional service with a personal touch, an attribute that has earned it recognition within the industry.

"We've received a number of 'supplier of excellence' awards from our customers," stated Teresa Casale, vice president who administers the human resources, financial, legal, and administration ends of the company. "That's how we've stayed in business all these years—by getting the job done right, on time, and at a competitive price."

The experience of Qual-Tronix's employees has also played an important role in contributing to its success. The company's purchasing staff links customers with a vast array of suppliers and assists in locating hard to find components; the engineering department documents internal design layouts, wiring and operational functions of products, and develops blue prints for prototypes; and the manufacturing personnel are at their customers' service from parts requisition through the assembly process and final test.

The subcontracting company, which provides custom manufacturing and installation of wiring and component

*Rick Evans,
operations manager.*

products, is also geared to meet its customers' needs for small, medium, or large size production runs. "Our production system allows for great flexibility to turn out products quickly and efficiently to accommodate our customers' demanding schedules," stated Rick Evans, operations manager. And the company has earned and continues to enjoy the highest reputation for reliability and holds certifications in major industry categories, including ISO 9002.

It's important to remember that, when thinking of Qual-Tronix, "quality" and "electronics" go hand-in-hand with the company's business philosophy and with its name. Qual-Tronix continues to refine its processes—to achieve zero product defects—and its relationships with customers—to provide superior service and support. ■

*Teresa Casale,
vice president, and
Frank Casale, president
and CEO.*

Working in Silicon Valley can be a wild roller coaster ride of fortunes and flops, with some companies hiring anyone with a heartbeat one minute and laying off everyone in sight the next—an unstable, kaleidoscopic land where annual employee turnover rates of 30 percent, 40 percent, 50 percent, and higher are the norm? Right?

Wrong—that is, if you're talking about California Eastern Laboratories (CEL). CEL's annual turnover is only 20 percent.

Founded in 1959, CEL is the exclusive North American sales, marketing, and product development organization for more than 900 RF, microwave, optoelectronic semiconductors, and fiber-optic products manufactured by NEC of Japan—one of the world's largest semiconductor manufacturers. From its headquarters in Santa Clara, CEL maintains over 17 field sales offices throughout the country, and in 2000 approximately 434 million devices were shipped through its Santa Clara warehouse.

"The components we provide are used in cellular telephones, pagers, satellites, direct broadcast TV, wireless security systems, and literally hundreds of other products used by consumers and businesses," says Jenifer Jacobs, CEL's manager of corporate communications.

This firm is one of the oldest technology companies in Silicon Valley and has never had an unprofitable year. With its employee count rapidly approaching 200, this $200 million (and fast-growing) company is exceptional in many ways.

California Eastern Laboratories, located in Santa Clara, California, is one of the oldest technology companies in Silicon Valley.

For example, CEL is 50 percent owned by its employees through its Employee Stock Ownership Plan (ESOP), established in 1983. That makes it one of the largest private, employee-owned companies in California.

And, although the ESOP is a valuable tool in attracting and retaining talent, the company also supplements its ESOP plan with an impressively broad range of other benefits. "We need to increase our workforce to keep up with the demands for our products", said Jacobs. "We expect to maintain this pace of growth well into the 21st century."

With 80 percent of the world still without telephone service, and less developed countries scrambling to build their wireless infrastructures, the telecommunications business has skyrocketed. This is creating a global shortage of wireless communications design and other engineers. These days, competition for technical talent in the microwave industry is so heated that firms have been known to fly banners from airplanes to offer huge signing bonuses to engineers and technicians.

"The window of market opportunity is wide open for us, but we need people," Jacobs said.

CEL is one of the few "swords to ploughshares" success stories, but it has transitioned from selling primarily to the military to selling to companies that produce cutting-edge consumer electronic products. And, unlike most others who have made that shift, it did it with nary a hiccup in performance or profits.

Running a business where the employees are also the owners, requires much more open communication about financial details than is the norm at most companies. "We post graphs of financial performance on hallway walls and report other news through an e-mail ESOP bulletin board," explained Jerry Arden, CEL's chairman and CEO. "At quarterly all-employee meetings, I never know what pointed questions may be asked. Employees take their ownership role to heart."

Not being publicly traded allows management to take the long view in its business decisions.

"We are not constantly looking over our shoulders—or worrying about a blip in quarterly numbers," Arden stated. "The same ability to focus also applies to employees, who aren't bouncing off the walls every time the market takes a drop—morale and productivity are much steadier in our environment than in a public company." ∎

ISG started in 1997 as the Integrated Solutions Group of California Eastern Laboratories or CEL, a Silicon Valley technology company since 1959. CEL is the exclusive North American sales, marketing, and product development organization for products manufactured by NEC of Japan, world-renown manufacturer of semiconductors.

In '97 CEL recognized a growing market for transceivers, and in order to meet the need for better and faster Internet connection, CEL created the ISG separate organization, and "it has taken off like a rocket."

ISG designs and markets RF gateway products designed to enable broadband communications to be delivered to homes. As the world is moving away from the old means of Internet access, and more and more consumers are wanting faster and more efficient broadband communications for their at-home use, ISG couldn't have entered the market at a better time. In fact, over the past four years the company has become well established, now boasting transceivers in over a million homes worldwide, and with 100,000 new ones being installed monthly.

With the increasing popularity of broadband communications, ISG has grown dramatically, from its incorporation in 2000 to its recent move from CEL's facilities in Santa Clara to its own new plant in Milpitas. "Now that we are in our new facilities, we'll be ramping up production," said President Don Alfson. This optimism is well founded, as the company has been experiencing record sales and an ever-increasing product demand.

Yet the company work force is remarkably lean. Alfson explained that ISG stresses design work and has a staff of only 32—all hard at work on developing new products and improvements to existing ones. This dedication to the design phase has a payoff of a steady flow of fresh technology, essential to success especially in the Silicon Valley. A testimony to this success is the recent announcement of the addition of an ultra miniature MMIC-based RF transceiver module, the ISG3350, half the size of other modules. Just 1.8 x 1.9 x 0.4 inches, it simplifies the operation of RF and digital sides of cable modems. In May of 2001 ISG added a new generation, a low-cost miniature RFIC-based transceiver module for cable and IP telephony. This device measures a mere 4.6 x 4.85 x 1.1 centimeters, smaller than "single chip" tuner designs. It interfaces well with Texas Instruments' equipment, saving time and expense for the network designers, the manufacturers and the system integrators.

With this obvious array of products and the solid backing of a long-established company like CEL, ISG is sure to be around for a long time, inventing, creating, and serving residents of the Silicon Valley and the entire world by enhancing broadband communications service through advanced technology and innovation. ∎

The original ISG3300 became an industry model for miniature, integrated RF transceivers. The new generation ISG3350, shown here above the ISG3300, is less than half the size of the original.

Donald G. Alfson, President and CEO, ISG Broadband, Inc.

CISCO SYSTEMS

Leaders from hundreds of companies and governments worldwide visit Cisco Systems' San José headquarters each year.

One of the largest employers in San José, Cisco Systems' success as the worldwide leader in networking for the Internet is due, in part, to its strategic use of Internet technologies and an emphasis on business partnerships. Being a good corporate citizen means building strong communities, and Cisco uses similar business strategies to strengthen its Corporate Philanthropy initiatives.

Two legendary programs that combine the best of Internet technologies and partnerships to impact social change are the Cisco Networking Academy Program and Netaid. A partnership between Cisco, education, business, government, and community organizations around the world, the Cisco Networking Academy Program prepares students for the 21st century workplace, while serving as a valuable model for e-learning. A unique partnership between the United Nations and Cisco, the Netaid.org Foundation's mission is to use the power of the Internet to end the cycle of extreme poverty through online volunteerism and education.

Cisco Systems has forged strong partnerships with local governments, companies, and non-profits to address the unique needs of San José, a growing metropolis. Photos provided by Cisco Systems, Inc.

While Cisco will continue to develop ground-breaking global programs as part of its e-philanthropy initiative, the company is committed to supporting the numerous investments employees wish to make in their local communities, including financial contributions, volunteerism, and special projects.

To make cash donations easier, the company partnered automatic payroll deduction with a matching gift program. And as part of its Technology in Non-Profits initiative, Cisco makes product grants and matches technical volunteers with non-profits to help install and maintain their networks. In this way, non-profits can enjoy the same technological benefits as businesses.

Cisco engages employees in special projects as well. The Global Holiday Food Drive has become the most visible grass-roots project at Cisco, raising funds for hungry families worldwide. Last year's drive netted $3 million—double the previous year—for food banks in many countries, including Second Harvest in San José. Employees also help to select the recipients of community grants bestowed twice yearly by the Cisco Foundation. Created in 1997, the foundation is dedicated to incubating and developing programs in e-philanthropy, education, and basic needs.

Overall, Cisco technologies have connected the world, fostering a greater ability to understand global issues. Cisco will continue to build partnerships and identify inventive ways to use Internet technology to create strong, healthy communities. ■

Founded in 1990 and considered to be one of the fastest-growing providers of multi channel customer interaction solutions in the world, the Edify Corporation's number one goal is to provide its over 1,100 enterprise customers worldwide with the highest level of customer satisfaction possible. To achieve this, the company carries out monthly evaluations and surveys and finds that its Global 2,000 customers consistently score it over 90 percent for customer satisfaction.

Edify's other crucial goal is to provide its enterprise customers with unique technology that allows them to supply their own customers with a consistent sales and service experience regardless of the touch point used. Whether people are communicating and seeking information over the telephone, e-mail, Web, wireless, at a kiosk or at an ATM, Edify is taking self-service to the next level of efficiency.

This is accomplished with Edify Natural Language—a complex language engine that was developed for the Edify Interactive Center and Virtual Customer Service Representative (vCSR) applications. It is capable of understanding grammar and the intent and meaning of multiple-topic sentences and has speech recognition in 21 languages along with an advanced text-to-speech conversion for 11 languages. Thanks to this system, about half of all customer interactions, written or voice, can be managed accurately and immediately without those customers ever being directed to a human.

The vCSR contains a number of different components. These include the E-mail Correspondent, which automates responses based on content analysis using Edify Natural Language, and the Voice Analyst that uses speech recognition and speaker verification to complete customer transactions while improving the quality and effectiveness of service.

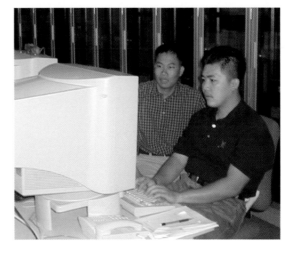

Enabling the interactive enterprise.

The Web Navigation Monitor collects multiple queries from a Web page, parses the text for the proper application, and then builds a response page to provide the customers with the information they need. The Chat Monitor and Respondent also uses the Edify natural language engine to interpret the meaning of a customer chat request on the Web in order to help the live agent answer questions properly and quickly.

Automating answers to customer questions and concerns increases the speed of response and reduces enterprise costs while actually increasing customer satisfaction. However, not all concerns can be handled automatically and when appropriate the vCSR will route requests to a human agent for resolution. To save both time and the need for the customer to repeat information already given, the system supplies all customer background data and transaction history to the agent's screen immediately.

When a call is handled by an agent, that contact is further streamlined by another vCSR application, the Wrap-Up Assistant. This software incorporates a company's workflow and business rules needs in order to automatically perform the necessary tasks required to complete a customer interaction. Consequently, the agent can promptly wrap up the call and quickly serve another customer in the queue.

Edify's CRM solutions touch literally millions of customers each day. As a result multi-channel interactions are more efficient and satisfying for customers and more productive and profitable for the companies that serve them. ■

Edify's home office, Santa Clara, Califonia.

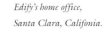

IKOS SYSTEMS, INC.

*IKOS' corporate head-
quarters is strategically
located in San Jose to
attract the world's best-
qualified technology
professionals.*

IKOS Systems, Inc., an integral part of the Silicon Valley technology community since its founding in 1984, develops and delivers high-performance, hardware-assisted, design verification solutions for chip design.

Chip design verification is the most critical element in chip development. If the functionality of the design is not verified correctly and goes into the manufacturing process, finding bugs later can be costly and time consuming, not to mention the lost opportunities resulting from flawed chips. Unlike their predecessors, today's chips are extremely complicated and are more like complete electrical systems than the single function chips previously used. The requirement to verify both hardware and software together further complicates the verification process.

*The mayor of San Jose
along with members
of IKOS executive
staff cut the ribbon
on the new corporate
headquarters.*

Because verification is so critical, engineers spend 60 to 70 percent of their development time performing verification. Historically verification has been accomplished using specialized software. As chip designs have become larger and more complex the performance of software-only solutions is insufficient to accomplish enough verification to reduce sufficient risk prior to manufacturing. That's where IKOS comes in. IKOS produces verification systems that can be as much as 100,000 times faster than verification software.

The company currently offers its products to leading electronics firms including: Nvidia, Lucent, Philips, ST Miroelectronics, Toshiba, SIS, Infineon, Motorola, Texas Instruments, Nokia, and many others. IKOS strategic partners include such IP and EDA companies as ARM, Novas, Verisity, Cadence, Mentor Graphics, and Synopsys.

IKOS has experienced steady growth, usually at an annual rate of approximately 30 percent. As this growth continues, IKOS is increasingly becoming an important global corporation. IKOS has already established a strategic presence in key market areas in North America, Europe, Japan, and the rest of Asia. IKOS is also a global company from a development standpoint with major research and development centers in San Jose, California; Waltham, Massachusetts; and Noida, India.

IKOS can credit much of its success to the fact that it offers unique technologies. One example of this is IKOS' "VirtualWires" patent. This technology enables engineers to program or model the design of the chip on a hardware platform that consists of advanced, standard Field Programmable Gate Arrays (FPGAs). The FPGA's are re-configurable, so the engineer can program the platform to take on the personality of the design—weeks or even months before the chip is available.

IKOS believes that chip development will continue to grow at a rapid pace and expects the size and complexity of chip designs to double every 18 to 24 months. Design engineers will continue to demand verification systems that can handle very large designs at very high performance levels, and IKOS is well positioned to address their needs, now and in the future. ∎

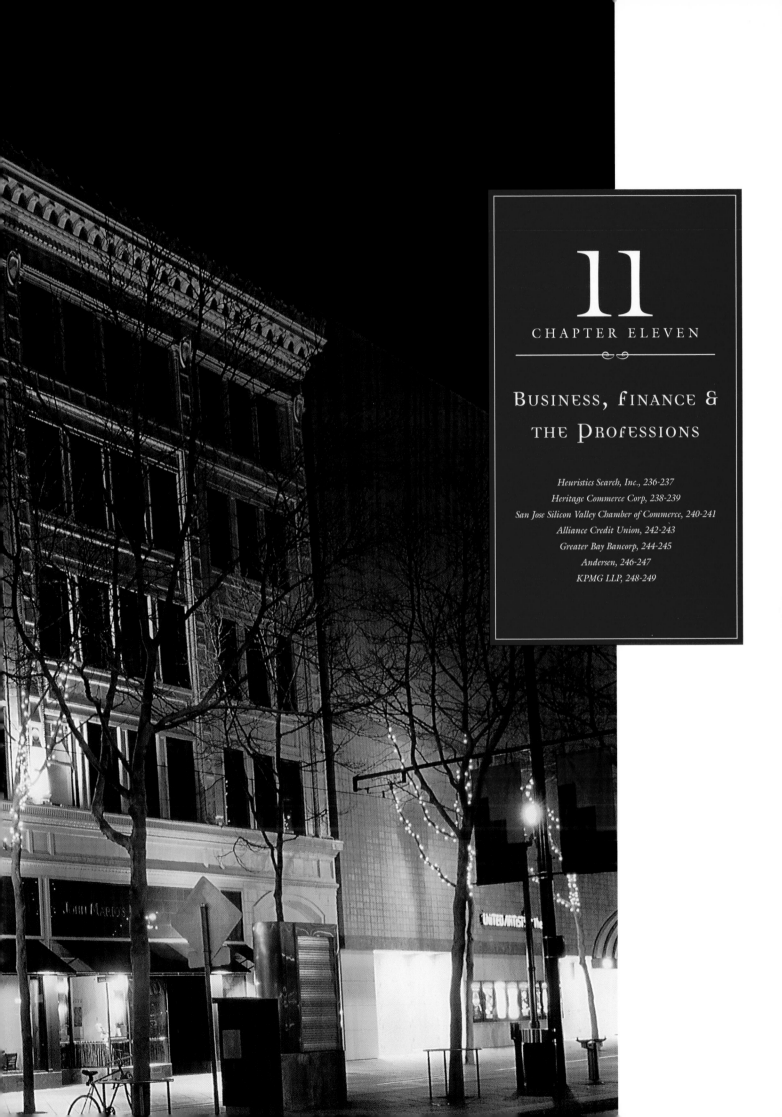

11
CHAPTER ELEVEN

Business, finance & the Professions

HEURISTICS SEARCH, INC.

A group of visionaries founded Heuristics Search Inc. more than two decades ago with the idea that a personalized approach to staffing the fledgling software-development industry would keep the company in the forefront of the now-crowded recruitment field.

Time has proved them right.

Top: Heuristics Search, Inc., 2001.
Right: Sales managers discuss the week's job orders at their daily morning meetings.
Photos by Joel Moses Photography

The name Heuristics comes from the Greek word meaning aiding or guiding in discovery. It is also a term for an algorithm in computer science, and in business schools Heuristics refers to continued and varied approach to solving problems.

Heuristics Search now is the nation's largest recruitment firm specializing in placing software engineers and technology specialists in everything from Fortune 500 companies to the most successful start-ups.

Founded in 1979 by President Elizabeth Patrick, Heuristcs Search is still striving to be true to its name. It offers a continuous and varied approach to solving recruitment needs for corporate clients looking for employees with cutting-edge ideas and the talent to implement those ideas.

"I knew that software was going to be in everything, in every product," Patrick says. "I thought that software development deserved to have its own recruitment firm, and from that, we became the leader."

Based in San Jose, Heuristics has branch offices in Boston and Seattle. The company's 16,000-square-foot corporate office in downtown San Jose offers spectacular views of the

Silicon Valley. Heuristics has eight interview rooms where candidates meet as professionals, watch videos on how to succeed in the interview process, and discuss their future with experts.

"I think what sets us apart is that we focus on personalized attention," says Yvonne Demos, vice president of sales. "We meet all of our candidates, which isn't the normal practice in the industry, and we meet most of our clients. We're really performing personal introductions."

Heuristics invites local high-tech firms to conferences with its recruiters where they explain their products and specific employee needs. That's how the Heuristics team, which can include as many as two-dozen representatives for every position, ensures everyone is working together to find the right candidate for each job.

"Clients don't have just one account manager representing them," comments Farri Ouraie, senior technical recruiter. "They have the entire company working for them."

It is a process that can require the staff to make hundreds of contacts to find one candidate. Such a lengthy endeavor could consume vast amounts of a high-tech company's precious time, which is why so many of them turn to Heuristics to fill critical positions. Because of Heuristics' contacts and expertise, they are able to streamline the process for client companies.

"Many times a high-tech company is so busy concentrating on getting the product out to market that it becomes a burden to do all of the interviewing necessary

to fill their positions," Joseph J. Strate, vice president of business development says. "We can help facilitate the process and make it seamless. The client's management staff can use our offices and interview several qualified candidates in a three-hour block of time, in comfort, and in privacy and free from distractions."

These clients also are spared the time required to check employee references and perform background checks. Once again, that's part of the full service Heuristics offers its clients.

Heuristics doesn't just find the perfect employee match for its corporate clients. Heuristics also helps high-tech firms with short-term project placement by maintaining a group of contractors on staff who can start work at a moment's notice. For some clients, Heuristics has built an entire team, including architects, designers, testers, and quality assurance specialists.

How does Heuristics come up with these perfect matches? Well, it takes well-trained and experienced recruiters who never stop trying to find qualified candidates to fill positions corporate clients may not even know they need yet. And that means Heuristics recruiters do not rely on a cold database: "Everyone in our database has been interviewed and pre-screened in our office," Patrick says.

Behind the human system is a huge engine—a Seibel database, and Heuristics continues to invest in leading-edge technology to provide the best and fastest service to its clients. This database allows the account executives to make hundreds of contacts they need to complete each day.

Another useful tool Heuristics provides is a fun, informative Web site (www.heur.com), which takes a humorous approach to the serious process of finding a job. Its services include offering client companies tips on attracting employees and industry salary surveys. There is also useful information such as career tips, and complete

access to an online search engine for available candidates and jobs. Filled with cartoons, jokes, and other forms of entertainment, the site is a valuable resource of employment trends in the software industry.

With its success in introducing companies to the employees who will make a difference, Heuristics hasn't forgotten its obligations as a corporate citizen. Heuristics supports the San Jose Symphony, the San Jose Cleveland Ballet, San Jose public television, and several non-profit community agencies.

"We have grown with the local industry and the community," Patrick says. "We want to tell everyone how proud and grateful we are to be part of this wonderful, exciting valley." ■

Prospective candidates complete profile forms before meeting with their recruiter.
Photo by Joel Moses Photography

There is never a quiet moment on the Heuristics sales floor.
Photo by Joel Moses Photography

Brad L. Smith, Chairman and CEO of Heritage Commerce Corp, next to a sculpture by a local artist in the Heritage Bank of Commerce lobby.

Today, Heritage Commerce Corp, a bank holding company created in 1998, is the parent company of four thriving subsidiary banks with assets totaling over $860 million.

The company's original bank, Heritage Bank of Commerce, located in downtown San Jose, was founded in 1994 by a group of prominent San Jose entrepreneurs concerned by what was happening to the area's banking industry. Several San Jose banks had been absorbed by larger entities, and savings and loan institutions were filing for bankruptcy. When the dust had settled, the group saw a glaring need for a highly personalized, local community bank with products and services geared especially to small- and medium-sized businesses. This was Silicon Valley after all, and companies still needed "seed money."

The group's primary vision was to establish a local bank, with well-connected and enthusiastic local founders and directors, that defined itself around the needs of its customers and the community. They were successful— the founder's list reads like a who's who of San Jose area leaders—men and women who represent a diverse cross-section of the business community and are highly involved in civic affairs. This philosophy of local, independent banks, each with its own local group of high-profile investors and directors, would serve as the business model for each of the future Heritage banks.

The Heritage Building is a familiar site in the heart of downtown San Jose—located in Park Center Plaza. It is the headquarters for Heritage Commerce Corp, and the home of Heritage Bank of Commerce.

William J. Del Biaggio, Jr., a well-known beverage distributor and third generation Californian with over 40 years of San Jose business experience, became the organizing committee's leader and ultimately the first chairman of the Heritage Bank of Commerce Board of Directors. Mr. Del Biaggio recalls, "There were 21 of us in the beginning, and we each chipped in $15,000. Later we upped it to $60,000. We were aiming to raise $12 million with our first stock offering and instead raised over $14 million, the largest bank capitalization in the history of Silicon Valley." Within six months, assets had jumped to over $50 million, expanding to $132 million by the end of the first full year of operations. This would be typical of Heritage's growth.

Heritage Bank of Commerce first opened its doors in the former Security Bank building at 195 Almaden Boulevard. Within days, the San Jose Redevelopment Agency announced it was going to buy and demolish the one-story structure. This proved to be an opportunity in disguise—the bank quickly secured its present site, a much more visible high rise located directly across the street at 150 Almaden.

As the bank's assets steadily grew, the board of directors cast their eyes toward new projects. They were eager to bring the Heritage style of relationship banking to new and expanding markets. The first step

From left: Brad L. Smith, Chairman and CEO, with Richard L. Conniff, President and Chief Operating Officer.

reinvestment is evidenced by each bank's contribution of time, money, and resources to a broad variety of charitable, economic, educational, and cultural groups.

Heritage has always taken a uniquely creative approach to community banking. Through its Fine Arts Collaborative, inaugurated in 1994 with the opening of the original bank, the artwork of local artists is displayed throughout the banks. Produced by a local art curator, the rotating shows allow promising artists to gain exposure and add a distinctive touch not commonly associated with the banking industry. This ingenuity has become a Heritage hallmark.

Despite its rapid growth, Heritage has managed to remain true to its vision—community-based banks in key markets with local management, staff, and boards of directors. Smith observes, "We realize that our strength lies not only in providing the best possible service, but in our investment in people and the community; that's what really sets us apart." ■

in their strategy was the formation of a holding company for Heritage Bank of Commerce and any future banks. In 1998, Heritage Commerce Corp was created and the company's common stock was approved for listing on the NASDAQ National Exchange under the symbol "HTBK."

Heritage next extended its reach into the rapidly growing East Bay and South Valley communities with the creation of "de novo" banks that would later become fully independent subsidiaries of the holding company. Heritage Bank East Bay opened for business in Fremont in 1998, followed by Heritage Bank South Valley in Morgan Hill during 2000. In October 2000, Western Holdings Bancorp, the holding company for Bank of Los Altos, merged into Heritage Commerce Corp, and Bank of Los Altos became the company's fourth independent bank. Under its present subsidiary bank structure, each Heritage bank delivers progressive, innovative, and highly personalized banking services to its clients including specialized SBA, asset-based, and residential mortgage lending products.

Under the current leadership of veteran community bankers, Chairman and Chief Executive Officer Brad L. Smith and President and Chief Operating Officer Richard L. Conniff, Heritage Commerce Corp continues to experience sound financial performance and strong community presence. Smith says, "The Heritage style of doing business is characterized by a powerful sense of quality service, integrity, and community—and that's been the foundation of our ongoing success." The company's unwavering commitment to community

The Heritage Bank of Commerce lobby. Unique architectural design is a trademark of Heritage Commerce Corp banks.

Right: The San Jose Public Library is the largest public library system between San Francisco and Los Angeles. The chamber has been a strong advocate for ballot measures to insure the expansion and improvement of the library system.

Bottom: Flood control has been a large part of the chamber's advocacy efforts. Over the years, the chamber has played a key role in several flood control initiatives to ensure waterways remain attractive, while protecting commerce against flooding.

As you leaf through the pages of this book and peruse stories about San Jose's unique history and innovative businesses, it's important to remember that the San Jose Silicon Valley Chamber of Commerce has and will continue to play an important role in the development of this valley.

The Board of Trade, the Chamber's predecessor organization, was formed in 1886 to attract people to the San Jose basin. Not unlike today, its efforts at the time were so successful that people rushed to settle the orchard filled area. This caused an unexpected population boom—land values soared and the county recorder's office was forced to quadruple its staff.

The group then turned its efforts toward developing the city's structure. "The Board of Trade promoted construction of the deluxe Vendome Hotel on North First Street and persuaded the citizenry to vote bonds for a new brick city hall on Market Street at San Antonio, park improvements, and a sewage system," reads their history record.

Although the valley has changed from the agriculturally-focused economy of 150 years ago to the high tech of today, the issues that the Chamber and its 2,000 member companies face today have remained the same—that of maintaining the valley's delicate balance between growth and infrastructure to support quality of life.

For example, going back to the '20s when the area's agricultural industry needed water, the leaders of the chamber were out there supporting the building of a dam. But in modern times, piping in adequate supplies for the burgeoning economy means chamber advocacy for the use of reclaimed and recycled water, ecology, and conservation.

One area of concern to the chamber has been the quality of the bay waters. "When you dump 120 million gallons of water into the bay each day, you're going to have an impact on the ecology of the area, especially on the south end where it's shallow," explained Jim Tucker, the Chamber's executive director of communications and economic development.

Initially, regulators were going after industry as the water's source of excessive levels of copper and nickel. Then the chamber helped found a coalition to take a more comprehensive look. "What they discovered," explained Tucker, "was that most metals were actually coming from brake linings, copper pipes, pesticides, mercury that washes down from the mountains, and root killers that people pour into their sewage systems."

Since the early days, the chamber has also been involved in regional transportation issues. As a matter of fact, it had a hand in building the San Jose International Airport, which was initially farmland leased from the city to a group of businessmen in 1945 to build a 1,900 foot runway, a hangar, and an office building. Ever since then, the chamber has had an ongoing interest in the airport and is presently the chief advocate for a $1.5 billion expansion plan for its overcrowded terminal buildings that now process 13 million domestic and international passengers a year, up from 2 million a decade and a half ago.

Land for business growth is another major area on which the chamber took an early stand. "A home-building boom in the '60s and '70s was filling up the open spaces," stated Tucker, "but you needed someone like the chamber to look long-term at areas like the Coyote Valley, which is probably our last industrial frontier." So back in 1975, the chamber began working with city governments on a general plan for development of industrial reserves.

As a result of its efforts to preserve land for future business growth, the chamber is now endorsing the building of a Cisco Systems campus in the North Coyote Valley. When finished, this site is expected to generate $2.8 billion annually for the region's economy. "Cisco was exactly the kind of company they were envisioning during that timeframe," stated Tucker. "A company that would come in and take a big chunk of land, put in a high-quality campus operation, and provide a lot of jobs."

Whatever the issue that impacts the valley, the chamber is a place where businesses come together to accomplish things they cannot do individually. Presently, the chamber has advocacy programs that monitor new laws and regulations to develop governmental policy on behalf of businesses; COMPAC, a political action committee representing business gets directly involved in local election campaigns; a Small Business Advisory Council that provides a focus on that sector's unique issues; and an Education Committee that looks at future workforce concerns.

It's apparent that ever since the early days, the chamber has taken on the role of "business caretaker of this valley." This is shown in its name, which was changed a few years ago to add the words "Silicon Valley" to reflect the true scope of its organization, membership, and geographic boundaries.

As the chamber now looks to celebrate its anniversary and reflects back over all its hard work, Tucker commented, "It's kind of fun to be 115 years old and still be viable in the 21st century." ■

Top: The San Jose Chamber of Commerce Building in downtown San Jose, circa 1912. The San Jose Silicon Valley Chamber of Commerce (still located in downtown San Jose) has been the voice of the business community for the past 115 years. The San Jose Silicon Valley Chamber of Commerce recently installed a new sign that shines brightly at the corner of First and San Carlos streets in downtown San Jose. Left: Jim Cunneen, former businessman and state assemblyman, was named President and CEO of the San Jose Silicon Valley Chamber of Commerce in 2001. Under his leadership, the Chamber's new mantra is, "The Real Economy Starts Here."
Photo courtesy of
San Jose Magazine

Pictured in front of the Curtner Avenue Branch is Mr. Norman Pudlack, the last remaining active member of the 14 original founders of the credit union. The credit union's charter was signed September 2, 1952 at the GE Motor Plant in San Jose; the cooperative financial institution will celebrate its 50th anniversary throughout 2002.

For almost 50 years, San Jose-based Alliance Credit Union has provided low-cost financial services to members in the Santa Clara Valley and in Wilmington, North Carolina. In July 2000, members overwhelmingly approved a charter change that allows the financial cooperative to provide services to anyone who lives, works, worships, or goes to school in Santa Clara, Alameda, or San Mateo counties in California, and three counties in North Carolina.

Alliance was founded in 1952 when 14 employees of General Electric's Motor Plant on Monterey Road sat down with two federal credit union examiners and, in the space of two hours, brought to reality an employees' credit union for the San Jose plant.

Since that time, Alliance has expanded to eight branch offices and a corporate headquarters, 119 employees serving over 46,000 member/owners, and has assets exceeding $300 million. The charter conversion, the biggest strategic change in recent years, allowed the credit union to expand its "field of membership" beyond the 400 employee groups previously served.

"Credit unions are unique in that they tend to be more people oriented than other financial institutions," stated Patsy Van Ouwerkerk, Alliance's president and CEO since 1997. Credit unions had their start in a small town in Germany in 1849 when the mayor encouraged residents to dig themselves out of a financial disaster by pooling their money and lending it to each other at favorable rates. The Federal Credit Union Act of 1934 was the catalyst that started the credit union movement in the U.S., which now boasts over 11,000 financial cooperatives and 77 million members who hold $367 billion in savings.

"As a non-profit institution, we give our earnings back to members in the form of higher savings rates, and lower fees and loan rates," said Van Ouwerkerk. "Our primary fiduciary responsibility is to our members, who own our institution.

The other big difference is that we are run by a volunteer board of directors, elected from the membership."

In 2000, Alliance Credit Union added to its range of services by joining the CU Service Centers Network, a nationwide system of over 525 shared branches where members can transact business. Brokerage and insurance services were added through the Credit Union National Association's MEMBERS Financial Services network. A new service, Webloan, was initiated to give members instant loan decisions over the Internet, and technological improvements have been made to its popular telephone banking system.

"The use of technology has enabled us to compete in a fast-paced marketplace," said Dan Joyce, Vice President, Marketing. "Everything we've done over the past few years, from our MasterMoney™ debit card program and telephone service center to our Internet Branch and Bill Payer products, has been designed to allow members access to their funds any way they want. Our goal is to build the Internet channel to the point where members can do all of their business that way if they choose to."

One of the reasons for Alliance's strong growth is the credit union's ability to serve members through all phases of their lives. The Scottie Savers Club, from newborns to age 13, trains youngsters on how to save and offers incentives for increasing their balances. A new program, *boom!*, was designed to meet the special needs of kids 13-21 and offers checking accounts, debit cards, Internet banking, and a first time loan program. The special newsletter and educational materials offered teach these younger members about good financial habits, along with details about student loan

Alliance's Community Involvement Committee makes many positive contributions to numerous community entities. One of the annual activities is the purchase and trimming of a Christmas tree for the residents of the Willow Glen Convalescent Hospital in San Jose.

Alliance is run by a volunteer board of directors elected from the membership. With the help of a dedicated staff, they develop the plans, policies, and strategic vision that keep the credit union strong and moving forward.

programs and the Rose M. Ratka Memorial Scholarship Program. This program, named after the credit union's former President/CEO from 1979-1996, awards scholarship funds to high school seniors who plan on continuing their educations.

Beyond financial services, however, Alliance Credit Union is an organization centered on helping people. The credit union has been involved in numerous community involvement activities over the years and will increase its focus on developing even stronger ties to the community in the future.

"We are very committed to helping the communities where we do business, and our involvement says so much about who we are as an organization," said Eileen M. Lewis, Executive Vice President/COO, and Alliance's longest-tenured employee. "We have a very active Community Involvement Committee, which plans activities and is always looking for organizations to help."

Employees reach out to those in need through fundraisers like "casual for a cause" days where they voluntarily donate $2 for dressing down at work. The proceeds then go into a fund for purchasing items like hats and safety vests for Santee School's safety patrol and Christmas decorations for the Willow Glen Convalescent Hospital. Some of the many activities that employees have donated their time to include packing canned goods at Second Harvest Food Bank, taking pledges during KTEH pledge drives, participating in Daffodil Days for the American Cancer Society, and collecting blankets and clothing for Old Republic Title's *Warmth Of Winter* campaign.

A full slate of member activities and celebrations will commemorate Alliance's 50th anniversary in 2002. "Although we will continue to develop products and services to meet members' needs in the future, we will not forget what has made us successful in the past," says Van Ouwerkerk. "The reason we are strong today is the continued support of our loyal members and our many dedicated volunteers and employees. To them we say a sincere, 'Thank You.'" ■

Future credit union leaders from a local Girl Scout Troop tour the Curtner Branch and demonstrate their cash counting skills!

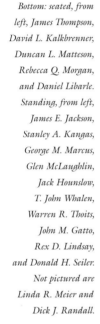

I n the land where newness is worshipped, an old practice has again taken hold and created a resounding success. Formed in late 1996 in the heart of California's Silicon Valley, Greater Bay Bancorp (NASDAQ: GBBK) has grown to become an over $6 billion business built on a foundation of relationships and personal service.

"The old notion of doing business directly with a banker had disappeared," recalls David L. Kalkbrenner, president and CEO. "Small to mid-sized business owners and managers were lost in the shuffle as large banks consolidated into megabanks. CFOs had a very difficult time trying to set up an appointment with someone knowledgeable. Service suffers because there were no real bankers in the traditional sense of the word."

Kalkbrenner saw the problem first hand. An executive with Crocker Bank when Wells Fargo bought Crocker, he left to fulfill a unique vision. "I saw that business people expected more from their bank. They needed the critical business services and credit capabilities of a large commercial bank. Yet they wanted to deal with a person who knew and cared about them and their business. Meeting and exceeding that expectation was a founding principal of Greater Bay Bancorp."

The vision became a strategy and the execution of that strategy became what Kalkbrenner calls Super-Community Banking.

On the surface, it's a relatively simple concept: combine the personal relationships built in local community banks with the extensive resources of a large commercial bank.

Bottom: seated, from left, James Thompson, David L. Kalkbrenner, Duncan L. Matteson, Rebecca Q. Morgan, and Daniel Libarle. Standing, from left, James E. Jackson, Stanley A. Kangas, George M. Marcus, Glen McLaughlin, Jack Hounslow, T. John Whalen, Warren R. Thoits, John M. Gatto, Rex D. Lindsay, and Donald H. Seiler. Not pictured are Linda R. Meier and Dick J. Randall.

At the same time, a "ring-the-bay" strategy would provide extensive geographical coverage in one of the country's fastest growing business markets: the Greater San Francisco/Silicon Valley area of Northern California. Of course turning the plan into reality would take some doing.

By all accounts Kalkbrenner and his team have done it. Greater Bay Bancorp is a holding company with 10 bank subsidiaries covering eight bay area counties. And while so many financial institutions choke on their mergers and acquisitions, Greater Bay has thrived. The key, according to Kalkbrenner, was to make certain each bank maintained its own identity and personality. No names were changed and local bankers were retained.

But perhaps more important was the fact that decision-making stayed at the local bank. Clients never hear that paperwork must be sent downtown. Nor do they have to pick from a fixed list of financing products. Says Susan K. Black, regional president for the San Francisco, Peninsula and North Bay Regions, "Our bankers don't just make decisions. They craft solutions that help business clients manage cash and credit. They guide their clients through referrals to specialists in such areas as SBA loans and international commerce. They are proactive on their clients' behalf so they must develop a real working relationship with each of their clients. They get to know the person as well as the business. This is why our bankers are different and why our bankers become partners with our clients."

With steady growth came Greater Bay Bancorp's ability to deliver the services typical of the banking giants. For instance, while local community banks are limited in their ability to provide financing, clients within

Active, too, is Greater Bay's Venture Banking Group, which specializes in emerging growth companies. Northern California is often called entrepreneur heaven and Greater Bay Bancorp has become a noted player helping start-ups become successful on-going businesses.

Greater Bay Bancorp has succeeded in bringing big bank resources to the local, personal level. Offices now reach from Petaluma to Carmel, covering many of the most important business markets in the world. Service offerings have been expanded to include asset-based financing (factoring) and industry-specific financing for dentists and veterinarians.

"We are constantly measuring ourselves against our clients' and our own expectations," says CEO Kalkbrenner. "The rule is that we must exceed those expectations in all areas—from providing extraordinary client service to delivering record setting corporate financial performance."

Greater Bay Bancorp has, perhaps, done the unexpected. The company has created a vision and made it real. ■

Left: David L. Kalkbrenner, president and chief executive officer, and Duncan L. Matteson, chairman of the board.

Bottom: seated, from left, David L. Kalkbrenner and Susan K. Black. Standing, from left, Byron A. Scordelis, Gregg A. Johnson, David R. Hood, and Steven C. Smith.

the Greater Bay family of banks have access to greater amounts of credit. This allows businesses to expand without growing beyond their bank's capabilities.

Service offerings increased in number and variety along with (and contributed to) Greater Bay's revenue growth. Access to these services is both local and immediate. Commercial services range from cash management and liquidity maximization to letters of credit and SBA loans. Complete depository and retirement services are available and specialized expertise is brought right to the local office when needed. This is particularly useful for global businesses. International commerce is a big part of Northern California's economy and guidance through the quagmire of international trade regulations is scarce for the average small to mid-sized business. One phone call from a banker in the Greater Bay family brings to the client an expert in such obscure international trade areas as harmonized codes and over-the-rail insurance costs. Greater Bay Bancorp's International Division is the recipient of the 2001 Small Business Bank of the Year Award from the Export-Import Bank of the United States (Ex-Im Bank) recognizing its contribution to the U.S. export effort and U.S. job creation.

Gary Matuszak, office managing partner.

With a Silicon Valley client list that reads like a Who's Who, Andersen could be billed as a star in the economic success story of hundreds of startup and long-established companies. Instead, its services are the backstage and supporting roles—consulting, assurance, tax, and corporate finance.

The Chicago-headquartered giant that began as an accounting and business advisory firm in 1913 took to the San Jose area stage about 30 years before the turn of the century. Focusing primarily on technology companies from startup ventures to Fortune 1,000 companies, Andersen grew to employ more than 1,200 professionals in the Valley and Bay Area by the beginning of the 21st century. Its client list at the new millennium includes dozens of high-tech headliners, from Oracle and Peoplesoft to Cadence Design Systems, Flextronics, and Brocade Communications, as well as emerging stars Epiphany, Documentum, and hundreds more.

Andersen's vast range of expertise covers everything from human capital to financial risk consulting, tax services, audits, and consulting on a range of corporate matters, such as process improvement and reengineering, supply chain management, and customer relationship management, among others.

Besides an expanded presence in the world of e-commerce, both business-to-business and business-to-consumer, Andersen is recognized for its expertise in the software industry throughout the Valley and in the industry as

a whole. The Firm also provides budgeting, auditing, tax planning, structure, supply chain management, and merger/acquisition services to area contract manufacturers, such as Flextronics and Sanmina.

Global Leader

Andersen's phenomenal growth in the Valley parallels its worldwide success. Long known as Arthur Andersen, the company shortened its name in 2001 to Andersen, creating a global brand.

Andersen is the youngest of what were once known as the Big 8 accounting/consulting firms—and at the end of the 20th century as the Big 5. Andersen was founded and remains headquartered in the United States and is the only firm to dramatically increase its size through internal growth rather than mergers.

Worldwide, Andersen employs over 85,000 at 400 locations in 84 countries. Besides the full range of services offered at its United States offices, in most countries outside the United States its offerings also include legal services. In the year 2000, its annual revenue topped $8.4 billion.

Framework For Success

A major contributor to Andersen's success is its structure as a truly global partnership rather than a group of franchises. Unlike other firms, Andersen's offices do not compete with each other. Instead, they work together to give clients the best access to the company's full resources, a key element in helping clients compete globally.

Silicon Valley Leadership Team, from left, Jeff Hank, Ann Moncus, Tom Broderick, Gary Matuszak.

In another break from old-school methods, Andersen turns away from the traditional accounting firm model of hiring staff right out of college and expecting turnover. Instead, it hires with the intention of retaining quality staff by offering extensive training, because today's business complexities demand greater specialization and experience.

A Community Partnership

Like its supporting role in the growth and success of its clients, Andersen also takes to the community stage, providing behind-the-scenes assistance to countless agencies and activities via financial and hands-on assistance.

In the Valley, these have included Junior Achievement, Special Olympics, Habitat for Humanity, United Way, Salvation Army, and many more. Employees, too, step into the spotlight, participating in fundraisers such as the AIDS Walk and Diabetes Walk, and contributing to the Second Harvest Food Bank, Dress for Success, and other social services. They're encouraged by Team Andersen, a program that invites all employees to participate in humanitarian programs.

Andersen has long been synonymous with quality professionalism, outstanding technical knowledge, and dedication to client service. The Firm is steadfastly committed to its people and serving as business advisors to many of Silicon Valley's most prominent companies and executives. ■

This worldwide partnership eliminates geographical barriers, allowing each office to share all of the Firm's assets and expertise through a single point of contact. This gives clients access to industry experts around the world who provide valuable insights into each market's unique requirements and regulations. And clients reap the benefits of responsive communication, which drives efficiency.

As a result, Andersen consistently ranks number one in independent customer service and satisfaction surveys.

Rated One Of The Best Places To Work

Besides top ratings for its performances for customers, Andersen ranks highly as an employer, too. It has been named one of the best places to work by leading publications, including *Fortune* magazine and others.

A dedication to diversity, including its leading-edge program, Growth and Retention of Women, is a contributing factor to Andersen's top ratings. By offering employment perks that include leaves of absence after childbirth, daycare assistance, and flexible work schedules, Andersen retains a higher percentage of women than the industry average. Other factors in its popularity as an employer include its dedication to helping workers achieve balance in their lives and its career-development mentoring program.

KPMG LLP

Mark A. Goodburn,
Silicon Valley Office
managing partner.

K PMG LLP's Silicon Valley office is rather distinct within the larger KPMG International, which has more than 109,000 professionals (including partners), in 159 countries. That's because it is the "engine" that drives its powerful high-technology practice—they call it information, communication, and entertainment, better known as ICE[SM].

In other words, this office's specialty is providing tax, assurance, and advisory services to the technology companies that have made this valley so successful. "We have tremendous strengths in serving technology-based companies," stated Mark A. Goodburn, managing partner of KPMG's Silicon Valley office. "While our sister offices assist with the serving financial-services, industrial, and consumer markets, as well as health-care and public-sector clients, the absolute center of our focus is high technology. The more we stay focused, the more value we provide."

KPMG recognized the value in a Silicon Valley office long before the other professional service firms, and long before the valley became a center for technology. The true history of the firm goes back to 1897 when Scottish-born accountants James Marwick and Roger Mitchell began the business, and later Sir William B. Peat joined in. A half-century later, in 1952, Peat, Marwick, Mitchell & Co. became the first international accounting firm with a presence in the San Jose area.

KPMG's office is located in Mountain View, at the very heart of Silicon Valley.

During the 1980s, KPMG was at the forefront of shaping the accounting and consulting profession as Peat, Marwick, Mitchell & Co. merged with KMG Main Hurdman to form KPMG International, the $13.5 billion organization well-known today.

KPMG now serves many of today's market leaders, and the Silicon Valley office leads the charge in serving technology companies. "We have strategically located our national and global leaders serving technology companies here in Silicon Valley," said Goodburn.

"So if one of our clients is wrestling with complex business or accounting issues, or needs assistance with an IPO or Securities and Exchange Commission filing, our entire team will go meet with the company on site. This allows us to fully understand our client's goals, reach conclusions, and develop a resulting plan very quickly."

Market research and studies performed on the professional services industry attests to the Silicon Valley office's exceptional reputation for quality client service. One high-tech senior executive is quoted as saying: "KPMG gives outstanding service, both technical and personal. It's obvious there is excellence in their personal skills, courtesy, follow up, accuracy, and intelligence."

To service its clients, KPMG's strategy is built on three pillars: people, priorities, and pace. The firm spends a great deal of time recruiting the best talent from leading

As a part of KPMG's *"Involve" program,*
employees get involved
and take part in many
local community
volunteer programs
and activities.

somebody who helps companies evaluate data and make focused decisions, and somebody who advises them on how to implement and act upon the decisions they've made to meet the challenges of tomorrow."

As KPMG concentrates on servicing the demands of its clients in the Bay Area, it also takes time to connect with its neighborhoods, keeping ever present the company's mission statement—"to turn knowledge into value for the benefit of our clients, our people, and our communities." Annually more than 200 nonprofit organizations in Northern California benefit from KPMG employee's volunteering and matching contributions to their cause.

Over the past half century, KPMG's Silicon Valley office has enjoyed the privilege of serving the valley's premier companies and their surrounding communities. With relentless focus on client service, coupled with outstanding training, KPMG will continue to provide its people with exciting challenges in a fast-paced, high-growth environment for decades to come. ∎

universities, and pulls in professionals with valuable industry experience in the accounting, law, finance, and merger and acquisition fields. "While many of our employees are home-grown," stated Goodburn further explaining the scope of their expertise, "we also have a big population that relocates here through an active training program. Employees will spend a few years here, then return to other KPMG offices in the U.S. or foreign priority markets, strengthening our ability to serve our global clients."

According to Goodburn, priority for the Silicon Valley office is really about picking the right clients and working with them long-term. KPMG's Silicon Valley office has strong relationships with venture capital firms, law firms, and the investment banking community, identifying emerging companies that are shaping the market, and who will be tomorrow's household names. "We have an outstanding list of clients—many high potential emerging companies as well as several of today's worldwide market leaders," he stated as KPMG helps guide companies in their ascent from inception to leadership.

When it comes to pace—there's no better place to be than Silicon Valley, the hub of the information universe where millions of new bits of information are processed every week. "Companies no longer want a public accounting firm that knows how business worked yesterday," explained Goodburn, "they want

An engagement team
at the forefront of
providing assurance
services to technology
clients. KPMG
professionals offer
creative solutions to
help clients succeed in
today's fast-moving
marketplace.

12
CHAPTER TWELVE

EMPLOYEE GIVING

Therma, Corp.

Therma, Corp., takes "giving" very seriously. The corporate logo includes the image of an outstretched hand designed into the Capital "T." "I like it both as the logo for our company and for our charity work," stated Joe Parisi, president and co-founder, along with his wife, Nicki, Therma's chief financial officer.

Therma, which has been a successful mechanical contractor in the valley for over 34 years, has a strong commitment to the local community. The company and its founders and employees have extended a helping hand to assist with fundraisers, serve on boards of foundations, hold officer posts in local associations, help employees in need, and donate equipment and labor for the renovation or construction of community buildings.

Therma employees are generous with not only their money but also their time. Here they man the phones at the KTEH Auction, a Therma-sponsored event.

Honey Meir-Levi, executive director of Stanford Hospital's famed Ronald McDonald House remembers Therma's generosity, when she called the company one day to get a bid to install air conditioning. She explained, "Joe answered the phone, and I said I was calling around getting bids. But before I could finish what I was saying, Joe replied 'Oh, we'll do it.'" Taken aback, she remembered asking with a cautious tone, "What do you mean we'll do it?" Joe simply stated, "We'll do it, and we won't charge you anything at all."

That was the start of what turned out to be a horrendous but heart-warming experience. The house, which has served thousands of families who stay there while their critically ill children are receiving medical care at Stanford, was originally designed in the '60s and was lacking drop ceilings and had pointy roofs. "We had to hide the ductwork outside under eaves," stated Joe Parisi, whose crew employed a bit of ingenuity to make today's technology fit into yesterday's architecture.

For several years, Therma was the corporate sponsor for the Cattle Baron's Ball, a fund raiser for the American Cancer Society, with employees designing, installing, and manning the booths.

"It was just an act of unexpected and stunning generosity," state Meir-Levi as she concluded. Original bids were all over a quarter million, so it must have ended up costing Therma close to half-a-million dollars.

Joe sits on the boards of many non-profit groups. It was through the VMC Foundation that the Parisis became involved in replacing an outdated pediatric clinic in San Martin with a new building. "Joe chaired the drive to raise the funds, and in fact wound up building the structure pretty much on his own," stated Jonathan Driscoll, executive director of the foundation, which raises awareness and funds to support Valley Medical Center and the health system in Santa Clara County.

The Karie Lyn Anchondo Childrens' Center, which the county named in loving memory after Joe and Nicki Parisis' late daughter, is now providing outpatient services to 15,000 low-income children a year (five times its original capacity).

Nicki Parisi was a very active partner in the McDonald house renovation. She also participates regularly in KTEH's annual fundraiser, strongly supports the Arthritis Foundation, is consistently a major sponsor of the American Cancer Society, and has several other charities that she holds dear to heart including the San Jose Ballet and the Kidney Foundation.

For years Nicki Parisi was a member of the Cattle Baron's Ball Committee (an annual fundraiser for the Cancer Society). Come summer Nicki would put Therma to work designing and building the elaborate theme environments. For one particular evening, Therma put its design engineering group to work on "Ram Bull" a computerized bovine that stood at the entrance stomping his hoof.

Therma contributed the full mechanical system for the Stanford Ronald McDonald House.

Alongside stood two life size stallions; a full-scale steam loco-motive completed the scene. Every year Therma employees assisted with the live auction and other events of the evening.

"I know Mrs. Parisi feels fortunate to have been in a position to have resources to help the Ball, which attracted 1,400 guests last year," stated Suzanne Oberman, a spokesperson for the Cancer Society. "Therma has not only donated money, they have donated time, manpower, ingenuity, and heart. They have helped make Cattle Baron's Ball what it is today."

Employees have also been motivated by their founders' good work. They have in turn helped out with local charities and donate their own time. From answering phones for the KTEH fundraisers, to participating in the various Cattle Baron Ball venues, Therma employees are encour-aged to give of themselves to benefit others.

From Therma's conception Joe and Nicki felt the need to contribute. In the early 80s, when Cabrini Center for the developmentally disabled in Tuolumne County was faced with a construction budget shortfall, Joe and Nicki donated the full mechanical and plumbing systems thus allowing construction to occur. The local Senior Centers, schools, and universities have all benefited from Therma's generosity.

At Therma, extending that helping hand is not just something done around the holidays. "Giving back," says Nicki, has become a way of life, a function of our business demeanor, and our personal lives. When asked for the reason behind their giving spirit, Joe Parisi simply replied, "We just like to help people." ■

Therma shows its care for employees through such programs as this health clinic, which provides cholesterol and blood sugar testing.

Intel Corporation is dedicated to being a good corporate citizen and neighbor. Not only does the company help drive the economy as the world's largest chip maker, they have also taken their innovativeness out of the cubicle and into the community where they apply it to the issues that concern us all.

Through both the corporation and its separate non-profit organization, the Intel Foundation, Intel donated worldwide a little more than $120 million in 2000 in goods, services, and cash. Of that amount, almost 90 percent went to help improve education, from elementary school to higher education.

"We focus our giving on education because of its importance to the future of our country and our industry," stated Peter Broffman, executive director of Intel Foundation. "It is also an area where we have expertise and can add value beyond just giving money or equipment."

Under the Intel Innovation in Education initiative, there are several outreach programs aimed at improving math, science, and technology education, increasing the number of people pursuing careers in those fields, and at expanding access to and effectiveness of technology in classrooms.

One program was an outgrowth of Intel ACE (Applying Computers in Education), a 1997 partnership between Intel, Microsoft Corporation, and Hewlett-Packard that trained teachers on the local level to use technology in an academic environment. After several years of refining the curriculum, Broffman explained, "In 1999, our chief executive officer and president, Craig R. Barrett, challenged us to expand the program to reach 100,000 teachers in the United States and a half-a-million around the world over the next three years."

The Intel Teach to the Future program was born out of that challenge. The dream is now becoming a reality in 20 countries. Master Teachers trained by Intel in countries like China and India facilitate 40-hour workshops where teachers learn not only how to operate computer equipment and software programs, but also get valuable tips on how to integrate technology into their classroom teaching to improve student performance.

As part of the course, teachers prepare actual lesson units that they can immediately implement. "We then place selected lesson units on a Web site, so educators anywhere in the world can access examples," stated Broffman. One success story is a teacher in Oregon who is now using technology to encourage interest in wetlands. She is collaborating with classrooms in Australia and Hawaii to create artificial wetlands based on their own natural environments.

Top: Sharkie—the mascot of the NHL franchise San Jose Sharks—poses outside the Intel Museum, where thousands of visitors come every year to see the beginnings of the high-tech industry and the magic of how chips are made. Right: In 2000, more than 2,000 Intel employees in Silicon Valley took part in the "Intel Involved" program, volunteering almost 22,000 hours with local charities and community-based organizations—one of the largest corporate volunteer programs in the Bay Area.

A second signature program is the Intel Computer Clubhouse Network, based on a highly successful learning model developed by Boston's Museum of Science and MIT's Media Lab. A collaborative effort to bridge the digital divide, Intel is investing $20 million over the next five years to establish 100 Intel Computer Clubhouses around the globe in community organizations. The first Intel Computer Clubhouse was opened in November 2000 at East Side San Jose Boys & Girls Club, and others are planned in locales around the country such as Sacramento, Washington DC, East St. Louis, New York, Los Angeles, and in other countries including Israel, the Philippines, and China.

Working with Intel to implement the clubhouse program are leading companies from the industry—Adobe Systems Inc., Macromedia, Hewlett-Packard, and Autodesk, Inc. They have donated high-end software programs that the kids then use to create personal projects using music, video, and animation. While they are having fun in this informal environment, the kids become experts on the use of the professional-level software without realizing it. "The Clubhouse operates on a 'learning-by-doing' philosophy that provides youth not only access to technology, but also meaningful skill-building opportunities to help them succeed," stated Barrett, who came up through the ranks of Intel over the past 25 years to become its CEO in 1998.

In order to promote math, science, and engineering, Intel also sponsors two of the best-known and most challenging pre-college competitions in the world. Originally sponsored by Westinghouse, the Intel Science Talent Search, now in

its 60th year, is the most prestigious science competition for high school seniors in the United States. The Intel International Science and Engineering Fair is the largest international science and engineering competition for high-school students, attracting competitors from 45 countries. Students develop projects in 14 different scientific categories, from biochemistry and environmental sciences to mathematics and physics.

At the local level, Intel invests funds and thousands of volunteer hours in local communities through their Intel Involved initiative. In 2000, a total of 1,800 Silicon Valley employees volunteered time to inspire students, clean parks, build affordable homes, and participate in charity events. A few local projects dear to their hearts are the Housing Trust Fund, which provides low-interest loans for first-time homebuyers and supports shelters; Intel Carver Scholars, a project aimed at increasing the number of African-Americans in the sciences; and San Jose's Tech Museum Endowment, which allows Intel to fund special exhibits.

Whether the company is striving to provide a better technology-driven education for the Einsteins of tomorrow, or being a good corporate neighbor to the global community, one thing is for sure as stated by their leader Craig Barrett: "Intel is committed to playing a positive role in preparing our youth for the demands of tomorrow." ∎

Intel Involved volunteer Walter Robe gets ready to help cut sheet rock at a Habitat for Humanity home build. Every year Intel Involved volunteers take part in several home building projects throughout the San Francisco Bay Area. At this site in Redwood City, Intel Involved volunteers joined with employees from other Silicon Valley companies to build eight homes during a one day "Rapid Build."

Comedian Sinbad joined Intel CEO Craig Barrett and Public Affairs Manager Rosalind Hudnell at the grand opening of the Intel Computer Clubhouse in East San Jose— part of a network of 100 such Clubhouses that aim to help bridge the "digital divide."

AIR SYSTEMS FOUNDATION, INC.

The Messenger II starship is an icon for the foundation with its interactive features getting Air System's message out to the community that "Together we can build our Children's Future."

Everywhere you see purple, think of us—people with passion for what we do in supporting children's programs and charities throughout Santa Clara County," stated Christine Davis, president of Air Systems Foundation, Inc.

Air Systems Foundation, Inc., was founded in 1997 through continuous fundraising efforts started in 1984 by Christine's husband, John Davis, when he decided to have a party for the employees and customers of his mechanical contractor business, Air Systems Inc. (now an Encompass Company). "We knew a number of people who owned special cars," stated John Davis, "so I said, 'Let's have a party and all bring our cars to show.'"

Out of this cozy gathering, which attracted 30 cars and about 250 attendees its first year, was born the Air Systems Car Show & Family Fun-Fest, an extravaganza that three years later became a private fundraiser for the San Jose Children's Discovery Museum.

"Now, after 17 years, we have grown from supporting 1 to over 38 different programs, giving more than $1 million to local children's charities—from handicapped situations to education programs and scholarships to feeding hungry children," stated Christine Davis, who came out of a short retirement from her career as president of a retail meat business and from raising her one-month-old son to head the Foundation.

At last count the biennial event attracted an incredible collection of 254 show cars with a total worth of more than $20 million dollars. Some cars are more unusual than others—like a '64 Ampicar that can be driven on land or through the water and a 1920 Rolls Royce specially built with a cannon for an African king.

In 1993 with the event hosting more than 2,500 guests, it outgrew Air Systems' property and was moved to San Jose History Park (formerly the San Jose Historical Museum). Silicon Valley leaders, their families, friends, and car enthusiasts, now stroll through the 14-acre site enjoying the events' old-fashioned country fair atmosphere that's filled with roaming funny-faced clowns and Hanna Barbera characters, live music, sports celebrities, rides, safety demonstrations, barbecue food, and a spectacular fireworks finale.

The Air Systems Car Show & Family Fun-Fest continues to be the foundation's largest fund-raising effort since its inception in 1984. Clowns, cars, and kids provide a unique and great combination to encourage the financial support, immeasurable memories, and keep kids as our driving force.

The foundation generously supports literacy programs and encourages under-privileged children to love school. Self-esteem and confidence play a large role in a child's desire and performance in the classroom. A backpack, school supplies, and a new pair of shoes puts a smile on their faces.

this, we're able to extend their passion to the people we serve, giving them the opportunity to grow and learn, and be the best they can be."

As a symbol to Air Systems Foundation's driving force, the Foundation even has a 14-foot diameter, 4,000-pound starship called the *Messenger II*, which was built by a team of ASI employee volunteers who are always eager to help when they see so many lives touched by their generous efforts. They also get into the act by donning purple spacesuits and guiding curious youngsters through the interactive craft that contains computers, voice synthesizers, blinking lights, and special sound effects.

The spaceship makes appearances at the Fun-Fest and is in high demand around the area. For example, it had a moment of glory in September of 2000 when it appeared on stage with John Glenn, former U.S. Senator and astronaut, at a San Jose Silicon Valley Chamber of Commerce event.

"The *Messenger II* spaceship is a vehicle to get our message out to the community that 'Together we can build our children's future,'" concluded Christine Davis. The Foundation does just that as it ties the color purple into its letterhead, newsletter, and clothing; and passionately brings together distinctive vehicles, attendees, volunteers, a board of community leaders, and business sponsors to raise funds to benefit children in the local community. ■

With over 98 percent of the Fun-Fest's net proceeds going to benefit Santa Clara County programs, Debbie McKenzie, who is development manager for the Children's Discovery Museum stated, "We're still one of the core beneficiaries of the Foundation, but now the money also goes to many other underserved organizations." Some of these charitable organizations include: the Boys & Girls Clubs of Santa Clara County, Packard Children's Health Van, City Team's "Back to School & Back on Track," Teens for a Healthier Tomorrow, Children's Shelter of Santa Clara County, and Via Rehabilitation Services Inc.

The Children's Discovery Museum is a special place where children of all economic walks of life can come on their own or through school field trips to enjoy a hands-on experience. "The Foundation was a major sponsor of our 'Magic Beans, Creative People' exhibit that demonstrated ways cultures use seeds," explained McKenize.

Another program that benefits from the Foundation's generosity is Via Rehabilitation Services, Inc., formerly known as Crippled Children's Society of Santa Clara County, Inc., a non-profit organization dedicated to helping children with disabilities. "We've been a recipient charity since 1998 with the Foundation funding testing materials and equipment for our first step program for premature babies, infants, and toddlers who show signs of being developmentally delayed," stated Kay Walker, Via's chief executive officer and president.

"The passion that the Foundation has in supporting organizations that serve children is obvious in everything they do. Even at the car show, volunteers wear tee shirts that say 'Kids are our Driving Force,'" stated Walker. "And because of

A portion of Air Systems Foundation's funds proudly supports programs where parents and their children engage in group therapy and counseling to help improve and educate developmentally delayed infants and toddlers.

Founded in 1981, Adaptec is a financially successful company engaged in the manufacturing of computer hardware storage devices and in the development of software to manage and protect data and digital content for e-business and internet applications. In recognition of its success, Adaptec is actively involved in giving back to the community to help those who are less fortunate. It has an active Corporate Contribution Program that makes grants to non-profit organizations to help benefit the communities where they operate. Funding priorities for the firm include education and research, and its goal is to help lower the dropout rate of youths in accredited schools and colleges. It also provides assistance to students particularly in engineering-related university programs.

Health and human services grants are designed to help find cures for degenerative and devastating illnesses as well as to provide help to the homeless, abused spouses and children, and drug and alcohol rehabilitation. Grants to cultural and artistic endeavors are also supplied in order to help people enjoy life more fully through music, dance, art, museums, and other similar pursuits.

To encourage its employees to help charitable organizations, Adaptec has a policy of matching dollar for dollar contributions made by its employees to organizations that reflect the funding criteria categories listed above. These matching contributions range from a minimum of $50 to a maximum of $1,000. The matching dollars given by Adaptec exceeds $600,000 each year for an average of about $400 per employee.

Examples of organizations that receive annual grants from the company are: Santa Clara University, the Silicon Valley Charity Ball, the American Red Cross, Child Advocates, Milpitas High School, the Children's Discovery Museum, the Technical Museum of Innovation, and the San Jose Repertory Theater. Adaptec also encourages continuing education and has a generous tuition assistance program. Adaptec also endows an annual undergraduate engineering scholarship at Santa Clara University.

In addition, employees are encouraged to do more than just donate money. They are given the opportunity to physically help in the community through a Community Service Day program. Staff is allowed to take one paid day off a year to help their charity of choice. In some instances, entire departments have taken off the same day so that they can all help with a particular project.

This culture of giving to the community, demonstrated by the company and its employees, results from a working environment that has a strong sense of values. Not only

A Community Service Day was designed to allow employees to take one paid day off per year to help their charity of choice.

does Adaptec value the community, but the company also values its own people and demonstrates respect for their needs and contributions. Dealings with employees, customers, and suppliers are based on ethics and integrity and the belief that teamwork and co-operation are vital to success. As a consequence, Adaptec is a favorable employer for working mothers in an industry that is known to burn out even its most energetic engineers.

New employees have commented that they went to work for Adaptec because of the fact that people in the company work together and are treated professionally. No one is expected to work around the clock and to never or rarely see their families and loved ones. There is employee flextime and the opportunity to telecommute. There is a liberal time-off policy beginning with 13 paid holidays each year including a week off at the end of the year and an additional 12 days of vacation.

In 2000, Adaptec created a recruitment campaign called "Work Smart, Go Home." As management believes that families come first, they make provisions for staff to attend to sick children or to participate in their children's school field trips. Employees are allowed up to 40 hours per year in paid time to attend to these responsibilities.

New parents are allowed two weeks off at 60 percent of their salary at the time of birth. This was originally designed to encourage new fathers to take time to bond with their newborn. The firm also participates in a Family Care Association to provide in-home health care for employees who need help with children or their aging parents. To help keep staff well informed on health matters, there is an annual health fair where various agencies and vendors provide advice and information to staff. Free flu shots and cholesterol testing are also offered.

As health-care questions concerning children can occur at anytime, Adaptec sponsors a toll-free number where parents can call and obtain advice from an experienced registered nurse. In addition, employees receive a $50 per year voucher that can be used towards a variety of family care needs. There is even a Pet Care Connection to help employees find various services for their pets.

To assist staff with their normal chores, Adaptec provides on-site services for its employees like an ATM, gift shops, dry cleaning, oil change facilities, dental services, a post office, take out meals, ticket agent, and a health club. ■

Adaptec's headquarters, Milpitas, California.

IBM

IBM is leading a revolution in corporate citizenship. This technology innovator is dedicated to solving specific problems and issues, by committing not only funding, but also leadership and hands-on assistance, demanding excellence from its people and from its grantees.

IBM's worldwide corporate philanthropy is helping individuals and communities in a variety of key areas, especially education. Chairman Louis Gerstner is committed to a systemic reform of education; so, IBM hosted the first two National Governors Summits on Education and will host the third in November 2001. Last year nationally,

Congressman Mike Honda admires the eMentoring of students by IBMers at the San Jose Academy, where he was formerly both student and later principal.

IBM donated over $120 million in grants and equipment, 75 percent of which supported educational initiatives, split almost evenly between K-12 and higher education.

IBM realizes that its success, and that of the American economy, depends upon the quality of our children's education. Students must be prepared to meet the exciting and demanding challenges of the future. Through its Reinventing Education program, IBM contributes its expertise and knowledge to schools.

IBM CEO Lou Gerstner's passionate commitment to education has inspired IBM's $40 million Reinventing Education grants program to systemically reform schools, recognized by President Clinton in May 2000 with the Ron Brown Award for Corporate Leadership, the nation's highest honor for corporate community relations.

Reinventing Education

In Northern California, IBM has awarded two Reinventing Education grants, one to San Francisco Unified School District and another to the San Jose Unified School District, to help every child succeed and every teacher to improve. IBM and the San Jose Unified School District have partnered to form a comprehensive, sustainable teacher support and professional development program. This innovative program helps teachers to become skilled at using technology to support all subject areas, while making learning exciting and inspiring.

A key component of this program is the Teacher Portfolio Tool, which helps novice teachers excel as they progress along a four-step continuum. This tool guides teachers, allowing them to document both their work and progress while collaborating with mentors and other new teachers.

E-Mentoring

IBM has partnered with neighboring San Jose Unified School District and East Side Union High School District to sponsor E-Mentoring. In this pilot program, IBM employees mentor students online, providing guidance on specific topics as well as with the broader skills necessary to succeed in school and in life. This structured opportunity to interact with adults through the Web is helping to increase attendance, improve social adjustment, and decrease the number of disciplinary referrals. At the Computer Academies of East Side High Schools, IBM awards qualified students continuing summer internships at the plant.

IBM also is a strategic partner with MESA (Math, Engineering, Science Achievement), an initiative of the University of California with all local schools to prepare students at risk for college and professional careers. Where half these students normally fail to complete high school, MESA graduates well over 90 percent of its students to higher education and rewarding jobs. To excite students in all grades with science, IBM partnered with science museums worldwide to create the TryScience website (www.TryScience.org), filled with interactive experiments.

EXITE Technology Camps

This summer IBM hosted an EXITE Summer Technology Camp to help middle school girls from diverse ethnic and academic backgrounds improve their skills in

math, science, engineering, and computers. This week-long summer day camp empowered female IBM staff to serve as role models to the girls and E-Mentor them throughout the next school year.

IBM also helps teachers during the summer. It is a founding member of IISME (Industry Initiative for Science and Math Education), a coalition of high-tech businesses that provide K-12 teachers in all disciplines an eight-week summer internship in companies. After attending the program, the teachers return to their schools with a commitment to share their new knowledge and skills in the classroom.

Collegiate Summer Programs

The IBM Almaden Research Center is involved with two very important programs in conjunction with The National Science Foundation. One is a $2.2 million grant to Stanford and U. C. Davis that enables students to work with IBM in the area of polymer films research. This research involves almost 90 post-doctoral researchers and includes a strong summer outreach for chemistry undergrads and high school teachers. An IBM-sponsored program also provides a post-doctoral instructor to The Tech Museum who offers support in chemistry for the museum's outreach programs.

Partnering with San Jose State University, IBM runs a summer program for college juniors majoring in surface chemistry, as well as for high school science teachers, allowing them to gain real lab experience working at IBM facilities. Part of the program includes input on making career decisions, because the junior year is the key year for deciding on a career.

Employee Partnership Programs

IBM employees have always been generous with their time and money, supporting local charities and service organizations. To encourage that involvement, IBM's Fund for Community Service program, rewards employee volunteerism with money or the latest hardware and software to these organizations. Through its Employee Charitable Contribution Campaign, IBM matches employee donations to health and human services agencies. Separately IBM is a prime contributor to the local United Way, donating cash and equipment to many local non-profits. IBM and its employees gave $1.7 million to local charities last year.

IBM has donated hundreds of Young Explorers (computers in plastic playstations) to Head Start programs to eliminate the digital divide. To encourage more giving, IBM's Matching Grants Program allows employees and retirees to donate selected IBM equipment and software to eligible schools of their choice.

Through these unique programs, IBM and its generous employees have had a powerful impact on their communities. It is a tradition that IBM will continue to promote, empowering a new generation of valley citizens. ■

CEO Gerstner greets a student who wants to succeed him. Lou wants to give him the education to do so.

As Co-Chair of Achieve.org, Gerstner advocates standards, assessments, and accountability to drive systemic reform of all U.S. schools.

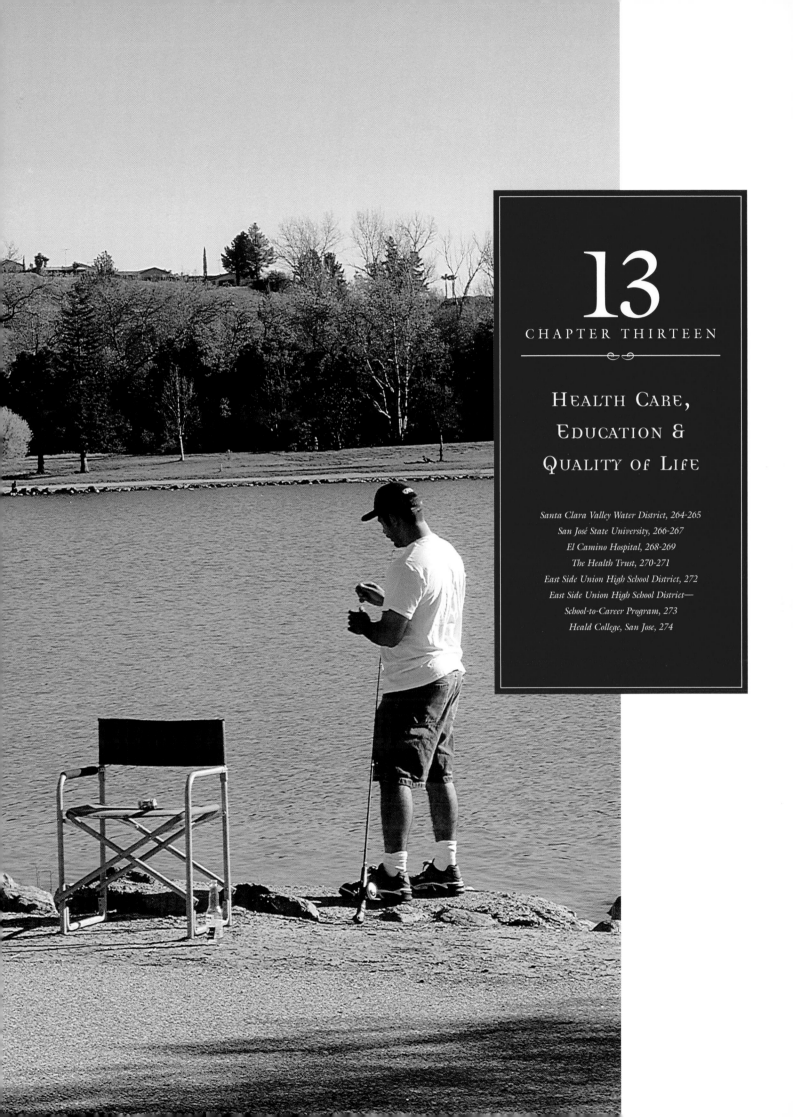

13

CHAPTER THIRTEEN

HEALTH CARE, EDUCATION & QUALITY OF LIFE

SANTA CLARA VALLEY WATER DISTRICT

The Santa Clara Valley Water District is the public agency responsible for comprehensive water resource management in Santa Clara County, including wholesale water supply, flood management, and stream stewardship. The district is governed by a seven-member board of directors, and encompasses all of the county's 1,300 square miles and 15 cities, including the 1.7 million residents and 200,000 commuters.

As much of the area has morphed from the Valley of Heart's Delight into Silicon Valley, so have the face and issues of water management become more complex. The roots of today's Santa Clara Valley Water District lie in the valley's agricultural heritage. In 1929, local farmers formed the Santa Clara Valley Water Conservation District in order to safeguard groundwater supplies. Since then, through several incarnations, today's water district is entrusted not only with providing an adequate supply of clean, safe drinking water for the county, but also with working to protect people and property from flooding in an environmentally sensitive manner.

Voters Approved Plans

In November 2000, county voters approved Measure B, mandating the water district to implement the "Clean, Safe Creeks and Natural Flood Protection" plan. The 15-year plan, funded by a special parcel tax, is part of the district's comprehensive flood protection and stream management plan that emphasizes working with rivers and floods rather than against them. Elements of the plan help to reduce property damage and disruption to business and ensure that people can travel to jobs and schools during even the wettest winters.

The plan helps improve the quality of life in Santa Clara County by incorporating new and increased services requested by residents. It also will work to improve water quality, restore habitat for wildlife, enhance creek aesthetics, and provide new recreational opportunities.

The special parcel tax will raise about $24.7 million annually and will sunset in 15 years. The sunset allows for evaluation of program effectiveness, reassessment of community needs, and the consideration of new projects in the future. The plan does not include debt financing to accelerate the construction of capital projects; rather, projects will be built as the money becomes available.

Flood Protection and Stream Stewardship

The "Clean, Safe Creeks and Natural Flood Protection" plan offers a multifaceted approach to achieving the district's flood protection and stream stewardship goals. For details, visit the district Web site at www.heynoah.com. Some highlights include:

• The addition of nine new flood protection projects that will safeguard 13,600 homes, 43 schools and public facilities, and 1,040 businesses and public buildings. Those projects are planned for Permanente, San Francisquito, Calabazas, Berryessa, Coyote, and Upper Llagas creeks, the Guadalupe River, and Sunnyvale East and West channels.

Top: Anderson Reservoir in Morgan Hill, an important piece of Santa Clara County's water supply picture, can hold more than 89,000 acre-feet of water. It also provides recreation opportunities for area water enthusiasts. Right: The Guadalupe Creek Trail in San Jose depicts the new face of flood management. The flood plain that can contain heavy flows from the river also features jogging trails and valuable habitat.

The district is also on the forefront of expanding available water supplies through conservation programs, water recycling, and additional banking, storage and water transfers at the state and regional level. All of these components are included in the district's Integrated Water Resource Plan, which maps a strategy for supply reliability through 2020 and is scheduled to be updated in 2001.

Clean, Safe Water

For more than 70 years, the district has delivered clean, safe drinking water to Santa Clara County. As new challenges to water quality arise, new programs and technologies are used to answer those challenges. Most notably:

• The district is in the midst of a $138 million, multi-year project to upgrade and modify the county's three drinking water treatment plants. The completed project will enable the district to continue to comply with upcoming new, more stringent water quality regulations; upgrade the seismic capabilities at each plant; increase the total daily treatment capacity; and enhance the taste and scent of the water delivered to the county's water retailers.

• The district board of directors and staff has been at the forefront of the move to ban the gasoline additive MTBE and prevent contamination of groundwater supplies.

• Several other district programs address urban runoff pollution, nitrates, source water quality, and other issues. For more information on any of these programs, visit the district's Web site at www.scvwd.dst.ca.us. ∎

A series of deep pools, formed by rock weirs, once again makes the Guadalupe River near Hillsdale Avenue in San Jose accessible to migrating Chinook salmon and steelhead trout. The water district worked with other local and state agencies to remove a concrete barrier and construct the plunge pools, which allow the native fish to return to historic spawning grounds upstream.

• Aggressive efforts to improve the quality of the water in the creeks and bays by concentrating on reducing or eliminating specific harmful pollutants, reducing illegal dumping of chemicals and debris, and removing trash and graffiti.

• Proactive work to protect the ecosystems of creeks and bays through endangered species protection; the protection, restoration, or creation of tidal and/or riparian habitats; removal of barriers to fish migration; and the removal of non-native, invasive plant species in favor of native species.

• An increase in recreational opportunities by providing public access to open space or trails along creeks where appropriate; providing bicycle paths for alternative transportation; and, where appropriate, incorporating open space, trails, and parks into flood protection projects.

Water for a Thirsty Valley

The district's other primary charge is to provide reliable, affordable, and high-quality water to the county's water retailers, who in turn supply water to residents and businesses.

To provide more than 275,000 acre-feet of water each year with maximum efficiency and flexibility, the district uses both local and imported water sources. Nearly half of the area's water comes from local sources, such as underground aquifers, and more than half is imported from the Sierra Nevada via state and federal water projects. All imported water is transported through the Sacramento-San Joaquin River Delta.

In its 2001 edition of "America's Best Colleges," U.S. News & World Report ranks San José State University among the Top 10 Regional Public Universities in the West. Shown here, SJSU's Tower Hall. Photo by Thomas Becker

In his welcoming address for the 2000-2001 academic year, President Robert L. Caret proclaimed that San José State University has truly become a "Metropolitan University." "For 144 years we have empowered the people of this valley to be successful," he stated, referring to its long history of serving the region and economy, its citizens and businesses.

SJSU was founded in 1857 as Minns' Evening Normal School in San Francisco as an institution for training teachers. But, during the term of President Ulysses S. Grant following the Civil War, the State Board of Education decided to move the school away from the clamor of the big city to a site that was termed "more quiet and with fewer temptations." In 1870 the sleepy town of San José with a population just over 9,000 was chosen as the new location—for its climate, available space, and as Superintendent of Public Instruction Oscar P. Fitzgerald noted, perhaps foreshadowing the future Silicon Valley, because "the people are intelligent, hospitable, and moral."

Since that time, the small teaching school has grown into a full-blown comprehensive public university with 134 degree programs ranging from anthropology and art to computer engineering. The oldest public institution of higher education on the West Coast, SJSU now has a student body just under 27,000 and a faculty of 1,700, with a budget of $319,000,000.

When Caret took over the administration of SJSU in 1995, he saw before him the elements for a great institution,

upon which he began to build: a mature university in a wonderful location, with a number of solid academic programs, and a fine faculty. At first he took small steps, making the campus "cleaner, safer, prettier, and happier" by washing windows again, trimming hedges, and picking up litter. He continued to promote a sense of pride by coining the phrase "the Metropolitan University of Silicon Valley," which clarified the school's identity and served as a stepping-stone for larger leaps and bounds.

Today, San José State University is earning strong regional and national recognition. A 2001 study by *U.S. News & World Report* ranked SJSU among the Top 10 Regional Public Universities in the West. And in July 2000, the *San Jose Mercury News* named Robert Caret one of Silicon Valley's top 40 most powerful individuals for his work in "strengthening its (the university's) ties to Silicon Valley and the larger community."

SJSU continues to be a pivotal player in one of the world's most rapidly evolving cultures by educating productive citizens who contribute much to this region. Silicon Valley companies employ more graduates from SJSU than from any other university in the nation—in engineering, science, education, health care, business, and the social services. And more than 130 of SJSU's attendees have gone on to found or lead area companies, like Ko Nishimura, chairman of the board and CEO of Solectron; and Larry Boucher, Silicon Valley entrepreneur and founder of three companies: Adaptec, Auspex Systems, and Alacritech.

"Few (institutions) have been as crucial to the region's success as (San José State), which trains many of the engineers, software designers, and tech-savvy businesspeople who keep the valley's technology machine running." San Jose Mercury News, November 26, 2000. *Shown here, SJSU's College of Engineering.* Photo by Sharon Hall

The university's roll call of famous alums includes Amy Tam, novelist and author of *The Joy Luck Club*; Peter Ueberroth, former baseball commissioner and 1984 Olympic organizer; and Gaylord Nelson who founded Earth Day. Former students who now immerse themselves in governmental affairs are Colorado senator Ben Nighthorse Campbell and Laurie Smith of Santa Clara County, the first female sheriff in California.

A key to the university's recent success is its ability to form creative partnerships with the city, with the region, and with the companies of Silicon Valley.

This includes projects like the $177.5 million collaborative library between the City of San José and SJSU, which is due to be completed in 2003. The new eight-story Dr. Martin Luther King, Jr., library will house both the city's main library collection and the university's traditional academic resources. When completed, it will be the largest library structure to be built "all at one time" west of the Mississippi. It will also become a business model for other institutions.

The NASA Ames Research Center at Moffett Field is the planned site for a shared project between SJSU, the University of California at Santa Cruz, and the Foothill-De Anza Community College District. There, the colleges will explore solutions to fulfilling the valley's high-tech work-force needs by training

residents from right here in the Bay Area. SJSU and NASA Ames have been partners for more than 25 years, with NASA funding more than $35 million in research grants and contracts to SJSU faculty.

SJSU has also expanded its reach into Silicon Valley through its eight academic colleges, which have programs that interact with surrounding communities. The College of Education received a five-year grant totaling $5.7 million from the U.S. Department of Education—the largest award given to an academic institution in California— for two GEAR-UP programs that are designed to assist underprivileged students prepare for college. And the Division of Continuing Education works with area corporations to deliver upwards of 60 customized in-house training programs that affect the lives of 1,200 Silicon Valley professionals.

President Caret's vision of a metropolitan campus is becoming a reality. "Thanks to the creativity and innovation that are part of this institution," Caret now states, "we are healthy and we are strong. We arc growing and we arc changing. We are ready to help California meet the challenges of the new century." ■

Where city streets once bisected the campus, tree-lined pedestrian malls with fountains and park benches now add to the attractiveness of the 144-year-old university. Photo by Sharon Hall

In 2003, San José State and the City of San José will open the doors to a $177.5 million new library, jointly funded, designed, and operated by the city and the university. Here SJSU President Robert Caret, former city mayor Susan Hammer, and current Mayor Ron Gonzales show off the building model. Photo by Sharon Hall

S ince September 1961, El Camino Hospital has been providing health care to residents of the El Camino Hospital District and surrounding areas. As the hospital celebrates its 40th anniversary, it is taking the time to reflect on both its proud past and its future potential.

Its long-time pioneering use of technology combined with a nurturing atmosphere has made it a "right-size" hospital for patients, says El Camino Hospital's Chief Executive Officer Lee Domanico. He says this will not change even as the hospital faces future challenges.

"El Camino has always had a reputation for being advanced, and ahead of its time, yet still being a very friendly, community-based hospital. I see so much potential here at El Camino Hospital. I consider it a privilege to lead this organization and help it achieve even more."

One of Domanico's major challenges will be to find a way for the hospital to comply with new earthquake safety standards enacted by the California State Legislature in 1994 following the Northridge Earthquake in Los Angeles. The laws state that all acute care hospitals must either retrofit or rebuild, many by as soon as 2008.

"Retrofitting does not seem to be a great option," Domanico states. "After four years of disruption and an estimated $133 million, we would have a seismically safe but functionally inadequate tower building."

The other option, which the hospital's board of directors has yet to finally decide upon, is to spend 15 to 20 percent more and build a new, state-of-the-art facility more oriented toward meeting the community's needs, he says. For example, rather than a 50s style hospital with long hallways and semi-private rooms, a new hospital could offer more private rooms centered around semi-circular nursing stations; larger rooms so that families could remain with patients overnight; an infrastructure built to accommodate more new technology; and improved access and parking.

The hospital is hopeful that its plans for a possible new structure will have the support of the community, just as it did 40 years ago. "People had faith even before it was built that a new hospital was something the community needed and would use, and that through the years the hospital would continue to be a vital resource for their community," says a hospital spokesperson.

Top: In 1971, El Camino Hospital was the first in the world to install a computerized medical information system. Today, the system is an indispensable part of patient care at the hospital. Right: The hospital is one of the area's largest employers and offers a wide range of medical and non-medical jobs. Photos by Dan Schofield (ECH staff photographer)

One of the hospital's highly regarded services is interventional cardiology. Photo by Dan Schofield (ECH staff photographer)

Today, that faith has been borne out. El Camino Hospital, with its 2,050 employees, is truly an exceptional hospital. In 1993 and again in 1994, the 426-bed hospital was noted as one of the Top 100 hospitals in the nation by HCIA, Inc., a data analysis and management company. In 1999, it received a double honor: the hospital was named a Top 100 Cardiac Hospital for its interventional cardiology services as well as being named as one of the country's Top 100 Orthopedic Hospitals. Its nursing satisfaction scores are consistently in the 93-94 percent range, one of the highest among the more than 130 client hospitals of Professional Research Consultants, a leading health-care survey organization.

Often referred to as the "Hospital of Silicon Valley," in part because of its location in the midst of the semiconductor industry, the hospital often takes advantage of technology developed right here in the area. For example, the hospital uses state-of-the-art telemetry systems and monitors developed by Hewlett Packard. Physicians here have been among the first to use prototypes of medical devices such as cardiac stents before these were put in widespread use. In the hospital's operating rooms, computer-aided instruments show three-dimensional images on monitors to guide surgeons through delicate operations.

El Camino even tied the Silicon Valley theme into the first of 4,400 births recorded in 2000. Born a little after midnight on January 1, 2000, nine-pound, four-ounce Marcus Victor Perlas was presented with a portfolio of Yahoo! and SGI stock to celebrate him as the first El Camino Hospital baby of 2000.

El Camino Hospital is just as proud of the caring, human touch provided to each patient. For example, the chaplain and her staff of volunteers visit and comfort patients daily. Volunteers check in every day by telephone with elderly or disabled people who live alone. Nurses give warm blankets to patients to make them feel a little less anxious and afraid while waiting for a procedure or to see the doctor. Anxious new moms are reassured after leaving the hospital when maternity nurses make follow-up calls to see how mom and baby are doing.

"The staff, physicians, and volunteers here all contribute to this," says a hospital spokesperson. "And over the years, we've become known for our personalized care. Every patient counts at El Camino Hospital." ■

Opened in 1961, El Camino Hospital is celebrating more than four decades of service to the community. Photo by Michael Ichikawa (former ECH staff photographer)

The Health Trust is a public charity that uses its resources to stimulate health in the greater Silicon Valley area.

The organization, which was formed from the proceeds of the sale of Good Samaritan Health System in 1996 and continues to prosper today through community donations, uses its resources to provide access to primary health-care and health education to the underserved population—the medically indigent, particularly children; the frail elderly; and vulnerable adults.

"We are a unique resource in the community that is 100 percent focused on health issues," stated The Health Trust's president, Gary Allen.

Allen sees the organization's role as identifying the root causes of health issues that fall through the gaps in the existing health-care system, then providing resources to facilitate and develop solutions to these problems. "If you come upon a sink that's overflowing, most people will invest in mops to clean the floor," Allen stated. "What we are trying to do, in the programs that we deliver and in the grants we make, is instill a thought process to creatively find ways to turn the faucet off and unplug the sink, from a community health perspective. We want to help people before the problem gets so bad that it requires expensive hospitalization and medical care."

One way The Health Trust accomplishes its vision is by offering Good Samaritan Grants for community-based health, prevention, and wellness activities; and Health Partnership Grants for medically related services by or through nonprofit or public hospitals. The current list of recipients includes organizations like the Santa Clara Valley Health & Hospital System to fund the first Fetal Alcohol Syndrome Diagnostic Clinic in the State of California and the Stanford Institute of Research in Disease Prevention, working through the Lucile Packard Foundation for Children's Health, to develop a community-based pediatric weight control network for overweight, low-income children in the county.

The Health Trust also manages seven health-related programs in Santa Clara County, among which are the Meals on Wheels program that serves hot meals to an average of 300 frail elderly and disabled clients a day and the School Health Centers program, which provides access to health care on 11 school campuses in six school districts, reaching more than 65,000 children from preschool through high school.

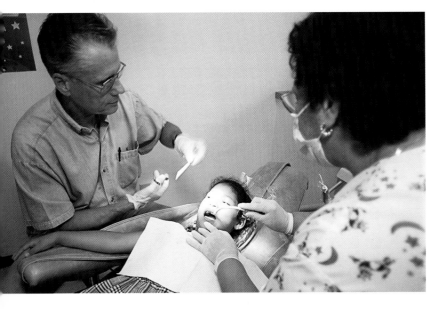

Top: Dr. William Comport, volunteer dentist, and Maria Campero, registered dental assistant, provide free dental services, to Maricruz Avila at The Health Trust's dental clinic at the Franklin McKinley School District Office. Right: Rolling Hills Middle School teacher Shelly Viramontez and learning specialist Carol Moran collaborate with parents and students to develop learning strategies that promote success in school.

*One learning strategy
that helps students
achieve success is
computer-assisted
instruction.*

"Very few schools have school nurses anymore," explained Peggy Gibbs, The Health Trusts' director of development, "and if they do, the nurse is typically shared by a whole school district." The Trust plays a vital role in keeping students healthy and ready to learn through its clinics, which offer physical exams, immunizations, treatment for minor illnesses and injuries, and health education.

*The Health Trust's
Children's Dental
Initiative Mobile Clinic.*

Other programs managed and partially funded by The Health Trust are the PlaneTree Health Library at 98 North 17th Street in San Jose, which houses 3,000 health- and medical-related books, 700 files of research articles, and a well-stocked collection of CDs, medical journals, and magazines to assist individuals in learning about their health or medical conditions and seeking treatment options; Health Connections AIDS Services; Community Wellness; Faith in Action; and a Family Health Insurance program that provides health-care to uninsured children and pregnant women in Santa Clara County.

But as The Health Trust goes about its work in the community, certain health issues rise to the surface as needing immediate attention, which are often bigger than one organization can solve by itself. "We then act as a 'convener,' bringing together individuals and organizations within the community to leverage our resources to solve these bigger issues," stated Gibbs.

Out of this role, two strategic initiatives were born. The first is the Children's Dental Health Initiative, which was designed to curb oral disease, the most prevalent disease among children, even ahead of asthma. Through this program, the Trust has partnered with the California Endowment to establish mobile dental clinics, prevention

programs with sealants and fluoride varnishes, and family educational programs.

The Health Trust's second initiative is aimed at creating an optimal learning environment for students who, because of learning differences, may be left behind in the traditional classroom setting. "The objective of the Silicon Valley Learning Alliance is to develop in these students positive mental health and to make radical changes to recapture them before they become vulnerable to the negative behaviors that lead to juvenile courts, rehabilitation, or welfare systems," stated Allen.

This 12-year project is aimed at a systemic change in the classroom learning environment by assessing children identified as slow learners, working with their parents, and training teachers to accommodate different learning modalities and school staff to be sensitive to the students' needs. Allen explained, "I can't tell you how many parents have told us, 'You don't know how many painful hours we've sat around the kitchen table with our children and fought to try to get adequate attention without success.'"

The many health issues the Trust faces in Silicon Valley did not develop overnight, nor will they go away in a twinkling, but The Health Trust plans to continue challenging itself and others to comprehensively improve the health of the local population. ∎

Superintendent Joe Coto congratulates East Side Academy graduates.

Preparing students for the 21st Century

The East Side Union High School District serves a population base of 434,000 people across a 180-square-mile area along the east side of San Jose. East Side Union is the largest 9-12 high school district in northern California.

More than 24,200 students attend the district's 15 high schools, including 10 comprehensive high schools with enrollments ranging from 1,400 to 4,300, and five alternative high schools with 100 to 550 students each. The district also operates one continuation high school and administers an adult education program that serves over 26,000 adults.

East Side Union has implemented a number of strategies to prepare its students for the changing global economy and the competitive job market they will face in the coming years. Such things as block scheduling, summer institutes for teachers, smaller student learning groups, expanded support services, and development of service learning opportunities for community service are aimed at improving student performance and increasing retention.

All ninth grade students are directed to enroll in college prep math, English, and science classes. Summer support

programs are offered to incoming freshmen, and year-round mentoring programs are being expanded.

East Side Union graduates comprise more than one-third of Silicon Valley's workforce. To better prepare the future workforce, the district established Electronics Academies at three high schools in 1985. The academies form partnerships with major companies in the electronics, computer, semiconductor, and telecommunications industries. This past year, more than 350 students at Independence, Silver Creek, and W. C. Overfelt took part in this innovative program. Graduation rates typically exceed 95 percent.

A Prime Example of Partnership

Exodus Communications® is the leading provider of complex Internet hosting and management services for companies with mission-critical Internet operations. The company manages its network infrastructure via a worldwide network of Internet Data Centers in North America, Europe, and Asia Pacific.

Exodus Communications is a major partner with East Side Union in the three electronics academies. Exodus went so far as to "loan" Mr. John T. Glover, an Exodus executive, to the East Side academy program on a full-time basis. Mr. Glover, with the support of Exodus Communications Chairman and Chief Executive Officer Ellen M. Hancock, has taken a leading role in further developing the electronics academy program.

Exodus has given East Side Union academies computer equipment, including a number of laptops, other equipment, and materials. Mr. Glover has provided curriculum support and career advice to keep the program active and current, as well as helping develop partnerships and support from other firms. His efforts have included soliciting donations for program support, lining up summer internships, and recruiting industry mentors for students. ■

Chairperson/ CEO of Exodus Communications, Inc., Ellen Hancock.

East Side Union High School District has worked hard to build a successful School-to-Career program providing career exploration in Pre-Engineering, Health and Medical, Telecommunications, Computer Science, Information Technology, Biotechnology, Animation, International Business, Teaching, Finance, and Aviation. Brenda Childress, Director of Career Services for East Side Union says, "students in these programs do better academically, are more committed to lifelong learning, and gain a better understanding of the skills needed to be successful. She says the goals for the district's School-to-Career Program are:

• To improve student achievement through the linking of academic and career-based studies.

• To provide incentives for students to complete their high school education and make a seamless transition to postsecondary study.

• To increase the employability of our students.

• To develop in our students responsible attitudes, workplace habits, and personal self-management.

Industry partners provide assistance with curriculum development, provide scholarships, mentors, summer internships, job shadowing and guest speakers, host student and teacher tours, and make cash and equipment donations.

Partnering with East Side's School-to-Career Program is Guidant Corporation, a world leader in the design and development of cardiovascular medical products. Although it is headquartered in Indianapolis, Guidant has California operations in Cupertino, Menlo Park, and Santa Clara. Guidant has been especially helpful by providing mentors, hosting steering committee meetings, and hosting tours for both teachers and students. The company also has given major cash donations to East Side Union.

Next fall, 1,600 East Side Union High School students will enter one of the nation's first information age high schools. The new Evergreen Valley High School in the Evergreen Foothills, overlooking Silicon Valley, will incorporate the latest in new technology. The spacious, 45-acre campus will focus on technology-oriented learning.

Today's employers want graduates with a good work ethic, appropriate social behavior, critical thinking skills, computer skills, good communication skills, and the ability to work with all types of people in a global economy. With the help of key partnerships with leading companies, East Side Union High School District is building the programs to meet those needs. Just last April, East Side Union Superintendent Joe Coto announced that 1,531 East Side

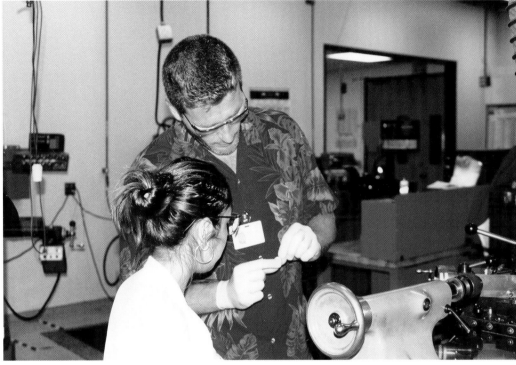

students were eligible for $1,000 Governor's Scholarship Awards. Those results testify to the district's success.

For more information on East Side Academies, contact Brenda Childress at 408-347-5249 or by email at childressb@esuhsd.org. ∎

Guidant employee Jeff McCabe coaches East Side intern.

Guidant employee Ralph Colon explains engineering prints to a student intern.

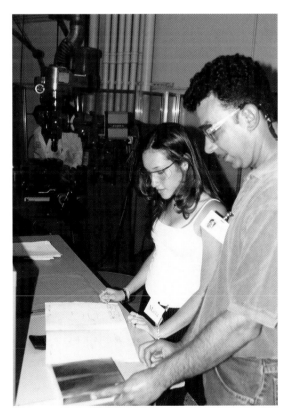

When companies look for new workers who have both the skills and maturity to succeed, Heald College, San Jose, is one of their first calls.

Industry leading firms and organizations know that Heald graduates have the practical skills needed to compete in today's fast-paced environment. Because of the school's concentrated focus on core business and technology subjects, Heald graduates are quick to pick up the pace of a new position and be productive faster.

Heald graduates have proven themselves to be valuable employees for some of the premier names in industry, such as Intel, Pacific Bell, Sony, Agilent Technologies, Lockheed-Martin, and many others. Major West Coast firms regularly recruit from Heald College.

Heald students gain the practical skills necessary to compete in today's workplace because they learn by doing. Students work on computers and equipment they're most likely to use in today's modern business environment. They have individual access to the latest in cutting-edge technology appropriate to their study program, whether accounting, business software, office administration, or networking technology.

Students have exposure to some of the best industry ideas in today's market because of Heald's dependence on corporate advisory boards to help develop curriculum. Local area employers provide expertise and input to help Heald administrators plan programs that are most relevant to industry needs.

Heald College, San Jose, offers 18-month associate degrees in applied science, with emphasis on both business and technology. Twelve-month diploma programs are available, or students can concentrate on six-to-nine-month

certification training in Cisco Systems or Microsoft® Windows® 2000 networking technology. Heald also has whole-program agreements with regional four-year institutions, whereby Heald graduates can transfer their coursework and continue on toward a bachelor's degree.

The Heald experience is a win-win situation for students and employers. During their course of study, students often receive job search assistance. When graduation nears, Heald career services personnel contact prospective employers and make referrals for students. Students receive counseling on career assessment, job search procedures, and interview techniques. The Heald program includes standards for professional appearance, attitude, and attendance, as well as for job performance.

Lifetime job placement assistance is available to Heald degree and diploma graduates. Degree and diploma graduates also have the privilege of returning to the campus to refresh their skills later in their career on a space-availablity and course availability basis.

Heald College, San Jose, is a nonprofit educational institution that specializes in career-focused education in business and technology. Heald is accredited by the Accrediting Commission for Community and Junior Colleges of the Western Association of Schools and Colleges (WASC). The school was founded by Edward Payson Heald in San Francisco in 1863. Today, Heald College serves more than 9,000 students at 11 campus locations and employs over 1,200 staff and faculty members.

Heald College, San Jose, is based in a modern, 56,000-square-foot technology center, fully networked for integrated training and education. Successful students who develop their marketable skills here refer to Heald College, San Jose, as "the high-speed connection to a great career." ■

14

CHAPTER FOURTEEN

MARKETPLACE, HOSPITALITY & TOURISM

STEVENS CREEK DODGE

*The entrepreneurial
spirit that drives the
executive management
team of Stevens Creek
Dodge is embodied in
its Founder and
Chairman N. Dwight
Goad (center), Chief
Financial Officer Jean
Haneke (left), and
Chief Operating Officer
Mark Lindeman.*

"I'm here every day, and I see what's going on," stated Dwight Goad, owner and founder of Stevens Creek Dodge, located on the auto row between Kiely and Saratoga in San Jose. "Customers can feel the difference between our family owned dealership and large conglomerates where everyone is a hired gun. That's why we have people that keep buying cars from us; as well as their children, grandchildren, and extended family."

What Goad is referring to is his dealership's commitment to treating customers, employees, and the community right. This value was ingrained in him as a child by his parents who ran a small general store in Patterson, Missouri; and later at Mike's Motors, a Midwestern dealership whose owner would turn his facility over to the church for the *Little Italy Festival*—chili was cooked and served in their showroom, while the service department hosted raffles and bingo games. Carrying on the same tradition, Stevens Creek Dodge is heavily involved today with the Santa Clara County Fair and the educational community.

As proof of Goad's and his 150 employees commitment to excellence, on the wall in the customer lounge hangs a letter from M. J. MacDonald, vice president of sales and service for Chrysler Motors Corporation congratulating them on being a Five Star dealership and on meeting high standards of facilities, training, and customer handling.

Certified since 1994, the letter reads, "Your dealership was one of the first in the country to meet those requirements…you have helped set the pace for the rest of the dealer body as we jointly work to provide the most customer focused retail process in the industry."

Of course, awards like this don't come easily, "We wear the Five Star insignia on our shirts with pride because we've earned it," stated body shop production foreman Gene Banks, referring to the yearly re-certification process,

which includes semi-annual facility inspections and customer satisfaction surveys that have given the dealership a 96 percent approval rating, far above the scores achieved by like-sized dealerships.

"We've also put together one of the strongest management teams in the Bay Area," stated Goad. Mark Lindeman, who serves as general manager, has a MBA and 19 years experience on the corporate side working for Chrysler Financial, which is headquartered in Detroit. And Chief Financial Officer Jean Haneke, with over 35 years in the business, has held many automotive dealership positions, from receptionist to general manager.

*Silicon Valley's largest,
most modern body shop
housed in a 40,000-
square-foot facility
situated on 3.5 acres
in the heart of Santa
Clara. Pictured from
left: Assistant Manager
Gene Banks, Manager
Bill Tiernan, and
Office Manager
Cherie Rudolph.*

With over 170 employees, a top management team is vital to success. Pictured from left: General Sales Manager Dan Wiseman, Sales Operations Manager Craig Dunn, Customer Relations Manager Sharon Mamola, Service/Body Shop Director Jim Garcia, Service Manager Leroy Sigler, Parts Manager Phil Murtey, Detail Manager David Estrada, and General Sales Manager Dan Rey (not pictured).

Goad also had a promising career with Chrysler Corporation as zone manager in Northern California, but when headquarters decided to move him and his family out of sunny California, he liquidated his Chrysler stock and refinanced his home to purchase an under-performing Jeep dealership on Capitol Expressway. "I remember the interim operator saying, 'I don't deal with techs because they're union,'" recalled Goad who had been a union member himself. "So when I took over, the first thing I did was sit down with the technicians and listen to their issues."

Within a few months after also bringing in a top crew and starting a creative finance department, the dealership turned around and eventually became the best selling Jeep-Eagle dealership in its zone, three years running.

In 1993, Goad sold Expressway Jeep and started Stevens Creek Dodge (www.stevenscreekdodge.com), which soon outgrew its 5.6-acre property. "We've been totally grid-locked the last few years," stated Goad, but after an exhaustive search, the dealership leased a 40,000-square-foot warehouse with 3.4 acres on Martin Avenue near the San Jose Airport and moved its body shop over there. Freeing up space at the main facility, the dealership now has 35 stalls to service the 2,770 repair jobs it averages each month. "Our wait for service used to be two weeks," stated Goad, "currently it's only two or three days."

Last summer the business poured $1.8 million of renovations into the palm tree lined body shop that serves as a direct repair facility for many insurance companies, performing body work on "all makes and models" in its ever-expanding 26 body stalls and 10 paint prep stations.

Having created one of the largest state-of-the-art body shops in the Bay Area, the new facility employs the latest in technology: Genesis laser alignment machines to calibrate damaged chassis; 35 lb. pressure stripping guns that use plastic button holes to sandblast vehicles in 60 minutes rather than eight hours; and an IRT (infrared technology system) that passes over automobiles like a car wash, fully drying paint in 20 minutes. "Rather than it taking three days to paint a car as it used to," commented Goad, "now you can bring your car in in the morning, and get it back that same evening."

"We're setting ourselves up for the future," Goad stated about Stevens Creek Dodge, who admits to being motivated by a sense of accomplishment. "I like being a Five Star dealer, seeing my management team develop and employees do well, and helping customers meet their needs." ■

Located on Stevens Creek Boulevard, the dealership facility spans 5.7 acres with room to display over 500 new and used vehicles for sale. The service department can accommodate up to 150 customer vehicles per day.

SILICON VALLEY
SPORTS & ENTERTAINMENT

D a dum...Da dum...Da dum. Sound familiar? Is it reminiscent of the *Jaws* movie theme that's played at Sharks games in the South Bay? Well, when you think of the Sharks, you should also think of Silicon Valley Sports & Entertainment. SVS&E is a business operations division that emerged in early 2000 from the hockey franchise's vast ocean of holdings to swim on its own.

In order for sports organizations to maximize their revenue potential, sometimes they have to venture into other waters. SVS&E does exactly this by first handling

the business operations for its prime holding, the Sharks; and then by managing special events and properties such as the Siebel Classic SENIOR PGA TOUR golf tournament, the Earthquakes MLS soccer team, Siebel Open ATP Tour tennis tournament, and Logitech Ice at San Jose.

"SVS&E was created as a single resource for our business partners to work with when planning their sport and event relationships," explained Greg Jamison, SVS&E's president and CEO. "Our partners can take full advantage of the expertise and capabilities involving all or part of the organization, including marketing, sponsorship sales, broadcast, ticket sales, event presentation, community programs, media relations, and many other areas of operations."

There are a great number of opportunities that are apparent in a team/event sponsorship. "It's much more than a simple media buy," stated Malcolm Bordelon, executive vice president for SVS&E. "Certainly you receive exceptional branding and promotional opportunities, reaching one of the most affluent audiences in the country and many of Silicon Valley's top decision-makers." Sponsors also enjoy intrinsic benefits from being associated with the Sharks and other such events—an emotional attachment not apparent in standard advertising buys. "Seinfeld, *Time* Magazine, a

Top: On game nights, San Jose Sharks players skate out of the shark head and take to the ice where a thunderous ovation from 17,496 "fin"atical fans await. Bottom: 2001 champion Hale Irwin (pictured) headlined a stellar field of players at the inaugural Siebel Classic in Silicon Valley, the South Bay's first SENIOR PGA TOUR golf tournament. The Siebel Classic is played annually at picturesque Coyote Creek Golf Club in San Jose.

radio station, or newspaper can't create that emotion," commented Bordelon, "nor can they win the Stanley Cup."

Six years ago, the Sharks had no sponsors within the High-Tech category. Now, after building the sponsorship end of the business, SVS&E has over 60 High-Tech corporate advertisers among their more than 115 partners. The crowning glory was this year when San Jose Arena was renamed *Compaq Center at San Jose.* "This unique 15-year partnership will provide funding toward technology upgrades to the building and enable the city to maintain the facility as one of the premier venues in Northern California or North America," explained Greg Elliott, SVS&E vice president of corporate partnerships. "In addition, this agreement will give $500,000 back to the Bay Area each year in support of local charities and community programs.

Companies also get to have fun with their advertising. Not only is the silver-studded venue with its 17,496 hockey seats and 64 luxury suites filled with slogans like Brainshark's "put teeth into your business communications," but also *Sharks* magazine and the team's Web site (sjsharks.com) are also hotbeds for parodies. One of the more imaginative advertisements in the magazine is Intersil's deep blue ocean scene with a silicon chipped shark fin breaking the wave. The tag line reads, "Top of the Food Chain—Bottom feeding is not an option."

But beyond all the fun and games is a serious organization with a dedication to excellence and a mindset to be responsive to the customers. "When you drive up to the Compaq Center, is the parking easily accessible?" asked Kent Russell, vice president sales and marketing. "How are you welcomed when you walk up to the building; is it safe; are your tickets at Will Call as they should be; are the bathrooms clean; are concession lines quick; are the hot dogs hot; are the drinks cold; and is the event entertaining?"

Like running an exceptional restaurant, SVS&E calls this customer service experience "setting the table." You can adjust the lighting and polish the silverware as SVS&E does along with Compaq Center Management, a separate division of the Sharks headed by Jim Goddard; but then you sometimes have to hope that the cook (the Sharks sports team or a special event) makes a good meal.

SVS&E is also involved in the human side of the business through community outreach. SVS&E sustains The Sharks Foundation with marketing services and other support in an effort to meet the educational, social, and cultural needs of the community. During the last six years, The Sharks Foundation has facilitated over 20 outreach programs, like Compaq's "Reading is Cool" program that is designed to encourage kids to read more, and Nike/NHL's "Sharks & Parks" street hockey program. The Sharks Foundation has donated more than $1.5 million to approximately 70 beneficiaries, including City Year, Boys & Girls Club, New Children's Shelter, and the Role Model Program.

Since September 7, 1993, when the Ringling Bros. and Barnum & Bailey Circus first opened its show at the Arena, the Sharks franchise, owned by George and Gordon Gund, has been an integral and important part of San Jose. And although the newly spawned Silicon Valley Sports & Entertainment remains in its infancy—"We're continuing to review and pursue management of a number of events and properties," stated Jamison. In the sea of entertainment, there's no telling where SVS&E will sail. ■

The world's greatest entertainers and performers have found their way to Compaq Center at San Jose including Barbra Streisand, The Rolling Stones, The 3 Tenors, Reba McEntire, Elton John, and Janet Jackson (pictured) amongst others.

The Siebel Open, Northern California's premiere ATP men's professional tennis tournament, returns annually to Compaq Center at San Jose bringing with it several of the top players in the world including four-time champion Andre Agassi (pictured).

The San Jose Arena Authority, the City of San Jose's agent in the oversight and operation of Compaq Center at San Jose, has been part of the South Bay's civic landscape since 1990. Compaq Center (formerly known as San Jose Arena) is owned by the City of San Jose and operated by the San Jose Sharks/Compaq Center Management. It is considered one of the country's most beautiful sports and entertainment facilities.

The San Jose Arena Authority, with its 19-member volunteer board of directors, serves on behalf of the mayor and city council in the ongoing administration of Compaq Center and acts as the community liaison to address the broader issues of the facility's day-to-day operations.

Today, thanks to the Authority, the 19,000-seat facility is a smooth-running center for major sporting events, concerts, family shows, and large-scale gatherings.

"San Jose has a reputation for great entertainment," reports Karen Danna, chairperson of the Arena Authority. "We are in a great location for entertainment, but we haven't always had the visibility we enjoy now with a quality arena."

Besides oversight responsibilities, the Arena Authority also contributes to a number of important community-based programs. These programs include the City and Community Events program, the San Jose Sports Hall of Fame program, and the Arena Ticket Distribution program.

The City and Community Events program allows for local community-based organizations to utilize the Compaq Center facilities at special rates packages. According to the Authority's executive director, Chris Morrisey, programs such as high school graduations, athletic events, concerts, fairs, and fund-raising events have been very successful in utilizing the Center. More specifically, City Events allow for locally-based nonprofit and service organizations to utilize the Compaq Center in San Jose free of rental fees, while Community Events allow for organizations to receive consideration for special rate packages. The Authority encourages any organization interested in the program to contact them directly.

In 1995, the Arena Authority introduced the San Jose Sports Hall of Fame program. The program was created to recognize local athletes who have excelled in their particular field of sport, while serving as role models for youths. Inductees honored by the program have included Peggy Fleming Jenkins, Jim Plunkett, Tommie Smith,

Compaq Center at San Jose.

The Board of Directors and Staff of the San Jose Arena Authority. From left, seated: Suzanne Salata, John Diquisto, Kelvin Peters, Henry Cord, Bill Clayton, Karen Danna, Kathryn Meier, Bert Bonanno, Bob Masch, Ken Yeager. Standing: Chris Morrisey, Linda Truelsen, George Shirakawa, Jr., Bob Martinez, Robert Hansen, Frank Fiscalini, Dave Salazar, Ray Purpur, Bill Ekern, Vicki Day, Mike O'Kane.

Jack and John Elway, Patty Sheehan, Bill Walsh, Bud Winter, Charlie and Lucy Wedemeyer, Donna DeVarona, and Millard Hampton. Compaq Center at San Jose was designed to display 76 bronze plaques of Sports Hall of Fame inductees along the public concourse. To date, over 30 athletes have been recognized by the San Jose Sports Hall of Fame, and their plaques are now permanently on display in Compaq Center.

In 1997, the Arena Authority introduced the Sports Hall of Fame High School Scholarship program, in which the high schools of Santa Clara County's top female and male athletes receive funds for their athletic programs. The scholarship program is widely recognized for its ongoing support of local youth sports.

The Arena Authority's Arena Ticket Distribution program has been a hugely successful community-based undertaking. As the program administrator, the Authority coordinates the use of the city suite located along the Center concourse, as well as 16 seats in the lower level seating area. Over the life of the program, more than 35,000 tickets have been distributed by Linda Truelsen, the Authority's suite and ticket administrator. The distribution of tickets is solely for municipal purposes, which include ceremonial occasions, economic development outreach, official welcoming of visiting dignitaries, and recognition for direct involvement in city-related projects and programs. Morrisey reports that over 85 percent of tickets distributed for the city suite and lower seating area are used in recognizing organizations and individuals for their involvement in city-related projects and programs. According to Danna, "It's a great way to get people into

Compaq Center who might never come to an event." The Authority greatly encourages participation in the program and will gladly respond to any inquiries.

Compaq Center at San Jose has been extremely successful and its operations largely problem-free, thanks in no small part to the San Jose Arena Authority.

"We serve as the city council's community liaison," Morrisey explained. "When there is an issue about the Center's operation, we typically identify it and find a solution. We are unique in that we have the ability and support to go to any city department or community agency and say, 'We need your help to accomplish this goal, to make this operation more efficient, and to minimize the impact on the surrounding neighborhoods.' We have been very successful in convening organizations to assist in finding solutions."

Recently, the city council entrusted the Authority with an additional responsibility: it will now oversee Logitech Ice at San Jose, the city-owned training facility and public ice rink, which is also managed and operated by the San Jose Sharks. No doubt, the Authority will bring success to the training facility just as it has to Compaq Center at San Jose. The organization and efficiency it provides are essential not only to the viability of these city-owned facilities, but also to their ability to serve Silicon Valley citizens and the general public. ■

The San Jose Arena Authority Executive Committee. From left, seated: Karen Danna, Kathryn Meier. Standing: Bob Masch, Bill Clayton, Bert Bonanno, Henry Cord.

The Executive Staff of the San Jose Arena Authority. From left: Linda Truelsen, Chris Morrisey, Mike O'Kane.

OAKWOOD WORLDWIDE

Oakwood's full-sized living rooms allow space for family time, business meetings, or just spreading out to relax.

Welcome to Oakwood, the world's largest and most experienced corporate housing provider," reads Oakwood Worldwide's homepage at www.oakwood.com. This simple expression says it all because everything about Oakwood Worldwide, from its uniformed front desk personnel to its 24-hour customer interactive center, exudes hospitality, comfort, and efficiency.

A perfect home away-from-home for corporate travelers, Oakwood Worldwide's accommodations include fully furnished apartments that will allow an office to be setup in one room and a crib in another. For the fitness conscious, exercise equipment can be brought in. The atmosphere is more residential than a hotel. Rather than having to dodge hordes of hotel guests, the discriminating Oakwood client can simply go home, stretch out on the couch, and relax in the comfort of his or her own apartment.

Oakwood Worldwide offers corporate housing locations virtually anywhere in the United States, plus select international locations including London, Toronto, Tokyo, Manila, Bangkok, Seoul, and more. In Silicon Valley and the San Francisco Bay Area, Oakwood has more than 2,000 apartment homes. The firm owns buildings—known by the brand Oakwood Apartments—in prime locations such as downtown San Francisco, Walnut Creek, Mountain View, and San Jose. Oakwood also subleases apartments from several other buildings. A company spokesperson stated, "The customer tells us

Oakwood's corporate apartments are furnished with all the comforts of home.

where they want to be, and we'll go find an apartment and furnish it for them."

Ever since Chairman Howard Ruby and two key partners founded Oakwood Worldwide in California back in 1960, its philosophy has been to provide apartments with something extra in the way of amenities, furnishings, and personal service. A huge clientele has responded to Oakwood's housing innovations, and the growing list of customers now includes Fortune 500 corporations, the IT industry, professional sports teams, government and military personnel, small businesses, the entertainment industry, leisure travelers, families, and seniors.

An example of a satisfied client is Federal Express (FedEx). The company's senior travel specialist remarked in *Business Travel Executive* magazine that, "The average cost per night (of Oakwood) is much less than a hotel room, and you also save a great deal on taxes and meals." She added, "There is a FedEx employee in an Oakwood apartment every day somewhere in the world," and that FedEx appreciates "Oakwood's willingness to customize services to meet the needs of different groups."

Oakwood Worldwide is continuing to grow its business, both in Northern California and around the globe, by building relationships with its clients and tirelessly enhancing its products and customer service.

"Our goal is nothing short of a perfect apartment every time," says Ruby. ■

Air Systems Strategic Partners have developed long time relationships and continue to grow with the company's core values always in mind by a strong bond and emphasis on communication. Pictured from left: Art Williams, vice president of marketing and construction; John Davis, CEO; Don Billups, vice president of service; Bill Wayker, CFO; and Tom Sosine, vice president of construction.

Now in its third decade of operation in the Bay Area, Air Systems Inc. is a business based on relationships. "I like to say, 'We have bank accounts with our customers,'" stated John Davis, ASI's president and chief executive officer. "We continually deposit good work ethics, on-time performance, superior installations, engineering practices, and we finish the job 100 percent. Then we follow up with services to take care of the customer on an ongoing basis."

As one of the nation's leading mechanical/electrical contracting businesses, ASI is constantly striving to maintain superior relationships by searching for ways to meet its customers' needs as the market and technology change. In 1999, ASI took a major step toward better serving its customers when the company merged with Encompass Services Corporation (ESC), which is clearly recognized as the nation's premier single-source provider of total facility solutions. ESC has over 33,000 employees at 250 locations nationwide. And in the third quarter of 2001, ASI officially changed its name to Encompass Facility Services of Northern California.

"We saw dramatic changes coming to the industry as a result of the desire for total facilities solutions and the rapid increase in the quality national accounts business," stated Davis, "and we were determined to take a leadership role in that change." Besides providing a competitive advantage with a wider range of services and locations for its customers, the merger into a publicly traded $4 billion dollar company also gave ASI employees stock options, training opportunities, better benefits, and a track for upward mobility, plus growth.

But before ASI began its rise to becoming a premier contracting business, it was simply an idea that came out of Davis's college experience. "I went to the placement office at San Jose State University one day and opened up a thick job listing book, right to the section on air conditioning and found a training position," recalled Davis who had received a degree in industrial technology. "My dad was an automobile mechanic and he was always talking about how great the automobile air conditioning business was. It stuck with me." Three days later Davis had the job; and three and a half years later in 1974, he and two former partners began their own venture, Air Systems Inc.

Internet Data Center—
220,000 square feet of
data floor served by
5,200 tons of rooftop
a/c units.

Bottom: Cisco Site 4—
19 buildings totaling
3.3 million square feet.
HVAC System by ASI
includes roof-mounted,
water-cooled, chilled
water systems with
custom air handlers.
Automated logic controls
system designed and
installed by ASI.

Business opened in a small 1,200-square-foot office in Mountain View with six employees. "The original idea was to set up an HVAC company that serviced and repaired air conditioning units," stated Davis. "We had a lot of energy and some good customers back then, but we didn't have a clue about what we were doing." So they hired the right union employees, educated themselves, and developed relationships that have been ongoing since. "Actually, I'm doing business with some of the same folks that I was doing business with 27 years ago," stated Davis as the names Renco, San Jose Construction, and Devcon Construction came to mind.

Over the last 27 years, ASI's HVAC business has branched out in other directions—into industrial and commercial plumbing, process piping, architectural sheet metal, and as an electrical contractor it also installs energy management systems. "As a product of Silicon Valley's growth we also do business in all different walks of life— biotech, semiconductor, mission critical facilities for the internet, and high-rise office buildings," stated Davis. "We haven't pigeon holed ourselves in any particular discipline or marketplace; the diversification has helped us grow."

ASI has remained a leader in HVAC where it builds, installs, and services air conditioning, heating, and ventilation systems using state-of-the-art equipment and technology that

include computerized plasma cutting and fully-automated CAD/Design systems to satisfy its customers' needs. In the plumbing area, ASI designs and engineers a variety of acid waste systems and treatment plants. And in ASI's high-purity processing piping division, the company operates certified clean rooms to manufacture gas stick fabrications in numerous configurations, gas boxes, ultra high purity systems, bulk chemical delivery systems, and deionized water systems.

Bayer Building 64—ASI installed the metal siding, metal roofing, metal column covers, soffit, general sheet metal, HVAC systems, plumbing, and controls.

The company's highly skilled workforce is also experienced at installing large metal roofs, expansion joints, metal siding, roof screens, custom copper work, flashing, and sheet metal. As a testament to their expertise, customer Ross Thomsen, senior estimator with Rudolph & Stetten, stated, "I have used ASI on probably almost all the large architectural projects we've had over the last 10 years. They were all

extremely complicated, more than just your average flashing sheet metal job, and on everyone of those jobs we've been extremely successful."

ASI has installed energy management systems in thousands of buildings. "We have guys that can talk to buildings through their computers and control the temperatures from remote sites," stated Davis. "If the temperature is too low or too high we can respond over the telephone lines by modem or in person in one of our 80 service vehicles."

This saves operating costs, allows ASI service technicians to diagnosis problems before they become critical, and it minimizes customer downtime. "As a matter of fact," stated Davis referring to his maintenance accounts, "because we monitor companies on a 24 hour basis, often times something will break, and the customer doesn't even know it because we can fix it even before they come back to work."

This level of exceptional service is the hallmark of ASI because the company is committed to meeting and exceeding its customers' needs—customers like Stanford Linear Accelerator, Fujitsu Software Corp., Sony, The Martin Group, Boston Scientific, Seagate Technology, Novellus Systems, Inc., Exodus Communications, and Cisco Systems...as well as hundreds of other customers throughout Northern California.

"We received a call from a long-time relationship at Exodus Communications requesting our immediate help with a project the company had that was behind schedule. We had several people onsite within a few hours and an entire crew onsite within a day, working seven days a week to complete the project," stated Davis. ASI's quick response and belief in building relationships led to helping Exodus construct over 3 million square feet at other project locations in Toronto, New Jersey, Boston, Atlanta, Miami, Austin, Dallas, Irvine, Los Angeles, and Seattle. It generated over $60 million in revenue for sister companies and fostered the sharing of resources and "best practices" within the Encompass organization.

"We've been doing work for Cisco since 1992 when it started a big expansion project into San Jose," recalled Art Williams, ASI's executive vice president of marketing and pre-construction services. "Site 1, Site 2...now we've assisted with new construction, remodels, retrofits, energy management, and preventative maintenance on about 50 buildings since then."

One particular Cisco project, nicknamed "Field of Dreams," required an unprecedented level of engineering expertise and technological specialization of ASI personnel. Working in conjunction with Devcon Construction as the general contractor, Alfa Tech Engineering, and ASI as the mechanical contractor, they were asked by Cisco to deliver one building a month for 19 months for a total of 3.3 million square feet. Now completed, the level of commitment this project took to build one of the largest campuses in the country, in such a short amount of time, far exceeded anything ASI had done previously.

Although ASI performs projects on a job-by-job basis, it develops and sustains customer relationships on a daily basis. It does this through its strong management team that includes the president and four executive vice presidents in accounting, sales and marketing, field operations, and service, who oversee every aspect of the business, and through employees who are oriented toward ASI's core values of integrity, vision and passion, quality and reliability, teamwork, financial success, personal growth, and community involvement.

"Building relationships, getting to know the people both on a business and personal level, and taking care of them is just inbred in us," stated Williams who has been with ASI for 16 years. "Even in the interviewing process for new employees, we spend a fair amount of time finding out how they build and manage their relationships. I don't mention the words 'building relationships' specifically, but if the person says it three or more times, they are already a long way toward making it in the door."

Once on board, however, ASI employees tend to stay and/or keep coming back. "We've started what we call our 'Boomerang Club,'" stated Davis with a funny little smile on his face, explaining that many employees return to ASI after leaving the company and how they receive a boomerang trophy for their desks.

"Obviously our employees are our biggest asset, and you have to treat your assets with care," stated Davis. "Assets can sit on a shelf and just be looked at, but we actually pull them off the shelf, dust them off on a regular basis, and tell them we care for them and that they are meaningful to the whole team."

Total Site Solutions— ASI constructed this Class 10 clean room for one of Silicon Valley's leading equipment manufacturers.

ASI employees are also a meaningful part of their community. "We tap into our employees all the time for our Air System's Car Show & Family FunFest, which the company started back in 1984. They volunteer for activities or make donations, and continually say 'How can I help,'" commented Christine Davis, John's wife and president of Air Systems Foundation, Inc., which manages distribution of the proceeds to 38 childrens' charities in Silicon Valley.

The important thing to remember about the personal aspects and best business practices of Air Systems Inc. as it begins this new era as part of Encompass Services Corporation is that although its name and truck colors have changed on the outside, the inside package—practices and people—remain the same.

John Davis, his executive team, and dedicated employees will still be helping Silicon Valley grow, one relationship at a time-they will just have a little more help. Locally, ASI is expected to expand by 40 percent to upwards of 1,400 employees as two other businesses in Sacramento and Oakland merge into the company. "Air Systems is going to become a platform company for Encompass," stated Davis. "We will then have the largest 'total site solution' business in Northern California." ■

ASI's process piping designers and technicians can meet the diverse needs of the bay area's high-technology industries.

Yahoo interior.
Photo by Marco Zecchin
Image Center

A prime example of Silicon Valley innovation and growth is the South Bay Construction Company, which specializes in building new high-tech facilities and renovating older ones for the area's booming companies.

When the two principals, Richard Furtado and David Russell, purchased the firm in 1993 it was doing a volume of $25 million annually. Today it is at over $400 million and heading higher. *The San Jose Business Journal* rates it as the fourth largest commercial builder in the highly competitive Silicon Valley, with 250 employees.

"A major reason for our success is because we understand that our customers need results," said John Aiassa, head of Marketing/Public Relations. "If we are late finishing a building for a new company, their products may be obsolete before they can gear up for production. We've always tried to maintain the personal atmosphere of a small company."

Because they operate in Silicon Valley, South Bay's specialized project managers can handle such technical work as large campus developments, "clean rooms," "explosion rooms" for companies working with sensitive chemicals, complex construction for biotech companies, tenant improvements, and any other needs of a high-tech company.

Macromedia exterior.
Photo by Marco Zecchin
Image Center

South Bay brings together its teams, including project managers, project superintendents, and subcontractors, with clients early in the design stage to review a project's requirements, estimates, and problems.

The staff has worked successfully with many architectural firms to ensure that all client requirements are clearly spelled out in the construction documents prior to the bidding of the project. They have over 150 years of combined estimating skills that through years of hands-on experience has enabled them to identify areas where significant cost-saving systems can be utilized to produce true savings for the client. South Bay Construction has produced and developed through its employees an estimating system that conforms to the Construction Specifications Institute (CSI). This accurately identifies every line item so they can compare their budget with the final estimate.

Months before a project starts, city officials are contacted to determine code, zoning, and other requirements.

It is a South Bay rule that "the teams who set your project up are the ones that are with you to completion." The client gets to know the team early, and there-fore, smooth working relationships are formed quickly. One staff member noted that, in many firms, clients deal with a contact person initially and are then "handed over" to other individuals who do the construction.

On a South Bay job, employees keep a "close eye" on every project. Daily inspections are made on each site by South Bay's staff, who look at both the

Epiphany Software, Inc.,
interior. Photo by Marco
Zecchin Image Center

The high school was an extremely difficult project because the site was at the top of a hill, located in San Jose and possessing a spectacular view of Silicon Valley. Because it is perched on the hilltop, it is visible for miles. However, the project was a difficult one. A road had to be built to the jobsite, grading of the site also was difficult, and all construction materials and equipment had to be hauled to the hilltop as the work was underway.

Although the majority of South Bay's work is in Silicon Valley, the firm also operates from an Oakland office to serve East Bay clients and a Petaluma office to supervise projects in the North Bay.

materials delivered by suppliers and the work completed by either the company's crews or the subs. Clients are alerted quickly to any problems to avoid potential costly errors. With their architects, the clients then are able to make change orders expeditiously.

Also South Bay has a reputation of working with an excellent group of subcontractors, using a team approach to accomplish a common goal—customer satisfaction.

When South Bay Development and Construction spun off its construction branch in 1993, both Furtado and Russell were company vice-presidents. Each had supervised several major departments and managed numerous projects for different companies. In the years since, they have seen the company grow from 40 to over 250 employees, and the volume of business has increased to 16 times its previous volume.

South Bay crews in that time have constructed more than 500 new buildings, ranging from structures as small as a 5,000-square-foot store to a 400,000-square-foot warehouse to mid-rise, steel framed office buildings. They have also completed more than 20 million square feet of interior improvements.

Clients have included such nationally known firms as General Electric; Apple Computer; Hewlett Packard, where they built "tenant improvements" with a full service cafeteria; Yahoo; and Ernst & Young, plus the N.E.T. campus of 300,000 square feet in Fremont; a retail center of 170,000 square feet, which anchors Ranch 99 in Milpitas; and the Valley Christian High School.

As the company grew, management stressed the need to retain the "small company" philosophy that is the benchmark of its success. A commitment to service, retaining and nurturing long term relationships, while creating new relationships, has caused its employees to prosper along with South Bay Construction. ■

Ernst & Young exterior.
Photo by Steve Whittaker
Photography

Colliers International provides superior commercial real estate services in California, Nevada, and Texas through its 12-office firm, as well as throughout 255 independent offices in 51 countries.

Colliers International's tag line of "global breadth, local depth" is reflected in the activities of its eight Northern California partnership offices headquartered in San Jose, California. First begun as a local and independent commercial real estate company by J. R. Parrish in 1974, the 12-office firm is now doing over $4 billion worth of business in California, Nevada, and Texas. In 1986, J. R. Parrish, Inc., became a member of Colliers International, joining other commercial firms in Europe, Asia, and the Americas to provide consistent and superior services in locations around the world. Today, they comprise 9,000 professionals in 255 independent offices in 51 different countries.

Despite the global breadth, local and regional business is still at the heart of what Colliers International refers to as a relationship business. Although networked with the latest technology and connected internationally, most of its local brokers are very attached to the Silicon Valley, have lived there for most of their lives, have deep roots in the area, and know the markets, the technology, and its leaders, owners, and developers. They are well positioned to provide real estate solutions for local people or international conglomerates.

The culture that defines the firm is based on dealing honestly and fairly with people, as well as trusting and sharing and putting other peoples' interests first. Colliers seeks to understand all the concerns before trying to advise clients of solution alternatives. Because of this culture, the firm is able to attract and keep the very best brokers in the business. Colliers is proud of the fact that it has never lost a Silicon Valley broker to any major competitor, and that length of service in an industry noted for its high turnover, averages 15 years. But then, unlike many other firms, Colliers goes to great lengths to provide a unique, professional business environment befitting the quality of the brokers it attracts. Notably, that includes private offices for its professionals

Based out of downtown San Jose, Colliers relocated to its prestigious 22,000-square-foot office building in June 2000. This location places Colliers in the optimum position to network with its local brokers and international clientele.

rather than cubicles. Colliers feels that each of its brokers is an independent business and that they need an office from which to conduct their business in the most professional manner. This environment enhances performance, rewards results, and helps the company attract and keep its highly competent staff.

The range of services offered is quite broad. It includes the leasing and sales of research and development; office, industrial, and retail property; investment sales and analysis; land disposition and acquisition; property management; construction management; build to suit brokerage; consulting; tenant and landlord representation; feasibility and market studies; property appraisal and valuation; financial services; and corporate advisory services, to name just a few.

In addition to the experienced team, customers benefit from the technological expertise of the firm. In order to ensure that the best and most timely answers, opportunities, and solutions are provided, the firm maintains a state-of-the-art proprietary database of present and historical market data. Much of this information is available online so that customers can access information in whatever part of the world they reside. Distance presents no obstacle to client solutions and satisfaction.

Clients also gain the benefit of long-term relationships. Colliers invests the time to understand the issues and objectives of its clients so that it can offer a realistic service and solution. Colliers' customers include such major Silicon Valley companies as Seagate Technologies, Adobe Systems, Oracle Corporation, Catellus Development Corporation, PMC-Sierra, and countless others.

These major national and international firms are comfortable doing business with Colliers International whether it is a local transaction or the negotiation of a lease on the East Coast or in another part of the world. Customers are confident in their expansion plans because they have been well briefed on all the alternatives available to them, and they have been provided with all the information they need in order to make a rational and safe decision. Colliers International has virtually dissolved geographic boundaries and language barriers and provides a single point of contact in its client's market, supported by English-speaking managers in each area of the globe.

"When you are working with Colliers, you are comfortable in the knowledge that you are represented by honest, hard-working professionals who understand the client's requirements," says a testimonial letter from Chrysler Corporation. General Foods, another satisfied customer, added that "Colliers' high standards show in the finished product."

This commitment to the importance of people and of forging long-term relationships extends beyond the business realm. Colliers' brokers and staff are very involved in helping the community in which they live. The company has adopted a local elementary school in a disadvantaged neighborhood and Colliers professionals donate their time reading to the children, acting as role models for them, and acquiring new equipment for them to upgrade their resources. Each year Colliers takes the entire second grade to a Christmas tree farm in the Santa Cruz Mountains, and donates enough trees to the school so that no family is left without.

In addition to the group giving, most everyone at Colliers donates his or her time and resources to a myriad of worthy causes throughout the community. In some cases, it's hands-on labor and in other cases they lend their business and management experience to help improve services for other non-profit organizations in their community.

The Colliers culture is alive and well in Silicon Valley, where the company started and where most of its professionals intend to finish their careers. Years ago, J. R. Parrish borrowed a phrase that he felt was the epitome of this culture. He called it "The Last Best Place." In San Jose, that is the standard measure from which all decisions are still made today. ∎

Defined by a culture and environment that is touted as "the last best place," the firm maintains high standards of professionalism and integrity in its business dealings. This culture is one reason Colliers is able to attract and keep the finest brokers in the business, while providing the best advice to its clients.

ICOM

Founded in 1981, ICOM Mechanical Inc. first began as a mechanical contractor, with the goal of providing its clients with the most professional and highest quality services possible in the building industry. Initially, ICOM served the industrial heating, ventilation, air conditioning, air, process piping, and maintenance and repair markets in the San Jose area as a mechanical subcontractor in a design/build capacity.

Until the late 1980s, the company focused on the needs of local real estate developers and contractors. However, when the building boom slowed, company officials decided to expand ICOM's design/build function into the high-technology, electronic, and biotechnology sector that was rapidly expanding in the Silicon Valley. Since then, ICOM has been increasing its activities in the provision of clean rooms for electronic, pharmaceutical, aerospace, biomedical, and photonics companies.

Today ICOM has expanded its services to include full turnkey solutions to the high-tech industry. ICOM acts as general contractor and mechanical contractor, as well as design and construction managers to provide from concept to completion construction services. ICOM projects typically include state-of-the-art clean rooms and process systems.

Offering both general construction and in-house mechanical design/build provides ICOM's customers with an efficient and effective method of getting facilities on line and products to market ahead of competitors. This is critical in today's world of short product cycles and competitive prices. Customers include a list of Who's Who in Silicon Valley, such as Apple Computer, Applied Materials, Inktomi, Lifescan (division of Johnson & Johnson), Amdahl, Fujitsu, Bayer, JDS Uniphase, and Teradyne. The company is also a leader in getting new start-up companies on line quickly and efficiently. ICOM's unique capabilities make it one of the leading design and construction firms in the Silicon Valley.

As a corporate citizen of the Silicon Valley, ICOM has a very active employee-run giving committee. This 12-person committee is charged with the responsibility of donating charitable money that ICOM allocates for this purpose each year. Their mission statement calls for them to try to enhance the quality of life in today's society, to reach out to

World Society for the Protection of Animals.

the disadvantaged and less fortunate, and to try to provide a better quality of life for those who are in need.

The committee meets on a quarterly basis to choose local charities that they feel could use help. One such project is the Silicon Valley Tech Museum in downtown San Jose that attracts many school children. The museum provides visitors with a history of the development of the high-tech industry in the area. There are displays and samples of products and how they are or were manufactured.

At Christmas, staff participate in the Children's Wish List. Poor, disadvantaged children put ornaments on a Christmas tree with their wish and ICOM staff collect them and purchase the gifts for them. Other organizations that receive benefits from ICOM employees are the local AIDS walk, the American Heart Association, local Ys, and a camp for children with diabetes. Money is also given to the National Institute for Transplantation to encourage donations of kidneys for transplant and the Alpha Pregnancy Center. This organization assists single mothers with the support necessary to keep their babies if they so desire.

Two animal welfare organizations are also aided by ICOM employees. Money is donated to the World Society for the Protection of Animals. This organization assists animals endangered as the result of natural disasters or who are treated cruelly. Another animal charity they support is PAWS. That is the Performing Animals Welfare Society that operates a ranch in California for "retired" performing animals from circuses and other entertainment avenues.

Decisions regarding which charities ICOM will support are based on the consensus of all giving committee members. Although the committee normally meets only quarterly to

Alpha Pregnancy Center.

disburse money, they will meet sooner if there is an emergency or need to make a decision ahead of schedule.

In addition to charitable giving, ICOM staff are encouraged to take an active role in civic activities and to participate in the democracy of the community by voting in public and union elections, by fulfilling social obligations such as jury duty, and by responding to every opportunity to make a contribution to society.

It is ICOM's intention to identify company interests with those of the community and to operate according to the highest standards of honesty and integrity to enhance and protect the physical environment and to support worthwhile projects. ■

ICOM Giving Committee.

GREENBRIAR HOMES COMMUNITIES^{SM}

Breathtaking foyers are a hallmark of Greenbriar Homes Communities^{SM}.

There are many reasons for Greenbriar Homes Communities' accolades and awards as one of Northern California's premier homebuilders. In more than a quarter century of business, Greenbriar has built almost 40 prime neighborhoods consisting of about 4,000 homes. It has a management team with close to two centuries of residential building experience, has won six Gold Nugget "Best Home" awards from the Pacific Coast Builders Conference, and, in a recent independent survey of San Jose home buyers, it was rated as having one of the strongest reputations for quality construction in the Bay Area.

These successes evolve out of the company's philosophy to "build our homes and communities as if they were intended for our own families" and "to build it right the first time." To do this, Greenbriar has a team consisting of highly qualified architectural and engineering professionals, competent craftsmen, and dedicated design, construction, and marketing personnel. Numerous meetings are held in order to maximize the design and construction of the homes as well as to enhance the attractiveness of the overall neighborhood. Small but important details get the care and attention they deserve.

The company's commitment to quality can be seen in the construction. Specially air-dried "k-d" studs are used to minimize interior wall warping. These may cost more but they do produce smoother and truer walls. Copper water supply lines and cast-iron plumbing drops are used because they are solid, quiet and extremely durable. They provide easy operation, worry-free performance, and extra long life.

Carnelian Heights in Silver Creek Valley.

In the kitchens and bathrooms, mortar-set tile is used rather than the less expensive gluing methods. This technique gives tiles better adherence and a greater resistance to moisture.

Different families have different lifestyles and needs, and Greenbriar recognizes that. The company listens carefully to what homebuyers want and therefore offers a variety of different floor plans to meet those differing needs. Two popular choices are the presence of home offices and workout spaces. In addition, Greenbriar recognizes that people's needs and lifestyles change over the years as families grow. Consequently, it provides for "flexible space" that can change with the changing needs of the residents. Some bedrooms, for example, have double doors so that they can be converted into dens in future years.

Other key interior elements in Greenbriar homes include spectacular architectural detailing, varied ceiling heights and window styles that enhance openness and luxury while conserving energy, walk-in closets in master bedrooms, and professional kitchens with top of the line appliances, abundant storage, superb custom cabinetry, and granite countertops. For those who wish to customize their own plans, Greenbriar will be opening its own design center in Fremont. Home buyers can chose from a wide variety of specialized cabinets, flooring, window coverings, and other accessories.

Spacious kitchens are designed by Greenbriar Homes Communities[SM] *with the epicurean in mind.*

a 10-bedroom complex (St. Joseph's Mens Worker House) to house more than 16 men and 4 counselors to offer job assistance, weekly counseling, and recreational facilities. Almost 95 percent of the men have successfully moved back into mainstream society. Working with the Cathedral Basilica of St. Joseph's in San Jose, Greenbriar has purchased four homes since 1998 to house almost two-dozen women, children, and counselors. The program is designed to help seriously distressed families to also make their way back into the community.

Greenbriar employees are also heavily involved in community work. They assist with the Emergency Housing Consortium's construction and reconstruction projects, the New Children's Shelter holiday season events, and the Second Harvest Food Drive.

Greenbriar's "premier living experience" can be found in the Bay Area's most desirable communities including Saratoga, Los Gatos, Cupertino, Mountain View, Pleasanton, Dublin, Alamo, Livermore, and the Silver Creek and Willow Glen areas of San Jose. ■

Just as important as the design and the materials used is the integrity of the construction, and Greenbriar's inspection program goes well beyond industry standards and that of its competitors. In addition to municipal inspections, a third-party structural engineer performs multiple inspections of the foundation and the wall and roof framing before, during, and after construction. Buyers are also given numerous walk-through and orientation tours during the course of the building. This is then followed up with a warranty program and a customer service organization in order to guarantee the family's long-term satisfaction with their purchase.

Greenbriar's commitment, however, goes beyond just the houses it builds. The company and it employees also pride themselves on building communities and they "strongly believe in enhancing the quality of life for all of our communities and neighbors." As a company and through its employees, Greenbriar contributes money, time, and construction expertise to community organizations. The company has been involved in the Bay Area daffodil-planting program for public spaces in the areas in which it builds. It supplied 50,000 bulbs and assisted with the planting. The daffodil is a symbol of hope that will bloom for many years to come.

Other community ventures include the construction management and supply of numerous building materials for a 132-resident public shelter for abandoned and abused children. Since 1997, Greenbriar has provided

Bridle Creek in Pleasanton.

The Villas at Town and Country, San Jose.

One of the largest home builders in Northern California, Citation Homes Central and its predecessor organizations, have built more than 50,000 superb homes in California over the past 40 years. As a family operated business, Citation is dedicated to successfully building and marketing homes in highly desirable areas, using the highest quality materials in appealing architectural styles. Its buyers are consistently assured optimum value and maximum satisfaction.

First founded after World War II as Besco Homes, the company became a general partnership in 1977 called Citation Homes and quickly established itself as the leading home builder in California. At that time, Citation Homes had three divisions in Northern, Central, and Southern California. With the death of the original founder, Wayne Valley, the partners each bought out their share of the company, and Stephen C. Schott took over Citation Homes Central in 1986.

Continuing in the family tradition, the three Schott children joined the company in the late 1980s. Son Stephen E. Schott heads the Land Acquisition and Development Department. Steve spearheads the search for land and is

actively involved with the various municipalities and governmental agencies affecting the business. Daughters Lisa Treadwell and Kristen Bowes play key rolls in the Marketing Department. Lisa directs the model home merchandising and Kristen directs the community signage and advertising. Wife Patricia is active with the many charitable organizations supported by the company.

One of their most prized projects is the Evergreen Specific Plan in San Jose that has been under development

Jasmine Heights in Evergreen, San Jose.

Park Paseo in the Evergreen Specific Plan.

since the late 1980s. This is the first master-planned community in the City of San Jose and, when complete, will provide 3,000 new homes for the area. Citation is in the process of building one third of the homes in this award-winning complex. In addition to the homes, there is a $75 million infrastructure of schools, roads, parks, lakes, and a European-style shopping village built around traffic circles. The flagship of Citation's developments in this area is Enchantment and The Legends. These single-family homes feature four to six bedrooms with many exciting options and upgrades and some of the best views of downtown San Jose in the area.

Other Citation developments provide its customers with a large variety of home styles and living concepts. Not only the traditional single-family homes, but town homes, courtyard homes, and apartment complexes. One of the newest endeavors is Cherywood, a new master-planned community of affordable homes in San Leanadro. This community offers three types of homes: courtyard, medium-sized single-family, and executive-sized single-family. Each of the individual communities offers a wide range of floor plans and amenities.

All of these housing communities are developed and built by a Citation team of experts and subcontractors who work together in a productive relationship to ensure that home buyers achieve a level of excellence and value that is second to none.

In addition to providing housing, the Schotts help support the community through their many charitable activities. In order to give back to the community, the Schott's support two major initiatives. The first, begun by Stephen C. Schott and other community leaders, is the Role Model Program. Participants visit local schools and act as models for the pupils to try to encourage them to stay in school and pursue education.

The Schotts' other major charitable activity is the Read to Exceed Program. Students are encouraged to read books and are rewarded if they achieve their reading goals. Money for this activity is raised by the employees of Citation

Homes via its annual golf tournament, as well as donations from the Schott family, who also contribute to the local YMCA and the San Jose Symphony.

Hard work and dedication are Stephen C. Schott's benchmarks. Born in San Jose and one of three children in a modest family, Stephen went to work in the orchards at the age of 11 to earn extra money, and then he worked on a survey crew during his teens. Educated on a partial baseball scholarship at Santa Clara University, Stephen served in the military and then became a cost accountant, all prior to his going into the home building business.

Because of his successes, Stephen C. Schott became a recipient of the Horatio Alger Award. Alger was an American author whose more than 120 books written after the Civil War had the inspiring theme of from rags to riches. His novels emphasized that perseverance and hard work will result in success. Distinguished Americans who exemplify this heritage and who are committed to sharing this message of hope with young people are honored with this award. Award winners come from all backgrounds, races, and creeds, and are innovators and entrepreneurs who are committed to sharing a message of hope with young people. Certainly, Stephen is an example of what can be achieved through perseverance and hard work. Citation Homes Central, his legacy, is dedicated to carrying on this tradition. ∎

Wisteria in Evergreen, San Jose.

Located in the Capital of Silicon Valley, the San José McEnery Convention Center is a natural home for technology-related conventions and trade shows that bring more than 600,000 visitors from around the world to San José each year.

City Manager, Del D. Borgsdorf (far right), and staff review plans for the new downtown library being built through a unique partnership between the City of San José and San José State University.

The city of San José has a rich history, one that has been shaped by dramatic growth and by the cultural and ethnic diversity of the people who call San José home.

Our residents speak 46 different languages and just under 50 percent of the city's population are Caucasian. Over 30 percent are of Hispanic origin, nearly 30 percent are Asian or Pacific Islander, and just under 4 percent are African American.

With a population of 918,800, San José is the third largest city in California and the 11th largest city in the United States. It has a thriving downtown with arts and cultural events, as well as nightlife. And for ten years, crime in San José has been the lowest of any of the nation's largest cities.

The City of San José is a customer-focused, results-driven organization. It has a nearly $1.3 billion operating budget and over 7,000 employees, making the City the seventh largest employer in the county. San José has been recognized as one of the best managed cities in the U.S. and recently received the highest credit rating of any large city in the state.

As the "Capital of Silicon Valley," San José, and its downtown in particular, serve as a magnet in attracting high-tech companies such as Cisco Systems, Inc., e-Bay, Adobe Systems, Inc., and a number of high-profile companies.

And while Silicon Valley annually receives more than one-third of the nation's total venture capital, on the international front, San José boasted over $29 billion in exports in 1998. In 1999, it grew to become the second largest exporting area in the United States.

Playing a major role in the exportation boom has been San José International Airport, which currently serves 13.1 million passengers each year, generates 75,000 jobs per year, and $4.2 billion a year in direct business revenue.

Another major City-owned facility, the San José McEnery Convention Center, draws visitors from throughout the world, who spend more than $160 million in San José each year. This includes money spent in local hotels, restaurants, attractions, and other businesses, which in turn generates 2,800 jobs locally.

Most importantly, the City of San José is committed to sustaining and improving its neighborhoods. In a recent community survey, two-thirds of those surveyed say their neighbors have pride in San José, and nearly 70 percent rate the quality of life here as good or better.

The City of San José has a reputation for creating innovative solutions and collaborative partnerships with businesses, schools, non-profits, and neighborhoods, to address local and regional needs and to strengthen the community. ■

The success stories of San Jose would not have come to fruition if it were not for the vision and commitment of the San José Redevelopment Agency. The Redevelopment Agency has been dedicated since its founding in 1956 to improving the quality of life for those who live, work, and play in San José.

The SJRA facilitates and implements a comprehensive program encompassing mixed-use, high-quality development to revitalize San José's downtown, neighborhoods, and industrial areas. Among its tasks are building affordable housing; upgrading transportation systems; preserving historic buildings; rejuvenating historic neighborhoods; and hosts of other undertakings to enhance the city.

The SJRA's Downtown program is modeled on the San José envisioned in the Greater Downtown Development Strategy 2000—a thriving core where San Jose lives, works, and shops. It has stimulated more than $1.7 billion in private investment in Downtown, creating an enviable quality of life. Within, and surrounding the oldest project, are: the Civic Plaza Redevelopment Project Area—construction has begun on a new $175 million City/San José State University Joint Library; a mixed-use parking facility with ground floor retail and banquet facilities; and a new school for Horace Mann Elementary.

Based on a recent study by the Urban Land Institute, the Redevelopment Agency is moving toward filling approximately 3 million square feet of downtown with mixed-use development including retail, residential, and office space.

The rebuilding of San José's neighborhoods began and continues with the Neighborhood Business District and Neighborhood Business Clusters programs to revitalize

and encourage private investment in San José's older commercial neighborhoods. The agency has invested more than $70 million in these areas, with the ultimate goal of creating flourishing, self-sustaining commercial centers within San José neighborhoods.

Working with the City, the Redevelopment Agency committed more than $100 million for neighborhood improvements based on the priorities of each community and launched the Strong Neighborhoods Initiative, which encompasses approximately 300,000 residents within 22 San José neighborhoods.

In addition to strengthening San José neighborhoods, the Agency is committed to increasing housing throughout the city by spending more than $550 million on housing, with $414 million of that amount set aside for affordable housing, and funded development for more than 3,000 for-sale and rental housing units.

As San José grows, and its needs change and expand, the Redevelopment Agency will continue to support San José communities by strengthening neighborhoods, increasing the housing supply, building world-class, accessible public facilities, and initiating and facilitating private development. ■

Top: The City of San José has the nation's best public safety record of any metropolitan area, a marvelous ethnic diversity, and a beautiful climate. Left: Following the Silicon Valley tradition of doing things in a way that's never been done before, The Tech Museum of Innovation opened October 31, 1998, in a dazzling mango and azure-colored domed building unlike any other in the world.

Visit Divco.com for more information.

This is a real estate investment, development, and management company with a portfolio of nine million square feet of West Coast properties, mostly located in the Silicon Valley. Founded by Stuart Shiff and David Taran, Divco has been headquartered in the heart of the Silicon Valley since 1993. Its business approach is "partnering," according to Michael A. Dumke, executive vice president and director of private equity capital. "Partnering with everyone involved—the tenants, the real estate people, investors, the lenders—is integral to our approach. This is the way Silicon Valley was built."

According to Dumke, while New York is the world's financial center, Silicon Valley is "the world's high-tech industry and venture capital center," and therefore an increasingly important area for the global real estate marketplace. "If you look at the pattern of investment in major new industries since WWII, all have been financed initially by venture capital. The center of the venture capital sector is now firmly based in Silicon Valley and a company looking to get a venture capitalist on its board of directors is in a much better position if it has a presence here." The nexus of capital, innovation, and growth industries such as technology has propelled Silicon Valley real estate into the ranks of the important locations in the world, making the region a firm focus of institutional investors.

Another Silicon Valley plus, according to Dumke, is the presence of "two of the world's greatest universities"—Stanford and University of California at Berkeley. "In addition to being in the midst of one of the deepest labor

Park Center Plaza, San Jose, an investment of Divco West and Charlesbank Capital Partners.

pools in the world," says Dumke, "UC and Stanford and a host of other schools around the bay are constantly turning out top-flight engineers, innovators, and business people." This talented, qualified workforce is eager to be employed by businesses located in the Silicon Valley area.

Start-up companies, as well as established companies new to the area, will find that Divco West's approach to leasing facilitates the process. "We're based in the valley and our leasing teams know this market very well and they are a tremendous resource to tenants and brokers."

Divco West has many properties from which to choose in Silicon Valley and throughout California. During 2000, the company purchased several properties in the valley, including an eight-building portfolio in Santa Clara, a two-building complex in Southern California's Manhattan Beach, and it is currently partnering with Gibson Speno, WestBrook Partners, and Cisco Systems to develop a 6.6 million-square-foot campus in the Coyote Valley, just south of San Jose. Information on these properties, as well as others, can be obtained at www.divco.com.

"There is significant opportunity here for companies located in this area," Dumke insisted. "There are companies that are going to continue to come out of the Stanfords and the Cals and companies like Cisco. There will always be engineers who will get together and say 'We can do this better, faster.' That's how this valley was founded and why it has developed so quickly." With this kind of innovation a normal occurrence, the Silicon Valley will keep its entrepreneurial traditions of growing new industries and companies, and it will remain "the place to be." ∎

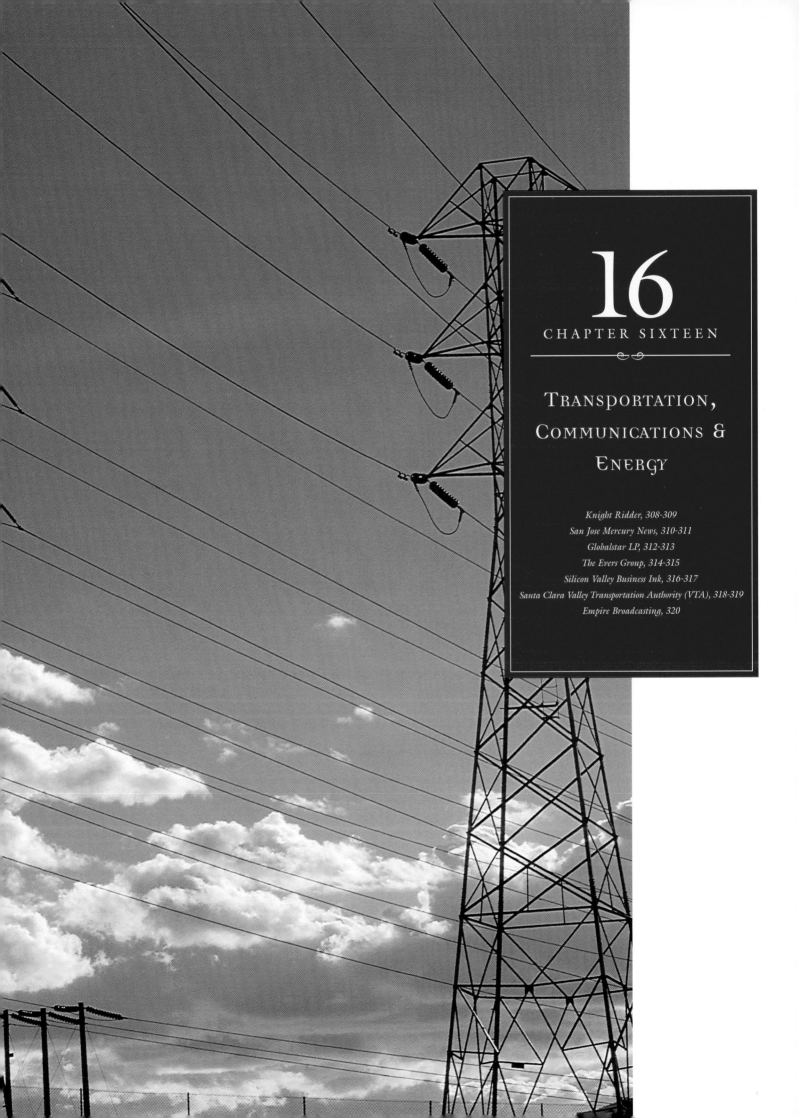

16
CHAPTER SIXTEEN

TRANSPORTATION, COMMUNICATIONS & ENERGY

Ever since Knight Ridder moved its headquarters from Miami to San Jose in 1998, this second-largest publisher of newspapers in the United States has found the innovative climate of Silicon Valley to be an ideal laboratory for seeking ways to grow its business.

With 32 dailies located in 28 U.S. markets, the company currently has a daily readership of 8.5 million, a Sunday readership of 12.6 million, and $3.2 billion in revenues. In 2000, the Philadelphia, Miami, and San Jose markets represented 40 percent of Knight Ridder's revenue. Together with its five other large markets—Detroit, Kansas City,

Fort Worth, Charlotte, and Contra Costa County—they brought in 75 percent of the company's annual revenue and 86 percent of its operating profit.

KnightRidder.com, the company's Internet subsidiary, is responsible for managing and growing a national network of regionally focused Web sites, or "hubs"—branded as the Real Cities network—and its strategy is to build that network into the leading provider of local content on the Web. These hubs represent 28 Knight Ridder markets and an expanding number of affiliate markets brought in by other media companies across the United States. Each site in the network offers a variety of online searchable services covering local news, sports, shopping, travel, career channels, interactive entertainment guides, classified ads, directories of local businesses, and civic institutions.

"KnightRidder.com's roots reach back to 1993," stated Polk Laffoon, vice president/corporate relations. "That's when the *San Jose Mercury News* launched Mercury Center, the country's first full-text online newspaper. Soon our other newspapers followed, eventually creating the Real Cities network. Today, we brand our sites by their regional names—BayArea.com, Philly.com, and all the others— because they offer so much more than just news. Our newspapers, with their well-known brand names, are available within those larger sites."

KnightRidder.com has expanded its reach through imaginative marketing deals with Palm, Yahoo, and Everstream, Inc. In September 2000, together with Tribune Co., it purchased CareerBuilder, Inc., a publicly

Top: Miami Herald Pulitzer Prize winners, from left: Gene Miller won for Local Investigative Specialized Reporting in 1967 and Local General Spot News Reporting in 1976; Liz Balmaseda for Commentary in 1993; Jim Morin for Editorial Cartooning in 1996; and Dave Barry for Commentary in 1988.
Photo by Jay Good
Right: Knight Ridder's headquarters in San Jose.

From left:
Dan Finnigan,
president/Knight
Ridder Digital;
Mary Jean Conners,
senior vice president/
human resources;
Tony Ritter, chairman
and CEO; Steve Rossi,
president/newspaper
division.

produced an extra 200,000 copies, with pressmen working three straight shifts, delivering to remote areas of the Santa Cruz mountains where people were without news.

Knight Ridder is an industry leader in diversity, having compiled a lengthy record for increasing the role of women and minorities in its businesses. In 1996, it won the prestigious Catalyst Award for advancement of women in the work-place. In 1999, it was named one of the 50 best companies for Asians, blacks, and Hispanics by *Fortune* magazine. In December 2000, Knight Ridder received top honors with *Working Woman Magazine*, placing among the "Top 25 Companies for Executive Women." Currently, 18 women serve as either publisher, general manager, executive editor, or as a corporate officer.

Ever vigilant to stay ahead of the changing world and business of news reporting, Knight Ridder will continue to strengthen its base in Silicon Valley and give exceptional service to its four stakeholders—its customers, its share-holders, its employees, and the communities they serve. ■

traded company in the business of providing recruitment services to other people's Web sites. The combination of CareerBuilder's own client "network," its proprietary search technologies, and the deep, local market presence and customer relationships of its new owners, will enable Knight Ridder to mount a serious challenge that rivals other online employment sites for leadership on the Web.

Progress on the Web sites is encouraging. By December 2000, the Real Cities sites were reaching 4 million unique visitors, up 40 percent from the year before, and they had a digital media reach of 5 percent, up 20 percent from the year before.

Knight Ridder was formed in 1974 by a merger between Knight Newspapers and Ridder Publications. The former, created in 1933 when John S. Knight took command of the Akron Beacon-Journal from his father, had made quality editorial content a hallmark of its operations. "There is no higher title than editor," Jack Knight often said—and that bias came to characterize all of the newspapers of the combined company.

Today, a commitment to public service is at the heart of Knight Ridder journalism—something in which its 20,000 reporters and staff take great pride. In 2001, the company won its 83nd Pulitzer Prize for journalistic excellence. And during the past decade, it won no fewer than three Pulitzers for meritorious public service, the highest honor in journalism: in 1993, for reporting on Hurricane Andrew in Miami; in 1994, for an examination of racial attitudes in Akron; and in 1998, for coverage of the Red River flood in Grand Forks, North Dakota.

In 1990, the *San Jose Mercury News* received accolades for reporting on the 1989 Loma Prieta earthquake. "We went to extra pains to publish who could offer help, who needed help, and what help was available," stated Rob Elder, the newspaper's editor. "Some people didn't have water, some were without electricity, and there were others whose houses were completely gone." Within 24 hours "the Merc"

KnightRidder.com is
responsible for managing
and growing a national
network of regionally
focused Web sites
branded as the Real
Cities network.

Mercury News
Publisher Joe Natoli.

Readers who turn to page 2A of the *Mercury News* find a unique declaration printed there every day:

"We are passionate about serving readers in Silicon Valley and its global electronic community, reporting and writing accurately and fairly, shining a light on injustice and defending the public's right to know. We will reflect the changing demographics of the community in both coverage and hiring, recognizing that diversity is a core component of accuracy. Two stories are central to our mission: the impact of technology and the changing demographic landscape of America. Those two stories create powerful connections between our community and others, both domestic and international."

This news mission, which serves both as a promise to readers and as a guide for the pages to follow, is notable for its emphasis on the international. As Executive Editor David Yarnold said in a recent speech, "You can look anywhere in the world and I can show you readers in the Bay Area who count on us to bring these places to them."

The *Mercury News* has recognized that "life outside Silicon Valley" is not only interconnected with the region's growth and technology-based economy, but also with the people from other lands who now call the Bay Area their home. Indians in Silicon Valley are just as likely to be CEOs, entrepreneurs, and venture capitalists as they are to be engineers and software designers. Chinese entrepreneurs were responsible for 29 percent of Silicon Valley start-ups in 1999. And since the 1990 census, the Asian population in Santa Clara County has grown an estimated 61 percent and the Hispanic community has blossomed by 34 percent.

"Our readers are among the most affluent, most wired, most diverse population in the country," agreed *Mercury News* Publisher Joe Natoli. "In a given week, 65 percent of adults here read the Mercury News. They are the movers and shakers of Silicon Valley, the people who created the computer chip, who built the Internet, who fund the new economy. They are the recent immigrants who traveled from around the world to be part of the technology revolution, and families who have lived here for generations. Together, they make up one of the most demanding readerships in the country, compelling us to reach for even higher standards," Natoli said.

In recognition of these demographics, the *Mercury News* has spread out beyond its local doorstep to cover the global community by establishing regional, national, and international bureaus in places like Sacramento, Los Angeles, Seattle, New York, and Hanoi, Vietnam. Its Hanoi office, opened in 1994, was the first post-war bureau in Vietnam established by an American newspaper. In addition, the *Mercury News* shares pool bureaus in Washington, D.C., Mexico City, Tokyo, and Jerusalem with its parent company, Knight Ridder, Inc.

The *Mercury News* was the first metropolitan newspaper in the nation to publish in three languages—English, Spanish, and Vietnamese. In 1996, the paper launched a free Spanish-language weekly publication called *Nuevo Mundo* to serve the sixth largest Hispanic market in the United States.

The Mercury News *is nationally known for its quality journalism.*

Nuevo Mundo is actually a separate newspaper from the *Mercury News*—with its own newsroom and editorial staff—but it operates under the same high journalistic standards as its mother publication as it brings readers "news you can use," sports, and special features.

Another ethnic publication of the *Mercury News* is the Vietnamese-language weekly *Viet Mercury*, which hit the stands two years ago to serve nearly 112,000 Vietnamese people who live locally—making up the second-largest Vietnamese community in the United States.

"*Viet Mercury* is a hybrid of Western-style objective news stories like what you would see on *CNN* or in the *New York Times* mixed with Vietnamese literary tradition of incorporating love poems and stories," stated De Tran, editor of *Viet Mercury*

The *Mercury News* also brings news of the world into its main publication and was recently named by the Columbia Journalism Review as one of the top 10 newspapers in the country. The paper has featured stories about abuses in the H-1B visa system; covered Mexico's recent historic presidential election; and, as one article put it, "There's the annual story for Norwegians who look forward to Sue Hutchison's holiday column on how much she despises Lutefisk, the traditional Christmas cod soaked in lye."

In 1985, the *Mercury News* won a Pulitzer Prize award for its international reporting of the Marcos regime in the Philippines. The Pulitzer board cited the three-part series entitled "Hidden Billions: The Draining of the Philippines" as having had a direct impact on subsequent political developments in the Philippines and in the United States.

Since the *Mercury News* was established in San Jose 150 years ago, it has built its reputation on recording the day-to-day history of the city's evolution from a tiny pueblo to the expansive Silicon Valley of today. Readers find the future written in its pages too, as the *Mercury News* brings moment-to-moment foreign news to the local community and strives to fulfill its destiny as a "top newspaper to watch out for the 21st century." ■

The Mercury News *publishes in three languages—English, Spanish, and Vietnamese.*

Globalstar LP

Right: GLOBALSTAR'S CONSTELLATION OF LOW EARTH ORBITING SATELLITES relay communication signals between the user and ground stations (known as GATEWAYS) by means of a simple, low cost "bent pipe" technology.

For anyone who has ever experienced the frustration of trying to make a cellular call where there is no signal, Globalstar is the answer," says Gloria Everett, executive vice president of sales and marketing for Globalstar.

As a matter of fact, the company's tag line is "Out of cell range, you are now in Globalstar range." That's because Globalstar LP, based in San Jose, California, is a consortium of leading international telecommunications companies and equipment manufacturers led by co-founding companies Loral Space & Communication and QUALCOMM, Inc., which has a product reminiscent of Star Trek technology.

In orbit 758 miles above the earth, Globalstar has a constellation of 48 satellites that beam caller signals to a global network of ground stations that then route the calls to earthly telecommunications systems.

"Globalstar phones work where cellular phones do not. In mountains or forest areas, at sea, in foreign countries… or even in cellular 'dead spots' in Marin County or along Interstate 80," explained Everett. But Globalstar is not in competition with cellular companies. Rather Globalstar wholesales time on satellite systems to more than 700 service providers in individual countries who then market and manage the systems as a "supplement" to cellular. For example, Elsacom is a provider for Italy and Eastern Europe, and in North America, Vodafone provides service under the name Globalstar USA.

In most cases, Globalstar's mobile and fixed phones—built by three of the world's top wireless manufacturers: Ericsson, QUALCOMM, and Telit—work in two modes. They first look for a cell to connect to and, if found, put the call through at a regular cell price. But if no cell is found, the phone can be switched to satellite mode to make the call. "Thus, users only pay for satellite service when they need it," commented Everett, who was recently named one of the top women in wireless by *Wireless Week* for her 30-plus years experience in the field.

Established in 1991, Globalstar currently provides service coverage through its network of 25 gateways

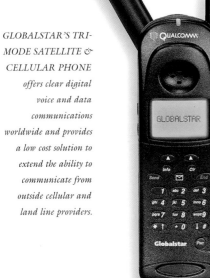

GLOBALSTAR'S TRI-MODE SATELLITE & CELLULAR PHONE offers clear digital voice and data communications worldwide and provides a low cost solution to extend the ability to communicate from outside cellular and land line providers.

(that consist of large dish antennas and switching stations) to 106 countries and their territorial waters, representing over 80 percent of the world's landmass, excluding Antarctica. In early 2001, the company's latest gateway was inaugurated in the heart of the Amazon basin, bringing wireless telephone service to vast stretches of northern Brazil where it had been almost non-existent.

Although Globalstar's market is potentially endless, the company has identified certain target areas that have an immediate demand for remote communication—maritime, transportation, utilities, agribusiness, natural resource exploration, and outdoor enthusiasts.

"Globalstar's maritime service now includes commercial maritime vessels transiting deep oceans and fishing fleets worldwide," stated Everett, "and recently we have started selling to cruise ship lines, enabling passengers to make phone calls from sea." Long-haul truck drivers use the service in areas where CB radios do not work to provide a reliable link to dispatchers, destination contacts, and weather information services.

Besides providing voice communications, Globalstar also has data transmission capabilities through its Packet Data Modem, which operates at 9,600 kbps. "This might seem slow for deskbound Web surfers, but for people on the move who largely want to send and receive e-mail or Internet-based information, it's quite adequate," stated Everett, who referred to its use in automatic retrieval of data from isolated locations as in-line voltage and load management monitoring for utility meter reading applications.

Agriculture businesses in countries like Australia, Brazil, and Argentina benefit from Globalstar's service to coordinate their operations, especially in buying and selling on the fluctuating commodities markets. The phones have become an indispensable business tool for forestry and fishery businesses; and oil, gas, and mining exploration companies that are housed in secluded communities that are underserved by conventional telephone lines and cellular markets.

GLOBALSTAR'S STATE-OF-THE-ART CONTROL CENTER, located in San Jose, California, and back up Control Center in El Dorado Hills, California, are comprised of two operating centers. The Space Operations Control Center (SOCC) commands and controls the satellite constellation, while the Ground Operations Control Center (GOCC) manages the communications networks for system performance.

And finally, outdoor enthusiasts—like lodge owners, hikers, hunters, and fishers—find Globalstar products to be an ideal form of communication. As a matter of fact, Globalstar has even provided service to the famed Iditarod Sled Dog Race that's held in Alaska each year.

The company installed fixed phones in Anchorage's Regal Alaskan Hotel for free use by the public and journalists that cover the race; gave the Iditarod Trail Committee mobile phones and car kits for use at 27 checkpoints; and loaned phones to USA Sports Network producers, pilots, and camera operators to assist with television coverage. "Alaska is a great place to demonstrate the quality and versatility of satellite telephone service," stated Dennis McSweeney, vice president and general manager for Globalstar USA.

The biggest advantages of Globalstar products are, however, its clarity and security. Globalstar was one of the first companies to adopt QUALCOMM's Code Division Multiple Access (CDMA) technology, which is being carried forward into third generation cellular applications. This CDMA signal provides a high level of security and crystal clear voice quality using digital encoding and frequency-to-frequency jumping based on mathematical algorithms.

Globalstar is a futuristic company doing business in the here and now. The company is bringing voice and data communication to areas that have never been covered before, and in so doing, it is expanding the global network and market. ■

GLOBALSTAR'S GATEWAYS, like the one located in Presidente Prudente, Brazil, South America, connect the Globalstar satellite constellation to the land-based switching equipment of terrestrial and cellular telecommunications service providers.

Communication can be as simple as a face-to-face meeting, or as sophisticated as a multimedia presentation with streaming video, animation, or a live digital broadcast.

In March of 2000, Jim Evers started The Evers Group.

The mission of The Evers Group is to assist both the public and private sector with their communication needs.

To accomplish this mission, Evers began assembling a diverse team of communication experts. "Our highly skilled specialists have more than 100 years of combined experience in corporate communications, engineering, television, and media relations," explained Evers. As a result, they can assist in the creation, production, distribution, and delivery of any message.

Before creating The Evers Group, Jim was part owner, president, and general manager at KICU Television in San Jose. "The sale of the station in 1999 provided me with the opportunity to realize a life long dream," said Evers, who holds the position of president and chief executive officer of The Evers Group.

The Evers Group consists of four primary divisions—Engineering, Production and New Media, Education and Distance Learning, and Government and Corporate Relations.

Director of Engineering David Lingenfelter along with Jim Boston, director of emerging technology, provide The Evers Group's clients with solutions for any portion or the entire process of their engineering project, including analysis and design, budgeting, management, installation, system integration, and training.

Like many top production companies, The Evers Group's award-winning Production and New Media Division creates and distributes content for video, television, CD-ROM, DVD, and the Internet. This division, led by Trent Tanaka, director of new media, out distances the competition by providing valuable consultation, support, and production services. Clients have access to state-of-the-art equipment including non-linear Avid post production. "Creatively we provide all aspects of production support from concept to completion," stated Evers. "This division has experience in creating short- and long-form traditional video used for corporate, academic, and broadcast applications. We also offer Web site creation, streaming video, and can assist in the domestic and international distribution of traditional broadcast material."

The Evers Group Education and Distance Learning Division works with educators and experts in various fields to produce and distribute high-quality educational content designed to enhance the learning process. "Our client base consists of a diverse group of organizations from technology and finance to medicine and public education," said Melissa Tench-Stevens, chief operating officer for The Evers Group.

"Too often, we underestimate or forget the importance of supportive relationships with the government, the media, and the community," Evers said. "These liaisons are vital to long-term success and growth." The Government and Corporate Relations Division, led by Director Barbara Zeitman-Olsen, supports clients in facing the delicate, yet

The Evers Group management team, from left: Jim Evers, Ray Madorin, Barbara Zeitman Olsen, Armon Mills, Marie Maionchi, David Lingenfelter, Trent Tanaka, Jim Boston, and Melissa Tench-Stevens.

critical challenge of building these relationships and creating strategic alliances. Services include media relations, executive training, crisis management, community outreach, business positioning, problem solving for business and government, and building liaisons with both the community and government.

And finally clients and employees are in good hands with Marie Maionchi, director of business operations for this diverse group, and Director of Human Resources Ray Madorin, who brings over 30 years experience in the high tech industry, as past vice president human resources for Xilinx, Inc.

In addition, The Evers Group is part of the management team for Silicon Valley Business Ink. Under the leadership of Armon Mills and with the support of a group of local investors, the inaugural issue of the highly successful weekly business publication Silicon Valley Business Ink launched on September 8, 2000. Touted as "the voice of the valley," this Evers Group partner company is a critical source of information to CEOs and technology leaders.

A visit to The Evers Group Web site (www.eversgroup.com) introduces a dazzling list of companies it has worked with over the years including motion picture studios, major television networks, high-tech giants such as Intel, iBlast, and Cisco, educational institutions, and many more.

"I'm proud of our team," Evers admits. "Their creativity, knowledge, and entrepreneurial spirit makes The Evers Group a stimulating and fun place to be each day."

"We're intrigued by communication on every level," Evers said. "That's why our structure is one of interactive divisions. Like good jazz, a great solo on the drums or bass or piano stands alone. But when you put it all together it's an art form like nothing else out there." ■

Top: The Evers Group offers a complete line of production services. Here Trent Tanaka prepares a video presentation using non-linear Avid technology that he will then burn onto a DVD. Left: The engineering division, headed up by David Lingenfelter (left) and Jim Boston, provides customized engineering solutions for corporate, educational, and broadcast communications facilities.

Silicon Valley Business Ink, a locally owned publication, is tucked away in the heart of downtown San Jose.
Photo by Scott Lewis

On September 8, 2000, Silicon Valley Business Ink launched its inaugural issue and became the first business publication to call "all of Silicon Valley" its home.

"Silicon Valley is pretty much a state of mind," explained Armon Mills, Biz Ink's publisher from his San Jose office. "I think anyone south of Market Street in San Francisco thinks they're in Silicon Valley. And I know companies in the tri-valley areas like Pleasanton and Dublin feel they reside there."

Before Biz Ink came on the scene, American City Business Journal's publications were practically the only game in town, with three separate sister publications in San Jose, San Francisco, and the East Bay.

"We felt there was room for competition," stated Mills, who was formerly president and COO of the American City Business Journal conglomerate out of Kansas City, owner of the Phoenix location, and publisher in San Jose.

Locally owned Biz Ink has differentiated itself from other newspapers by focusing primarily on technology but also covering finance, real estate, and lifestyles.

The staff has designed a visually appealing newspaper that adds sizzle to the Silicon Valley publishing menu.

"We've tailored Biz Ink, to some extent, after Crain Communications' publishing chain," Mills stated. "I like their dedication to editorial content and the slick look of their over 30 publications, among which are *Advertising Age* and *Crain's Chicago Business.*"

The guts of Biz Ink really come from its people—referring to both its concise, entertaining, and informative content and its edgy reporting. Rather than employing the staunch "news only" format that's used at traditional business publications, Biz Ink has a fresh approach. As the voice of the valley economy its reporters and columnists are encouraged to add a bit of humor or a bite of savvy to their writing, like when reporter Erik Linden compared the demise of dot-com companies to being "victims of cyber-Darwinism."

When Biz Ink's colorful cover is turned back, revealed inside is a package of provocative news stories and a lively set of weekly departments geared specifically for business people. You can tune into Biz Briefs to enter the playground of the gazelles of Silicon Valley and pick up the hottest news stories from the past week. Turning Point

Biz Ink's newsroom bustles every week as an experienced and dedicated staff cranks out the hottest new business newspaper in Silicon Valley.
Photo by Scott Lewis

offers introspective profiles of the valley's captains of industry. And, with Fast Track you can keep score of the corporate ladder—who's joined the rungs as new hires, and who's climbed ahead through promotions.

Sure, other publications run lists, but Biz Ink's Top 10 is different with a more comprehensive viewpoint, unique rankings, and color graphics that add value and context to the list.

"We'll not only list the top 10 valley public companies ranked by market cap on one page," stated Editor Vikki Bowes-Mok who oversees the newsroom and a team of experienced reporters, "but we'll take it far beyond that and stack them up against the top 50 in the Bay Area or even the world."

But the features that really put the "E" in entertainment are Biz Ink's crosswords, cartoons, and Ink Spots.

"We're really pleased to have Fred Piscop designing tech-related crossword puzzles for our publication," stated Bowes-Mok. Piscop is a regular contributor of crosswords to *Time* magazine. Biz Ink's staffers feed him Silicon Valley clues, and together they develop hometown questions. Also on the payroll is Scott Willis, a syndicate cartoonist formerly with the San Jose Mercury News, who occasionally taps funny bones with satirical cartoons on the opinion page. And a reader favorite is Ink Spots—all the news that's *almost* fit to print—juicy gossip, wacky pieces of information, and just plain interesting stuff.

Biz Ink's editorial staff has geared their publication to be a quick and concise read. After all, busy execs do not have a lot of time to wade through piles of data. Little wonder that 74 percent of their subscribers are CEOs, presidents, VPs, principle owners, and directors.

"We're up to 100 locations where the paper is now sold," stated Tom Jensen, associate publisher, "in news stands, vending boxes, and stores like Barnes & Nobles or Spartan Book Store." As a matter of fact, the new publication is so popular that Jensen, who worked with the American City chain before joining Biz Ink, commented, "Instead of having to solicit sales, we have people calling us."

What's the future hold for Biz Ink? It's very bright according to Armon Mills who claims the Internet is not going be replacing printed newspapers anytime soon—people still want to sit back on a brisk Sunday morning with a cup coffee in one hand and a newspaper in the other.

However, the technology that Biz Ink writes about does play an important part in today's business, even at Biz Ink. Mills stated, "We need to support our print product through technology," by getting stories up weekly on the company's Web site at www.svbizink.com. "That way, while you're riding BART to work," he added, "you can view our entire newspaper on your Palm VII." ■

The Biz Ink staff. First row (bottom), from left: Kathi McArthur, sales administrator; Veronica Ramos, sales coordinator; Steve Tanner, reporter; Jennifer Maragoni, associate editor; Erik Linden, reporter. Second row: Vikki Bowes-Mok, editor; Armon Mills, president and publisher; Jim Evers, co-chairman of the board; Rich Rutherford, account manager. Third row: Pam Valentine, circulation manager; Linda Baker, director of finance; Judy Dixon, director of advertising. Fourth row: Jill Arnone, account manager; Cassandra Moran, account manager; Sandra Mills, executive assistant, special projects; Robin Nakamura, account manager; Aldo Maragoni, Valley Scene editor; Christina Bellantoni, reporter; Lynn Graebner, reporter; Andrea Pusateri, administrative assistant; Sharon Michelson, circulation sales associate; Scott Lewis, photographer. Fifth row (top): Dennis Taylor, managing editor; Tom Jensen, associate publisher; Monique Martinez, researcher; Barbara Goodwin, graphic designer; Jeri Waxman, director of marketing; Clayton Moraga, production director; Dale Ganzow, account manager. Photo by Scott Lewis

SANTA CLARA VALLEY TRANSPORTATION AUTHORITY (VTA)

Transportation is a hot topic in Silicon Valley where traffic jams have surged to record levels and delays have cost motorists nearly $1.5 million a day in lost wages and wasted fuel. However, the Santa Clara Valley Transportation Authority, (known as VTA), is working to improve traffic conditions by providing transportation alternatives for all residents and visitors in the valley.

VTA provides many bus, light rail, and Caltrain connections for residents and commuters in downtown San Jose.

VTA is the result of a 1995 merger between two previously separate entities: the Santa Clara County Transit District and the Congestion Management Agency for Santa Clara County. VTA is also the successor organization to the former Santa Clara County Traffic Authority, which terminated in late 1997. This marked a new beginning for Santa Clara County with a comprehensive transportation authority for the first time. Today, VTA is an independent special district governed by its own Board of Directors. The Board consists of 12 elected city and county officials, appointed by the jurisdictions they represent.

All VTA Light Rail and Buses are equipped with bike racks.

VTA is making great strides toward fulfilling its vision of "providing a transportation system that allows anyone to go anywhere in the region easily and efficiently" as it administers light rail and bus operations; congestion management; transit, highway, and land-use planning; and regional transportation partnerships.

VTA currently operates a fleet of more than 500 buses that travel 79 routes a day in a 326-square-mile urbanized area with more than 4,600 stop locations. The scope of service includes local-route buses, express buses, paratransit service, special event (sports) buses, a free airport shuttle, and free shuttle services

to various employment centers and to local attractions such as Paramount's Great America Amusement Park and the Compaq Center at San Jose.

VTA also operates one of the longest light rail systems built in the United States in the last 50 years. The 30.5-mile system stretches among the cities of San Jose, Santa Clara, Sunnyvale, Mountain View, and Milpitas. VTA Light Rail is now branching southward into Campbell and Los Gatos, and eastward through San Jose.

In 1976, Santa Clara County voters approved an ongoing half-cent sales tax to help support public transportation service. Also in 1976, light rail was endorsed as the most efficient and effective form of rapid transit for Santa Clara County. Over the past 25 years, Santa Clara County voters have been extremely supportive of public transportation services by repeatedly funding transportation initiatives in 1976, 1996, and 2000. This fact can only be attributed to public foresight.

Although the current 1996 Measure B half-cent sales tax is scheduled to expire in 2006, funding for the future is secure. In November 2000, an overwhelming 70.4 percent of local voters passed Measure A to fund transit improvement projects with a half-cent sales tax for 30 years. This measure, which was put on the ballot by VTA, will provide for capital and operating funds for, among other things, a rapid transportation alternative for the Silicon Valley Rapid Transit Corridor, a rail connection to San Jose International Airport's passenger terminals, construction of two new light rail lines, electrification of Caltrain, and 750 zero emission buses to expand the fleet and replace diesel, and operating funds for the expanded system.

Through VTA's Congestion Mangement Program, VTA prepares and contributes to a variety of transportation planning and programming documents that link

The Almaden Lake Village project is a high-density rental housing project located adjacent to VTA's Almaden Light Rail Station and Park & Ride lot.

transportation with land-use considerations, and prioritizes transit and highway projects for local, state, and federal funding. VTA also partners with local cities to facilitate the creation of transit-oriented developments along existing and future corridors.

VTA annually reviews over 500 such proposed private development projects to ensure compatibility with existing transit services. For example, the area around the Middlefield Light Rail Station was redeveloped into an integrated office and transit facility, and VTA recently joined in opening 200 affordable apartments, a retail center, and daycare adjacent to the Ohlone/Chynoweth Light Rail Station.

Two highway-related projects (which are funded by the 1996 Measure B half-cent sales tax) are among those on VTA's priority list: the expansion of I-880 between Brokaw Road and Montague Expressway and U.S. 101 between San Jose and Morgan Hill. When completed in 2004, these projects are expected to provide relief for two of the worst bottlenecked highways in Silicon Valley, cutting commute time by as much as 18 minutes.

VTA is involved in coordinating regional commuter services as it partners with outside agencies to bring long-distance commuters into the area by rail. As a member of the Peninsula Corridor Joint Powers Board, VTA contributes $13.7 million annually to support Caltrain services between San Francisco and Gilroy. VTA's involved in a multi-agency cooperative effort with the Altamont Commuter Express (ACE) that carries workers to their jobs in Silicon Valley from San Joaquin, Contra Costa, and Alameda counties. And through the Capital Corridor Joint Powers Board, VTA governs trains that travel 150 miles a day between Oakland and Sacramento, with several continuing into San Jose.

VTA strives to be a "part of every trip you take" in Silicon Valley as it aggressively works to expand rail and bus lines, improve roadways, integrate transit and land-use planning into decision-making processes, and provide travelers with viable alternatives to the automobile. ∎

VTA provides accessible bus, light rail, and paratransit service for persons with disbilities and senior citizens.

At a time when all other Bay Area radio stations have been acquired by large national corporations, Empire Broadcasting Corporation stands out because its three stations (KLIV, KARA, and KRTY-FM) are virtually the only locally owned stations in the Bay Area.

This family atmosphere brings about several distinctions that the big boys can't enjoy. The first is that the company is not only locally owned, but 75 percent of the stock is held by its employees—people who go to work there every day and have a vested interest in the stations' success.

"At a time when generally speaking, radio people tend to hop around from market to market, from station to station, we're able to retain our employees long-term," stated Robert Kieve, 79, president and co-owner of Empire Broadcasting, who worked as a speechwriter for President Eisenhower and at CBS early in his career. Empire has a remarkable record for retaining employees like KLIV program director, Jane McMillan, 20 years with the company; KARA program director and Empire vice president, John McLeod, 34 years; KARA music director and now company Internet director, Mike Danberger, 21 years; and KARA morning personality, Kim Vestal, 21 years.

Another reason that Empire stands out is the energetic participation of its employees in their community. Frequently in leadership positions, Empire's employees have served on the boards of more than two-dozen nonprofit organizations. For example, Kieve and McLeod both have been president of the 450-member Rotary Club of San Jose. "Another more dramatic example," stated Kieve, "is Kim Vestal, who had a personal battle with breast cancer. She's now deeply involved with raising money for breast cancer research and in encouraging women, over the airwaves, to get mammograms."

Empire management also has the conviction that radio should broadcast controversial views, even on radio stations whose programming is based on music. Thus, not only news station KLIV, but also pop music KARA and country music KRTY regularly air commentaries by Kieve on subjects such as the City Council's rejection of the proposed power plant and the *Mercury News'* failure to include San Jose in its San Francisco edition's masthead; and all three stations frequently air "free speech messages" by members of the public.

Finally, Empire's most impressive distinction is perhaps its involvement in local politics, giving free air time to local office-seekers. In the primary election of 2000, the stations broadcasted a total of 842 such messages. ■

The people who own and operate Empire stations, seated, from left: Sheryl Semas-Ruth (6 years with Empire), KARA local sales manager; Jerry Durie (24 years), KARA sales staff; Tina Ferguson (9), KRTY local sales manager; Jan McMillan (20), KLIV program director. Standing, from left: Mike Danberger (20), air personality, KARA music director, and Internet director; Vince Lopopolo (34), executive vice president; Kim Vestal (21), KARA morning personality; John McLeod (34), vice president for programming; Nate Deaton (7), marketing director; Norma Roy (34), comptroller; Bob Kieve (34), president and founder. Not shown: Stuart Hinkle (17), national sales manager; Terry Rust (30), San Francisco sales manager; Dorothy Adam, former KARA traffic manager; Joanne Kilmartin, former KARA local sales manager.

Adaptec
691 South Milpitas Boulevard
Milpitas, California 95035
Phone: 408-957-4923
Fax: 408-957-5630
www.adaptec.com
Pages 200-201, 258-259

Adobe Systems Incorporated
345 Park Avenue
San Jose, California 95110
Phone: 408-536-6000
www.adobe.com
Page 225

Advantest America
3201 Scott Boulevard
Santa Clara, California 95054
Phone: 408-988-7700
Fax: 408-987-0691
E-mail: info@advantest.com
www.advantest.com
Pages 182-185

Air Systems Foundation, Inc.
940 Remillard Court
San Jose, California 95122
Phone: 408-918-5711
Fax: 408-918-5712
E-mail: asi4kids@airsystemsinc.com
www.asifoundation.org
Pages 256-257

Air Systems Inc., an Encompass Company
940 Remillard Court
San Jose, California 95121
Phone: 408-280-1666
Fax: 408-280-1020
www.encompserv.com
Pages 288-291

Alliance Credit Union
3315 Almaden Expressway, Suite 55
San Jose, California 95118
Phone: 408-445-3386
Fax: 408-445-9327
E-mail: service@alliancecreditunion.org
www.alliancecreditunion.org
Pages 242-243

Alteon WebSystems Inc.
50 Great Oaks Boulevard
San Jose, California 95119
Phone: 408-360-5500
Fax: 408-360-5762
E-mail: info@alteon.com
www.alteonwebsystems.com
Pages 222-223

Andersen
333 West San Carlos Street
River Park Tower, Suite 1500
San Jose, California 95110-2710
Phone: 408-998-2112
Fax: 408-998-2151
E-mail: gary.h.matuszak@us.andersen.com
www.andersen.com
Pages 246-247

Aspect Communications
1310 Ridder Park Road
San Jose, California 95131
Phone: 408-325-2200
Fax: 408-325-2260
E-mail:info@aspect.com
www.aspect.com
Pages 210-211

BEA Systems, Inc.
2315 North First Street
San Jose, California 95131
Phone: 408-570-8000
Fax: 408-570-8901
www.bea.com
Pages 208-209

Cadence Design Systems, Inc.
2655 Seely Avenue
San Jose, California 95134
Phone: 408-943-1234
Fax: 408-943-0513
www.cadence.com
Pages 196-197

Calico Commerce Inc.
River Park Towers
333 West San Carlos Street
San Jose, California 95110
Phone: 408-975-7400
Fax: 408-975-7410
E-mail: info@calico.com
www.calico.com
Pages 220-221

California Eastern Laboratories
4590 Patrick Henry Drive
Santa Clara, California 95054
Phone: 408-988-3500
Fax: 408-988-0279
www.cel.com
Page 228

Cisco Systems
170 West Tasman Drive
San Jose, California 95134
Phone: 408-526-4000
Fax: 408-526-4100
www.cisco.com
Page 230

Citation Homes Central
404 Saratoga Avenue, Suite 100
Santa Clara, California 95050
Phone: 408-985-6000
Fax: 408-985-6050
www.citation-homes.com
Pages 300-301

City of San José
801 North First Street
San Jose, California 95110
Phone: 408-277-5131
Fax: 408-277-3131
E-mail: tom.manheim@ci.sj.ca.us
www.ci.san-jose.ca.us
Page 302

Colliers International
450 West Santa Clara Street
San Jose, California 95113
Phone: 408-282-3800
Fax: 408-292-8100
E-mail: webmaster@colliersparrish.com
www.colliersparrish.com
Pages 294-295

Divco West Properties
150 Almaden Boulevard, Suite 700
San Jose, California 95113
Phone: 408-293-9600
Fax: 408-293-9690
E-mail: spilch@divco.com
www.divco.com
Page 304

East Side Union High School District
830 North Capitol Avenue
San Jose, California 95133
Phone: 408-347-5000
Fax: 408-347-5045
E-mail: cotoj@esuhsd.org
www.esuhsd.org
Page 272

**East Side Union High School District—
School-to-Career Program**
830 North Capitol Avenue
San Jose, California 95133
Fax: 408-347-5241
E-mail: childressb@esuhsd.org
www.esuhsd.org
Page 273

Edify Corporation
2840 San Tomas Expressway
Santa Clara, California 95051
Phone: 408-982-2000
Fax: 408-982-0777
E-mail: info@edify.com
www.edify.com
Page 231

El Camino Hospital
2500 Grant Road
Mountain View, California 94040
Phone: 650-940-7000
Fax: 650-988-8100
E-mail:
keeley_blanchette@elcaminohospital.org
www.elcaminohospital.org
Pages 268-269

Electroglas
6024 Silver Creek Valley Road
San Jose, California 95138
Phone: 408-528-3000
Fax: 408-528-3562
E-mail: info@electroglas.com
www.electroglas.com
Pages 214-215

Empire Broadcasting
PO Box 995
San Jose, California 95108
Phone: 408-293-8030
Fax: 408-293-6124
Page 320

The Evers Group
2055 Gateway Place, Suite 400
San Jose, California 95110-1015
Phone: 408-467-3855
Fax: 408-467-3817
E-mail: webmaster@eversgroup.com
www.eversgroup.com
Pages 314-315

Globalstar LP
3200 Zanker Road, Building 260
San Jose, California 95134
Phone: 408-933-4000
Fax: 408-933-4100
E-mail: sales@globalstar.com
E-mail: pr.group@globalstar.com
Pages 312-313

Greater Bay Bancorp
2860 West Bayshore Road
Palo Alto, California 94303
Phone: 650-813-8200
Fax: 650-494-9190
www.gbbk.com
Pages 244-245

Greenbriar Homes CommunitiesSM
4340 Stevens Creek Boulevard #240
San Jose, California 95129
Phone: 408-984-5900
Fax: 408-556-1860
www.greenbriarhomes.com
Pages 298-299

Heald College, San Jose
341 Great Mall Parkway
Milpitas, California 95035
Phone: 408-934-4900
Fax: 408-934-7777
www.heald.edu
Page 274

The Health Trust
2085 Hamilton Avenue, Suite 150
San Jose, California 95125
Phone: 408-559-9385
Fax: 408-559-9515
E-mail: garya@healthtrust.org
www.healthtrust.org
Pages 270-271

Heritage Commerce Corp
150 Almaden Boulevard
San Jose, California 95113
Phone: 408-947-6900
Fax: 408-947-6910
www.heritagecommercecorp.com
Pages 238-239

Heuristics Search, Inc.
160 West Santa Clara Street, 12th Floor
San Jose, California 95113
Phone: 408-925-9300
Fax: 408-918-0505
E-mail: hsi@heur.com
www.heur.com
Pages 236-237

IBM
Corporate Community Relations
5600 Cottle Road
San Jose, California 95193
Phone: 408-256-7899
Fax: 408-256-5466
E-mail: ccrwest@us.ibm.com
www.ibm.com/ibm/ibmgives
Pages 202-203, 260-261

ICOM
477 Burke Street
San Jose, California 95112
Phone: 408-792-2292
Fax: 408-292-4968
E-mail: doni@icominc.com
www.icominc.com
Pages 296-297

IKOS Systems, Inc.
79 Great Oaks Boulevard
San Jose, California 95119-1311
Phone: 408-284-0400
Fax: 408-284-0401
E-mail: info@ikos.com
www.ikos.com
Page 232

Infineon Technologies
1730 North First Street
San Jose, California 95112
Phone: 408-501-6000
Fax: 408-501-2424
www.infineon.com
Pages 212-213

Intel Corporation
2200 Mission College Boulevard
Santa Clara, California 95052
Phone: 408-765-8080
www.intel.com
Pages 198-199, 254-255

ISG Broadband, Inc.
1567 Centre Pointe Drive
Milpitas, California 95035
Phone: 408-957-8000
Fax: 408-957-8008
www.isgbroadband.com
Page 229

Knight Ridder
50 West San Fernando Street, 15th Floor
San Jose, California 95113
Phone: 408-938-7700
www.kri.com
www.knightridder.com
Pages 308-309

KPMG LLP
500 East Middlefield Road
Mountain View, California 94043
Phone: 650-404-5000
Fax: 650-960-1325
www.us.kpmg.com
Pages 248-249

NEC Electronics Inc.
2880 Scott Boulevard
Santa Clara, California 95052
Phone: 408-588-6000
Fax: 800-729-9288
www.necel.com
Pages 204-205

Oak Technology Inc.
1390 Kifer Road
Sunnyvale, California 94086
Phone: 408-737-0888
Fax: 408-774-5395
E-mail: pr@oaktech.com
www.oaktech.com
Pages 216-217

Oakwood Worldwide
2222 Corinth Avenue
Los Angeles, California 90064
Phone: 310-478-1021
www.oakwood.com
Page 284

PEMSTAR Inc.
1877 Senter Road
San Jose, California 95112
Phone: 408-282-4800
Fax: 408-282-4890
www.pemstar.com
Pages 218-219

Qual-Tronix
2215 Oakland Road
San Jose, California 95131
Phone: 408-943-9380
Fax: 408-435-1485
E-mail: ricevans@pacbell.net
www.qualtronix.com
Page 227

San Jose Arena Authority
PO Box 90207
San Jose, California 95109
Phone: 408-977-4780
Fax: 408-977-4784
E-mail: linda@sjaa.com
Pages 282-283

San Jose Mercury News
750 Ridder Park Drive
San Jose, California 95190
Phone: 408-920-5000
www.bayarea.com
Pages 310-311

San Jose Redevelopment Agency
50 West San Fernando Street
San Jose, California 95113
Phone: 408-794-1064
Fax: 408-277-3153
E-mail: peggy.flynn@ci.sj.ca.us
www.sjredevelopment.org
Pages 303

San Jose Silicon Valley Chamber of Commerce
310 South First Street
San Jose, California 95113
Phone: 408-291-5250
Fax: 408-286-5019
E-mail: info@sjchamber.com
www.sjchamber.com
Pages 240-241

San José State University
One Washington Square
San Jose, California 95192
Phone: 408-924-1000
Fax: 408-924-1118
E-mail: sjsupao@sjsu.edu
www.sjsu.edu
Pages 266-267

Santa Clara Valley Transportation Authority (VTA)
3331 North First Street
San Jose, California 95134-1906
Phone: 408-321-2300
E-mail: customer.service@vta.org
www.vta.org
Pages 318-319

Santa Clara Valley Water District
5750 Almaden Expressway
San Jose, California 95118-3686
Phone: 408-265-2600
Fax: 408-266-0271
E-mail: pubinfo@scvwd.dst.ca.us
www.heynoah.com
Pages 264-265

Silicon Valley Business Ink
300 South First Street, Suite 50
San Jose, California 95113
Phone: 408-993-1500
Fax: 408-293-2515
E-mail: amills@svbizink.com
www.svbizink.com
Pages 316-317

Silicon Valley Sports & Entertainment
525 West Santa Clara Street
San Jose, California 95113
Phone: 408-287-7070
Fax: 408-999-5797
E-mail: mbordelon@svse.net
www.compaqcenteratsanjose.com
www.sjsharks.com
Pages 280-281

Smart Products, Inc., a division of Smart Pumps, Inc.
1710 Ringwood Avenue
San Jose, California 95131
Phone: 408-436-0740
Toll-free: 800-338-0404
Fax: 408-436-0744
E-mail: sales@smartproducts.com
www.smartproducts.com
Page 224

Sony Electronics Inc.
3300 Zanker Road
San Jose, California 95134-1901
Phone: 408-432-1600
www.sonyjobs.com
www.sony.com
Pages 186-189

South Bay Construction
511 Division Street
Campbell, California 95008
Phone: 408-379-5500
Fax: 408-379-3256
E-mail: jaiassa@sbci.com
www.sbci.com
Pages 292-293

Spectra-Physics
1335 Terra Bella Avenue
Mountain View, California 94043
Phone: 650-961-2550
Fax: 650-968-5215
www.spectra-physics.com
Pages 206-207

Stevens Creek Dodge
4100 Stevens Creek Boulevard
San Jose, California 95129
Phone: 408-248-1800
www.stevenscreekdodge.com
Pages 278-279

Therma, Corp.
1601 Las Plumas
San Jose, California 95133-3418
Phone: 408-347-3400
Fax: 408-347-3434
E-Mail: jparisi@therma.com
www.therma.com
Pages 194-195, 252-253

United Defense, LP
1205 Coleman Avenue
Santa Clara, California 95050
Phone: 408-289-0111
Fax: 408-289-4294
www.udlp.com
Page 226

VERITAS Software
350 Ellis Street
Mountain View, California 94043
Phone: 650-527-8000
Fax: 650-527-1021
www.veritas.com
Pages 190-193

BIBLIOGRAPHY

Web sites used in the production of this book:

Alviso—www.alviso.com

City of San José—www.ci.san-jose.ca.us

County of Santa Clara—claraweb.co.santa-clara.ca.us/index.html

Evergreen Valley College—www.evc.edu

FIRST—www.usfirst.org

Fairmont Hotel—www.fairmont.com/FA/en/CDA/Home/CDHomePage

Guadalupe River Park and Gardens—www.grpg.org

Hakone Japanese Gardens—www.hakone.com

Happy Hollow Park and Zoo—www.happyhollowzoo.org

History San José—www.historysanjose.org

Japanese Friendship Garden—www.ci.san-jose.ca.us/cae/parks/kp/jfg.html

Japantown San Jose—www.japantownsanjose.org

Kaiser Permanente—www.kaiserpermanente.org

Kwanzaa—www.globalindex.com/kwanzaa

Northside Theatre Company—home.netcom.com/~rto2/ntc.html

Opera San Jose—www.operasj.org

Palo Alto Medical Foundation—www.pamf.org/copyright.html

Paramount's Great America—www.pgathrills.com/events.jsp

Rosicrucian Museum—www.rosicrucian.org

San Jose Chamber of Commerce—www.sjchamber.com

San José Convention and Visitors Bureau—www.sanjose.org

San Jose Downtown Association—www.sjdowntown.com

San Jose Earthquakes—www.sjearthquakes.com

San Jose International Airport—www.sjc.org

San Jose Medical Center—www.sanjosemedicalcenter.com

San Jose Redevelopment Agency—www.sjredevelopment.com

San Jose Repertory Theatre—www.sjrep.com

San Jose Stage—www.sanjosestage.com

San José State University—www.sjsu.edu

San Jose Symphony—www.sanjosesymphony.org

San Jose Unified School District—www.sjusd.k12.ca.us

Santa Clara County Office of Education—www.sccoe.org

Santa Clara Valley Wine Growers Association—www.scvwga.com/index.html

Shark Byte Art—www.sharkbyteart.com

Silicon Valley Charity Ball—www.svcb.org

Stanford University—www.stanford.edu

Stanford University Medical Center—medcenter.stanford.edu

Tech Museum of Innovation—www.thetech.org

Winchester Mystery House—www.winchestermysteryhouse.com

Contributing Editorial Writers

Jake Bowman

Jake was among the first students in San Jose High School's International Baccalaureate program, and continued his education at Ohio State University and the University of Tartu in the Republic of Estonia. Immersed in the start-up technology culture of Silicon Valley from an early age, he pursues a career in Market Intelligence, covering the data-communications, biotechnology, and alternative energy industries, while serving as a repository for local folk history.

Susan Ditz

Susan's family was among California's Gold Rush-era settlers, and she grew up in the San Jose area. After graduating from Boston University, she worked on the McDonald's, Nabisco, and Puma Public Relations accounts, also serving as public information officer for the American Cancer Society and other nonprofits. She was San Francisco Zoo's Marcom Director, and a columnist with *San Jose Mercury News.* Susan is a frequent contributor to a variety of publications, and raises lavender on her farm in Pescadero, California.

Connie Young Yu

A third generation Californian and Mills College graduate, Connie Yu is the author of the *San Jose, Chinatown, USA,* (History/San Jose,) and has long been involved with historical projects such as the restoration of the immigration barracks on Angel Island, and more recently, the Woolen Mills Chinatown uncovered by expansion of San Jose's Route 87. She was a founding member of Asian Americans for Community Involvement, Inc., and is a coach at The Fencing Center of San Jose.

Contributing Profile Writers

Gary Burchfield

Gary Burchfield has worked in corporate communications and for ad agencies in California and Nebraska. He has been a freelance writer since 1982, specializing in business and industry articles and publicity. He has written on such diverse topics as agriculture, landscape and turf management, travel destinations, and military history. He has been a contributing writer for Community Communications since 1999.

Richard S. (Dick) Cox

Dick Cox, a writer and teacher, is a fourth generation resident of Silicon Valley, whose family came to the area in covered wagons in 1852, where they became orchardists along Saratoga's Cox Avenue.

After graduating from the San José State University Journalism School, he was a *San Jose Mercury News* reporter for many years, and then the public relations representative for the County Executive of Santa Clara County for thirteen years. Following work for two private public relations agencies, he combined independent PR consulting for non-profits and businesses, free-lance writing and reporting, and teaching writing and journalism. Dick was a journalism lecturer at San José State University for fifteen years, and he has written and sold over 100 articles to magazines.

Danek S. Kaus

Dan Kaus is a veteran journalist and publicist. His work has been featured in dozens of publications around the U.S., and two of his screenplays have been optioned by Hollywood producers.

Kathy Mayer

Kathy Mayer has been writing about businesses since 1987, when she opened her own writing business in Lafayette, Indiana. Besides corporate profiles, she writes magazine articles, newsletters, brochures, and media releases. Kathy holds a bachelor's degree in journalism and political science from the University of New Mexico.

Marvin Ross

Marvin Ross writes for many specialty and consumer magazines, newspapers, and Web sites throughout North America, as well as doing press releases and corporate profiles. He is a regular columnist and features editor for *Business Executive* newspaper. Marvin was the profile writer for *Hamilton: A New City for a New Millennium,* produced by Community Communications in 2000.

Bob Serata

Bob Serata, an award-winning writer, writes for fun and money from Los Gatos, California and Islamorada, Florida.

Barbara Stahura

Barbara Stahura is a freelance writer based in Tucson, Arizona. Her articles and essays on subjects ranging from the Internet and e-commerce to spirituality and art have been published in many print and online publications.

INDEX